ABOUT THE COV___

The cover of this book
is an electronic painting by Sabra Stein entitled
The Cycles of Self-Discovery.
Based on a 16th century woodcut,
it represents humankind's courage
in the Journey through the veil
to understand the Joy of Knowing that We Are One.
It is symbolic of
the teachings of universal mastership
expressed in this book.

What a Few Pre-viewers have said about this book

*So very, very good, so much food for thought!

**This has been a <u>most</u> difficult book to edit. The temptation
to stop and meditate on different passages
is overpowering!*

**Would you please let us keep the manuscript? We just
don't want to have to wait for the book to savor it.
There is a hunger, a <u>need</u>!*

Alice Bryant, author of
The Message of the Crystal Skull

Some may feel the book is heavy and will stop reading after a few pages. But in the fullness of their time, they will return to it.

Said differently, this is not Metaphysics 101. This is Graduate Level Material! But it truly is neither ponderous nor heavy. It is just good!

As I read the material, I kept hearing a Zen Buddhist saying which appears in many of the sutras. The saying is, "Thus have I heard." It fits this work well!

Reverend John W. Groff, Jr.
Episcopal Priest

I wish to thank you and the Masters for sharing this important message with us. It is vital information beyond anything I have read to date. The guidance contained within is truly from unmanifest God brought through the dimensions.

Reverend Linda Seebach

There were times when I would feel myself to be absolutely hypnotized by the words!

I underlined so many passages which would be perfect for the back cover of this book that I think we will need several back covers!

Sabra Stein, founding Co-editor of
Aquarius, A Sign of the Times

THE JOY
OF KNOWING

WE
ARE
ONE

TRANSFORMATIONAL CONVERSATIONS

AMONG THE MASTERS AND

ERIK MYRMO

Compiled and Edited by

Dr. L. David Moore

PENDULUM
PLUS

PENDULUM PLUS PRESS
ATLANTA, GA

The editor wishes to thank Erik Myrmo for the transformational channeling, and for his agreement to publish this material. The editor also acknowledges the tremendous help and encouragement given by his wife Jan, and by those who gave their honest appraisals in the preview of this work: *viz.* Reverend John W. Groff, Jr., Alice Bryant, Reverend Linda Seebach and Sabra Stein. The editor also acknowledges that he was constantly guided by those who stayed with him during all the effort expanded in this editing job. "They" were here, "they" still are here, and "they" are always in my heart, seen or unseen.

First Edition, 1996

ISBN 0-9635665-4-7

Library of Congress Catalog Card Number 96-92577

Published by
PENDULUM PLUS PRESS
3232 COBB PARKWAY
SUITE 414
ATLANTA, GA 30339

Printed in the United States of America
10 9 8 7 6 5 4 3 2 1

TABLE OF CONTENTS

DEDICATION

This book is dedicated to all
who are transformed by:

We Say Unto Ourselves

and

Thus Have We Heard

that

We Are One with God

and

There is True Joy

in the

Knowing!

PREFACE

T his is the fourth book published by Pendulum Plus Press. The first book was *Christianity and the New Age Religion*, published in the summer of 1993. It was an attempt to build a bridge between two groups who should support each other in their love for God, but who tend to fight each other. For many people, the book has served to open their mind to the expanded thoughts of God, rather than to the restrictive thoughts which the established religions have tended to teach about Him/Her.

The second book was *The Christian Conspiracy*, published in the fall of 1994. This book tells "how the teachings of Christ have been altered by Christians," and was intended to answer those of the Christian faith who expressed their belief that the author of *Christianity and the New Age Religion* did not understand Christianity. After more than fifty years in mainstream Christianity, including almost thirty years in adult Sunday School and Lay Ministry activities, I felt that I understood the teachings of the Church very well. I also felt that few Christians knew where those teachings came from, for most of the teachings of the Church are from the Early Church Fathers such as Athanasius, Tertullian, Augustine, Hippolitus, Irenaeus, Jerome and others rather than from the Christ. However, few of the Christians in the pew have been told that truth, even though their ministers know it.

The third book was *A Personal Pathway to God*, published in the fall of 1995. This book was written to answer the numerous calls and letters which said, "We understand the problem, but where do we go from here?" The answer is to develop and follow the personal pathway which is meant for you alone, for there is no institutional pathway into oneness with God which everyone must follow. Instead, each individual is a unique expression of God, and each follows an individualized and unique pathway into the oneness which is the heart's desire of so many.

The first two books used generally accepted information as their background. This information was drawn from resource material such as *The Encyclopaedia Britannica, New Catholic Encyclopedia*, Williston Walker's *A History of the Christian Church*, and other sources whose acceptance can hardly be challenged. The third book used similar resource material to which was added a small amount of channeled information.

This book is different. It is almost totally based on information which has been channeled through Erik Myrmo. Although channeled information is being accepted by more and more people as a source for learning and for understanding who we are, it has not, as yet, reached the level of general acceptance represented by the resource material used in the previous three books.

The purpose of this *Preface* is to indicate the type of information presented in this book, to explain the format of the book's presentation, and to indicate something of the source of the channeled material.

This *Preface* is immediately followed by an *Introduction* to the book. The major purpose of the *Introduction* is to present some general information about channeling for those who know little or nothing about it. The *Introduction* also presents the admonition that it is up to each individual to accept or reject the relevance of the channeled information to him or to her. Finally, the *Introduction* presents an introduction to the book which was channeled by Maitreya. This channeled introduction contains an important message.

As humanity continues to evolve, more and more channeled information is being received. Parts of this information are very meaningful for some individuals, but not for others; and parts are possibly mis-leading for some individuals, but not for others. The acceptance of channeled information is somewhat like accepting the belief that each pathway is an individual and unique one; for if the concept of an individual pathway resonates with you as an individualized experience, then channeled information also may resonate with you as an individualized message.

The *Introduction* is followed by eight chapters of channeled information. The chapters are generally divided into four sections. The first section is a short Introduction to the subject material of the chapter, telling, in a general way, what the established religions of the world have taught about that particular subject. These Introductions tend to emphasize the Christian viewpoint. This is done not because Christianity is a preeminent religion for those who would be interested in channeled information, but because this book is being published in the United States and consequently may attract an audience which would want to compare the channeled material to the teachings of orthodox Christianity.

The next section is the Channeled Information. This material was selected from fifty-eight separate channeling sessions, and is offered as a typical presentation of the subject material. The third section in most chapters is a series of specific questions which were asked in order to more fully explain the subject material. This section presents Channeled Answers to Specific Questions. The final section in each chapter is a Summary of what the channelings have said about the specific subject. The first seven chapters present information on the following specific subjects: Ascension; Creation; Divine Will and Free Will; Manifestation and Prosperity; Christ Consciousness; Jesus the Christ; and Physicality. The eighth chapter presents Miscellaneous Information.

The eight chapters on channeled material are followed by a short chapter entitled *Summary and Conclusions*. This chapter is a concise presentation of the summaries presented at the end of each chapter. It is presented as an overview of the teachings and as a ready reference for those who would accept the channeled material as being meaningful to their lives.

The book ends with five Appendixes and an *Index. Appendix A* presents a description of the each channeling session. Material from many of these channeling sessions is presented in the eight major chapters. The numbers and dates presented in those chapters correspond to the number for each session presented in *Appendix A*.

Appendix B presents a description of the Ascended Masters who presented information during these channelings. The descriptions were presented in a channeling session with Maitreya on April 30, 1996. In some cases, small amounts of additional information as presented by other New Age sources are included in this Appendix. *Appendix C* presents the definitions of some of the terms as they were used in the channelings. These definitions also were channeled by Maitreya. Since the definitions of these terms differ greatly from the generally accepted definitions as presented in a standard dictionary, it was felt that this Appendix was needed to provide clarification. Because the channeled material uses traditional English words in an unusual way, it is highly recommended that *Appendix C* be understood before any of the channeled material is read, and it is further recommended that this Appendix be referred to often during the reading of the channeled material. *Appendix D* presents a personal experience which occurred during a channeling session with Kuthumi on April 18, 1996. Its message was so beautiful and profound that I felt it had to be included in this book. *Appendix E* presents a short bibliography of publications which were used in the development of this book, or which present additional channeled information or additional information about channeling.

This *Preface* will end with a word about the channeled information from which this book was excerpted. All of the channelings came through Erik Myrmo and were channeled in the Atlanta area between April, 1992 and July, 1996. Most channelings were two to three hours in length, with some thirty or forty minutes of that time being devoted to energy flow. All of the channelings were recorded, transcribed, and shared with those who attended. Most of the channelings had about fifteen people in attendance, with a low of five and a high of over forty in fifty-five of the transcribed channelings. The other three channelings consist of one private session given directly to Erik Myrmo as he was flying cross-country, and two channelings concerned with definitions or the answers to specific questions. These latter sessions were attended by only three people: Erik Myrmo and Jan and Dave Moore.

The transcribed channelings total almost 600 pages of single-spaced, 12 point typing. It was surprising to this editor to note the consistency throughout all of this channeled material. Often identical words and phrases would be used to describe a particular subject in two different channelings, even though the channelings might be three or four years apart. Less than one-fifth of the channeled information is presented in the pages of this book. Almost all of the personal information has been omitted, as have the comments made to an individual during an energy flow. The major subjects were chosen because each was addressed in several different channelings. In the early channelings, many Ascended Masters came forth. The later channelings came mostly from energies identified as either Kuthumi, Maitreya or St. George, although quite often a blend of energies channeled in order to give *"a blended consciousness that will help to facilitate the openings in ways that are specific for the unique way each of you perform; for within each person is a unique aspect of the Christ Consciousness."* [see page 149]

Although the channelings have been edited for clarity, all who heard the channelings and have reviewed their presentation in this book agree that they represent the information which was channeled through Erik Myrmo. Some of the channelings may seem to use archaic language, or archaic terminology, or archaic sentence structure in their presentation. That is as it should be, for the editing did not disturb that aspect of the information. In the channelings which has been presented in Roman type, italics have been used to indicate a question or a comment by someone other than the channeler. This is especially noticeable in the "Channeled Answers to Specific Questions" section of most chapters. Italics are also used for other purposes such as the title of books or chapters and for long quotations in which a comment from the audience is presented in Roman type. The editor feels that it will be obvious when there has been audience participation.

Erik Myrmo has been channeling as an avocation for a number of years. Possibly his best known effort was the channeling of Maitreya at the *Conclave of Michael*, a meeting of some 800 Lightworkers which was held in Banff, Canada during March, 1994. About 200 were present at that channeling, and all felt enlightened by what occurred. We, Jan and Dave Moore, were privileged to be at that particular channeling, as well as at fifty-seven of the channelings represented in this book. We have heard many channelers all over the world. It is our opinion that Erik has been able to channel without interference from his own ego to an extent which is superior to many channelers whom we have heard. As mentioned in the *Introduction*, all channelers, even the trance channelers, probably have to have a part of themselves present as they channel, else there would be no reason for their service. One problem which this introduces is that the ego of the channeler can interfere with the message being channeled. The editor sees a remarkable divorce of ego-involvement in the channelings of Erik Myrmo.

It has been my pleasure to compile and edit these channelings. I have learned while being involved in this project, and I have felt myself to be enlightened at each editing session. In fact, one problem in working on these channelings was the tendency to feel myself being pulled into them by their extraordinary power. Since that would interfere with my third-dimensional editing, I would have to reluctantly pull myself back.

I sincerely hope you have similar feelings as you experience the power of these channelings from the Ascended Masters!

INTRODUCTION

Channeling is a greatly misunderstood phenomenon, for some very religious people reject it without realizing that most religions have been based on channeled information. As one example, if the Bible is the inspired word of God, then it was channeled information which served as its basis, for the teachings were not handed directly to a third-dimensional being. Instead, the revered ones heard the voice of God or the voice of the Holy Spirit and, therefore, served as a channel for God's information. Many people served in this capacity. Among the many are names such as Noah, Abraham, Moses, Isaiah, Mary and others, not the least of whom were the Disciples at Pentecost. As another example, the Koran could be considered channeled information, for it is believed to have been dictated to Muhammad directly from God. Further, the enlightenment of Buddha was given during a meditative trance similar to that in which modern channelers are given information. Finally, the spirit religions of the Americas are based on stories channeled to the elders by the departed spirits. Consequently, channeling has been an integral part of mankind's religious experience.

Modern channeled information generates different reactions in different people. Some people of the New Age tend to accept all channeling as being a presentation of truth to which they subscribe. Others of the New Age accept some channeling, but reject other channeled information by using their discernment to decide what to accept and what to reject. Most of the general population know very little about channeled information; and some who have studied it, reject it out-of-hand.

But what, specifically, is channeling or channeled information? The Royal book [see *Appendix E*] defines channeling as *"the process of receiving communication from an infinite number of dimensional realities. The communication can be expressed via writing, verbal relay, artwork, music composition, and any creative expression."* In this definition, Royal implies that the "dimensional realities" could be angels, or nature spirits, or extraterrestrials, or discarnate entities, or "Ascended Masters," with this term referring to those who have ascended to another dimension from the third-dimensionality of planet Earth. This ascension is said by some to occur during the sixth initiation of that entity. On page 27 of his book [see *Appendix E*], Joshua David Stone describes the sixth initiation; and on page 275 he lists specific numbers of Ascended Masters by saying:

"As of September 1994 there were five hundred Ascended Masters on the surface of Planet Earth who had completed their ascension...[and] another three hundred ... in the hollow Earth. There is a grand total of somewhere between one thousand eight hundred and two thousand five hundred Ascended Masters if you include the etheric Ascended Masters who no longer retain physical vehicles.... Melchizedek told us that there would be approximately 30,000 Ascended Masters on the planet by the year 2000...[and] after the year 2000, there is the potential for this number to jump at a much larger rate."

Since most channelers tend to agree that some of the "dimensional realities" mentioned as the communicative source by Royal are the Ascended Masters mentioned by Stone, then if Stones's numbers are correct, this would account for the significantly increased amount of channeled information which is being received by those via this medium. Stone's numbers also confirm a significant increase in humanity's awareness, a belief which is echoed strongly in many of the channelings presented in this book.

The Young-Sowers book [see *Appendix E*] has been considered a classic of the channeling literature since it first appeared in 1984. In the Preface, the author says:

"The book Argatha *is the chronicle of my extraordinary dialogues with an angelic messenger of the Divine, a spiritually-evolved mentor whose guidance is meant to give us hope that by choosing love rather than chaos*

in our daily lives, we forever alter the course of human history and create love rather than chaos on the Earth."

Whether the "angelic messenger" of *Argatha* is an Ascended Master is a moot point, for whether an Ascended Master or an angel, either would represent one of the "dimensional realities" mentioned by Royal.

As a final point of interest about those who generate information for the channelers to bring through, on page 19 of the Westen book [see *Appendix E*] there is a quotation by Thomas A. Edison. On October 20, 1920, he was quoted by *Scientific American* as saying:

"If our personality survives, then it is strictly logical and scientific to assume that it retains memory, intellect, and other faculties and knowledge that we acquire on this earth. Therefore, if personality exists after what we call death, it's reasonable to conclude that those who leave this earth would like to communicate with those they have left here."

Therefore, one of America's most noted scientists has stated that if you believe in life after death, then it is not difficult to believe that the departed one would try to present information to you. They would also, therefore, be a part of the "dimensional realities" mentioned by Royal, for they no longer are of an Earth-level dimension but are real in another dimension.

There is a remarkable similarity between this statement of Edison's and an explanation of faith which is presented in the *New Catholic Encyclopedia* [see *Appendix E*]. On page 471 of Volume 13 of this very orthodox encyclopedia, it is stated:

"The existence of the soul after death does not contradict the belief that the soul did not exist before birth, since after death the soul retains previously acquired knowledge, a transcendental relation to matter, and even a certain exigency to be united with matter."

It would seem that a soul which retains its knowledge and has an urgent need to be united with matter is exactly the kind of source which would speak to us through a channel. It would, therefore, seem that one of America's greatest scientists and one of its most orthodox religious publications would agree that the departed souls of those who have recently left us represent a possible source for the communication of information to us.

If this descriptive material helps to understand where the channeled information comes from, then the next question is probably,

"Who can be a channel for this information?" In his excellent book, *The Seat of the Soul*, Gary Zukav [see *Appendix E*] describes how humanity has used "external power" in the past, and how it is now moving toward "authentic power" as a part of our evolutionary process. He describes "external power" in a number of ways, one of which is the domination of another by a variety of techniques. He describes "authentic power," on the other hand, as being a humble experience, based totally on internal love and including no domination whatsoever. Zukav states that our conversion from external power to authentic power is happening by our leaving behind the physical world as our sole means of evolution. By this effort, we will be evolving from "five-sensory humans" into "multi-sensory humans." What Zukav means is that although in the past we have felt that reality exists only in that which we can see, hear, smell, taste or touch by our using our five physical senses, in the future it will be a common occurrence to determine reality by utilizing senses other than the five physical ones. In developing these other senses, we will become multi-sensory humans.

Those who channel communications from other "dimensional realities" are using senses other than their five physical senses. They are some of the ones who are becoming multi-sensory, or multi-dimensional humans.

Dr. Norma Milanovich is a noted channel, and a personal friend. In the Spring 1996 edition of *Mount Shasta's Directory* [see *Appendix E*] she gave a long interview about channeling. In this interview, she stated that her first channeled information came from Tracy, a niece who had just died. This is similar to the source mentioned by Edison above and is a very distinct possibility of a post-death soul activity as described by the orthodox Catholic viewpoint as mentioned above. Tracy introduced Norma to fifth-dimensional beings known as the Arcturians, which then led to Norma's classic book of channeling, *We, The Arcturians, A True Experience* [see *Appendix E*]. As she followed the directions from these beings, she reached a certain frequency that allowed her to be introduced to the Ascended Masters, especially Kuthumi whom she has channeled for several years. During 1996, she is due to be introduced to beings of light known as the Ancient Gods and Goddesses, and will receive information pertaining to futuristic concepts not presently on this planet. In this way, she has progressed up the frequency steps toward dimensions beyond the first stages of Zukav's multi-sensory human.

Dr. Milanovich says that everyone can be and is a channel, for most of what is said on a regular basis is actually divinely inspired through connection to our higher self even though we might not be conscious that this is so. This belief is also presented by Erik Myrmo in a later paragraph. Further, Dr. Milanovich states that the channeling skill can be pushed a bit further with a conscious awareness that we are connected to a higher mind through which we are able to bring this information. And finally, it is her belief that channeling is a part of the Journey we take to understand the real power we have within us. As an example, Dr. Milanovich feels that through this process she has developed the ability to travel interdimensionally, to access Ascended Masters and to access information. None of this would have been possible as a five-sensory human.

And so, channeling is a skill which everyone has whether they realize it or not. In addition, it is a skill which can be further developed. Finally, in that development it can lead to additional skills not associated with humans who remain convinced that the five physical senses are all that is ever available to them.

Those who channel are generally divided into two types of channelers: trance channelers and conscious channelers. The difference is that a trance channel feels that he/she is completely absent and remembers nothing of the communications; whereas a conscious channeler is conscious of all that occurs during the channeling. A conscious channeler may feel that he/she is outside the physical body watching what is happening, but is, nevertheless, aware of the communications that have transpired.

On March 26, 1996, before the actual channeling started, Erik Myrmo said the following:

"Some of you may have some questions about channeling. What most people view as channeling is that someone with a given name comes in, takes over, and presents energy or information or whatever. That is not my experience of channeling. It may be the experience of other people, but for me, my experience is that I am fully present and I am conscious of everything that is going on even when the energy is working through me. I

tend to believe that this is true for all information that comes through in this way. I feel that there is always a funneling through the person. That is why you cannot ask, "What is going to be the level of the stock market in five days?" Maybe that answer is not appropriate to give or maybe I just do not have the clarity to allow that to come through. That is why, at least in this stage of myself, I could not sit here and channel in a foreign language because I would not be able to let that come through. So, you would like to think that channeling is perfectly clear information from another source, but it definitely comes through me and it is subject to my limitations. Are there any questions about that?

Is there a band that you particularly channel from? *That is an interesting question. All of us are multi-dimensional beings. We span from our physicality to our God-consciousness which is that part of ourselves that sits with unmanifest God. And so we span all bands. Therefore, any of us can bring in any information or energy or whatever from any level throughout creation. In fact, I would like to propose something that may seem a little strange. I would suggest that <u>everybody in this room is a channel</u>. What that means is that you are always channeling who you are, because what you see in your physicality is just a part of who you are. And so when you see this part of who you are expressing all of these multi-dimensional concepts, you are really channeling you. It is no different from what I am doing. You do it every day. That is a strange concept isn't it? But really that is what it is all about—everybody being who they are, being you, being conscious and being conscious in all those dimensions in which you exist, or at least which you are conscious of at this time. But you do definitely exist in all of them. Maybe we should just all channel together! [Laughter]"*

Before a channeling session on May 28, 1996, Erik Myrmo said the following:

To me, channeling is something that everybody does. I look at it as a cooperative venture. As individuals, we are working with not only ourselves but with other humans and the Earth and the animals and the living species on the planet as well as God-energies and soul-energies that are not necessarily in physical form. Just because we have a physical body, that does not mean that other energies and beings do not reside here. There are angels and other members of the Devic kingdom who are all around us and participating in this experience with us, but we don't normally see them or communicate with them in a waking way. A part of our evolution at this time is to be more aware and to experience their presence in a really conscious way. Channeling is one way to do that.

In a channeling on November 6, 1995, a blend of the energies of Maitreya and St. George gave the following statement about the information they present through a channeler. This statement is repeated in context in Chapter Eight.

"I may sometimes present a semantic problem in the clarity of my speech because each ear hears differently and each ear needs to hear differently. As a result, the words that are chosen are due to the audience as well as the ability of the channel that the words come through. Remember that every experience of channeling includes the experience of the person who is providing the vehicle for the channeling. No consciousness leaves the vehicle for another to come in and fill that body, because this is like kidnapping and this is not allowed. Even for those who are trance channels, their channeling is a shared participation, and the vehicle is very present. Although some may not think so, they are always very present. The need for their physicality is not only to allow the channeling to occur, but also for the education and advancement of the channel.

It is because the words may mean different things to different people that the clarity will always vary from what you hear, and what you know within yourself is right for you. Believe me, the Masters will be more than happy to provide you with every information you need to fulfill your balancing act of energy. In other words, if you wish to hear from a Master something which leads you on your merry way away from your purpose because that is what you need to accomplish to come into balance, it will be provided. I guarantee it! We will just channel that information right in so that what you need to learn in the most purposeful way will be available. That is why you must always check within yourself to know, and not automatically accept everything that is channeled to you; for you cannot give away your responsibility of clarity within yourself. You must always know within yourself.

I will give you the truth that is best for you as an experience, but you must understand that truth is subjective. Truth for one is not truth for another. You might then ask, "Are there absolute truths?" Well, there is always a deeper truth; but since God is creating anew each moment, then truth is being created as we speak. I can now hear some saying, "Oh, this spoils my conception of the grand truth of the universe!"; but the truths of God are ever-present, ever-available, and as loving and as magnificent as you ever imagined them to be. But just as it is a challenge to know what God is at any moment because God is ever-growing, it is also a challenge to understand a greater basis of truth. For even in your total clarification of your spiritual being in your physical body to where God is manifest here and now, that is just the beginning. That is just to get the motor running!

There is a grand plan for humanity in which you have a great part to play if you so choose. Many of you will not, because you did not come here to experience that. You came to help quick-start this planet and then to leave. Perhaps an entirely new dimension is where you will next be challenged to increase your vessel of God. But whatever you do next, the experience of love which is in this physicality is something that will expand your vessel of Light and Love, and is something that you will always take with you. Love has a quality in physicality that is not felt in other dimensions. So what you gain in this life is a rich reward, for when you take your body into other dimensions, there will be those who will say, "Tell me, please tell me about it." You will have experience that others do not have; for Love not only has a special quality in this dimension, it is felt according to the magnitude of the vessel you create for it. That is why you are here. The reward is so great and if any channeling helps you to realize this, then that channeling has served a very great purpose. But always remember to check within to know for yourself whether the channeler is relating a truth that is a truth unto you. That is very important!"

And so, in this portion of the *Introduction*, we have tried to present some thoughts on channeling: what channeling is, what the source of the channeled information is, what a channel is, and how the channeling experience benefits not only the audience, but also the channeler. Finally, we have attempted to give an indication of the channeling process from the source's viewpoint. With the exception of the channeled information presented above, all of the other information on channeling presented so far in this *Introduction* has been generated by third-dimensional people through their books, articles or speeches.

The following is a different kind of introduction. It is an introduction as presented by an Ascended Master in response to a specific request in a private channeling session with Erik Myrmo. The being who speaks is one who has been with all of the editing and other work put into the book to date. His introduction to the book is as follows:

I pose a question unto you which is, "What is that which is most often missing when experiencing the energy of God-self?" The most dramatic missing element of these experiences is the feeling of being comfortable, because the question in the back of many minds is, "If I were in this energy all of the time, how could I hold my life together, and how could I function in the every-day world?" Often it is hard enough just to be in this energy, and so I state the missing element as "being comfortable," with that term meaning an every-day experience that is peaceful and familiar. The gift of familiarity is one of the gifts that is happening at this time. It is a shift in degrees of energy consciousness so that the energies are integrated in a way which feels odd and yet is still functional. As familiarity develops, the energetic feeling of the God-self will soon become quite ordinary.

That will also happen when individuals read this book. Some may read it to gain knowledge, but the true nature of those who come to this book will be those who are wishing transformation. This book is living transformational energy. Those who allow themselves to be in their created experience by virtue of being with the energy upon these pages will become transformed. They will be one with God! Whether it is many people or only a few is not relevant. What is relevant is the transformation energy of those who allow it to be their created experience. It is not the Masters who do it for them, it is they as a Master who comes forward to participate with a group of Masters in mutual evolution of their consciousness and multi-dimensional awareness.

The lessons of this book are the lessons of life. Those who come to feed upon these pages will create opportunities in their life for expansion of their being. There is no set pattern for this expansion, just as there is no set pattern to life. Each is a constantly created experience. The words and energies within this book will allow one to open to the fullness of God that is available to them, and they will know that they are not alone. They have often felt alone, but there will be no mistake for those who come to this energy that there is help in the universe for them.

And so as they read these pages, soon they will say, "I say unto myself these very words," for self-creation is the recognition of self in all things, the recognition of Christ in oneself.

We support self-creation. Self-creation is God-creation. Whatever be the result of individual creativity, and the experience in awareness, it is for fulfillment of All That Is, for All That Is has given permission for all of Itself to create consciously, whatever path is chosen. There is always an avenue of God-consciousness open to all that is of God. One of the purposes of this book is to provide some road signs and some avenues that would turn one to the recognition of this God-consciousness avenue for themselves. It is not for me or any other aspect of God to preach to another. It is merely to work in service and fulfillment of the energy of God that moves in manifest reality.

And so it is that this work was created. It has been created in fulfillment of this desire and shall reach those who would humbly come to themselves and say, "God, I love you, and God, **I am ready to be you!***"*

Are you saying that this book does a service for humanity and should be published? *You know the answer to this because of what it has done for you! What it has done for you, it will do to others who merely touch the book. My* [i.e. Kuthumi's] *energy will be in every page and in every book. Maitreya's energy will be on every page and in every book. Sananda's energy will be on every page and in every book. There is a grand learning opportunity for those who will take the time to read such a complicated dissertation. The reason that so much of it is complicated is that it is purposeful that the mind will have difficulty at times, for when the mind has a little difficulty, then in a very loving manner we move in to help. It is unfortunate that the mass of humanity is not yet ready to feel the energy of the pages, but it will have a profound effect on those who will take the time, and it will be perfect for those who do so. Even if it is but one person, which has already been accomplished, it has been a worthwhile effort.*

CHAPTER ONE
ASCENSION

INTRODUCTION

Humanity has constantly looked to the heavens as a source of inspiration for its fondest dreams. In the earliest parts of our recorded history, the stars presented a chaotic picture to humanity. Then an enterprising human grouped the stars into pictures or constellations in order to generate some sort of order out of the chaos. Later, as humanity developed its insight into the orderly motion of many heavenly bodies through these constellations, the earlier thoughts of a chaotic universe were replaced by an understanding that the heavens were very orderly indeed—possibly even more orderly than Earth. This led to an increasing belief in "something" which was greater than man, for this "something" had created the heavenly bodies and had placed them into such an exact order that they would continue to return to a certain position as a function of "time." That "something" which was so powerful and mysterious, was called "God."

Although this description of pre-history is not the only way that humanity could have gained its first knowledge of God, it is one possibility. But in whatever way the concept of God dawned upon humanity, God was always "out there"; for God was always unreachable—as unreachable as the stars. Nevertheless, humanity continued to worship that unreachable God, that Being which was so powerful that He had created all things. After the continued passage of time, stories started to develop about those who had become great during their sojourn on Earth, so great that God had called them to be at His right hand. But since the only way to reach God was to go "out there," it was said that these great Earth beings had "ascended," because they had risen in order to be accepted into the presence of God. Before long, some of those who had "ascended" became worshipped in a manner very similar to that which previously had been reserved only for God.

Such a procedure has been repeated many times in many different religions. As one example, although the prophet Muhammad never was worshipped as a God, Islamic tradition states that he made his ascent to heaven from the rock in Jerusalem upon which Solomon's Temple previously had stood. Therefore, he became a specific "ascended one," believed in by those of Islam. As another example, the Christian Church teaches that Jesus Christ made his ascent into heaven on the fortieth day after his resurrection, and that he ascended from the mount called Olivet near Jerusalem [Acts, Chapter 1]. He became a specific ascended one believed in by those of Christianity. Other ascensions which are reported in the Bible are those of Enoch [Gen. 5:24], Melchizedek [Hebrews 7:3], Elijah [2 Kings 2:11], and Lazarus [Luke 16:22-3]. In Zoroasterism, the morning of the fourth day is the most sacred time in the death ritual of one who has left life, for this is the time when the departed soul ascends to meet Ahura Mazda in heaven. Many other examples from many other religions could be cited; and even the concept of Nirvana in Buddhism is thought to be beyond any terms of finite experience of human life, for its reality transcends the realm of birth and death and is, therefore, "out there."

But of all the religious or spiritual practices, possibly the "New Age" is most attuned to ascension; for one of the major beliefs of this non-uniform system of beliefs is the acceptance of a large number of "Ascended Masters." These beings are those who have gathered so many experiences into their "vessel of experience" that they have "ascended" to dimensions outside of the dense, third-dimensional physical plane upon which humanity presently exists.

Most belief systems which accept ascension do so because they believe that Earth is a place of learning, and that to come into the presence of God, we must pass the tests of this life. A basic concept of Hinduism is that we are trapped in the physical and are required to go through a series of incarnations until the cycle of birth-death-rebirth is broken by disinterested action, true knowledge and intense devotion to God. The Cathars [or Albigenses] also believed that they were trapped in the same physical cycle of birth-death-rebirth, but that through the personal [as opposed to church] worship of Jesus Christ, the cycle could be broken. The Church committed genocide against them for this belief. The Buddhists also feel that they are trapped in the physical, but believe that the enlightenment which comes from practices such as following the Four Noble Truths and the Eightfold Path will lead them out of their entrapment. Manichaeism, a third century Near East religion, believed that the physical world was evil and could be escaped only by coming into a spiritual existence by obtaining special knowledge. In this belief, they were similar to the Gnostics of the first and second centuries. In more recent times, Christianity and Islam accept life on Earth as a "training ground" for spiritual advancement; and so does the New Age. Although this discussion could go on and on, these few examples would serve to make the point that many religions tend to consider Earth to be only a "stepping stone" to something which is on an ascended level from Earth.

Another major point to be made is that in all of these cases, it is believed that physicality is a "lower order," and that from this lower state, we are to rise up or ascend to something higher. In the belief system of Christianity, that ascension would happen only after the "second coming of Christ" at which time the resurrection of all faithful bodies would occur. In the belief system of the New Age, ascensions are being made from this lower state to a higher dimension at all times, and many formerly physical beings have already ascended. In Christianity, and in much of the New Age, ascension is generally considered to be a one-time, somewhat spectacular event. It could be called a "giant leap forward," and once ascension has occurred, the conscious being is forever changed. Some channelers of the New Age have said that there will be waves of ascensions during which many will "go up" all at once; others have said that it will be an individual occurrence. No one knows with certainty which will happen, for that event is still being created. Most channelers have indicated that physicality is a stage to get through, and that it is not as desirable as the higher stages to come; and many New Agers tend to accept the belief that ascension will lead us to some place "out there."

These channelings paint a somewhat different picture. Their message is more nearly that of "humanity is in spirit on Earth to seek a physical adventure" rather than being that of "humanity is in physicality on Earth to seek a spiritual adventure." In this way, ascension would be more nearly an "in here" experience rather than an "out there" one. One channeling [see Channeling 52 on pages 31-3] even states that this Earth experience is the culmination, rather than the beginning, of our journey. Excerpts from some of those channelings are presented in the following section.

CHANNELED INFORMATION
Kahil Gibran, Channeling 6 [8/3/92]

Your process of ascension is merely removing the detours from the experience of self. When you ascend, you have merely enabled the consciousness of three dimensional living to travel beyond the first exit. When viewed from a cosmic perspective, ascension is the baby standing up and beginning to walk, for there is much beyond what we see and experience in third-dimensional life. It is easy for you to look at a child and understand that to walk, the child must merely stand up and move one foot after another in balance, in direction of intent for a specific purpose. That is what we all are doing in our various experiences. We are learning to walk, cosmically. As you find your walk, clearly walk with divine intent in balance and in the direction of your divine purpose. You, as the child who physically walks, are merely walking in greater energy.

From that perspective, a divine being in ascension is merely following Divine Will at all times. There is no separation between your intent and divine intent on the conscious level. You discern at each moment that which is your divine guidance. There is no battle between your personal self and your divine self. There is no questioning, for you are in perfect alignment with divine self.

You get to that state by responding to your divine guidance at every moment. How often during each day and each moment do you battle between that which you know is your divine guidance, and that which your personality wishes to experience? How often do we follow the personality when our core impulse is to allow the divine to move within us?

In concept, ascension is very simple. It is merely being the divine being that you are. In practice, it takes constant healing and clearing of those aspects that we have created which are not balanced and in alignment with spiritual self. We created some of these imbalances for the experience, and others because the world was not quite ready for thousands and thousands of Ascended Masters to appear at one time. And so, as Ascended Masters, some chose to forget; whereas others placed imbalances in order to ripen at the perfect time. Each is ripening and coming into balance in perfect order. Every aspect of self that is not of divine, creative impulse will come to your remembrance, will come to your understanding for balance. When balance is there, ascension is automatic.

Blend of Energies, Channeling 7 [8/17/92]

Is it not time to acknowledge your mastery? There is not one here who could not ascend by a step-by-step procedure of coming into the wholeness of your divine being. And yet, you will hear the words of Melchizedek who has said "From the level of the divine, ascension is like the toddler who stands up and walks," for there are grand universes and experiences beyond your ascension. The ascension is your entry requirement to those experiences. It is your ticket at the gate. But know you are the ticket-taker, and you are also the gate.

Think of those things from your heart and know that there is no separation that you did not create. Therefore, there is no separation that you cannot remove. However, in the physical it takes time to manifest changes; and if you have generated changes which were not in the desired direction, it may take time to remove those particular manifestations, whether they be fears, issues, or physical properties. It is those things which have created the separation in consciousness between your divine self and your conscious self and which prohibit your ascension. You put them there. You can take them away, and all it requires is willingness and intention and consistent application of the laws of healing and balance. It is really quite simple to ascend.

Serapis Bey, Channeling 9 [8/31/92]

I am who you have known as Serapis Bey. I have come to work with the energies of ascension; for a major reason why you are on this planet at this time is to work with the energy of ascension. Ascension is a natural by-product of your spiritual evolution.

There is nothing unusual about ascension. In fact, it will be quite commonplace in short order. Throughout the history of this planet, many beings have ascended. Some who came to demonstrate the process of ascension, ascended with a very small amount of experience in this realm. Others came to go to the depths of human experience, and through their love, they, too, gained their ascension.

The energies on this planet are now such that we again can have numerous ascensions. This is not the first time the energies have supported tremendous ascension possibilities; for there were times on this planet when the energies were quite conducive and the mass consciousness accepted ascension as the normal path of going and coming. It is only in man's ignorance that ascension has ever been forgotten.

You can make an analogy. In going from one room to another, the natural thing to do would be to open the door and to walk from one room to the other. Mankind has forgotten how to open that door; and so it searches for every other possible means to go into the next room, often taking apart the wall piece by piece without knowing there is a door.

How many times in your learning have you realized there was an easier way than the one you took? That does not mean the method of your evolvement is incorrect. Instead, it is always perfect for many of you to have chosen to experience the density of those walls and to experience the process to uncover your visions of possibilities.

Ascension is a natural state of where you currently are. You are already an ascended being, but you do not realize this because there resides within your body only a portion of your total consciousness. It is a portion that you have sent forth to learn and to grow by gaining the experiences of this realm. You have done this without remembering that there is a greater, a more divine aspect of your self beyond the human consciousness. The question now becomes: How does one attain that recognition of the ascended being that you are? I will suggest the following twelve step process:

1. Recognition of who you are;	7. Balance;
2. Intention;	8. Nowness;
3. Diligence;	9. Empowerment;
4. Attention;	10. Wisdom;
5. Allowance;	11. Beingness; and
6. Healing;	12. Integration

Recognition of who you are is the first step. You are a divine being, and a part of you is much greater than the human consciousness that often dwells alone. The **intention** of coming to full recognition means you fully become the creator God that you are by bringing forth all of your experiences and **diligently** accepting your recognition, intention and lessons; for ascension takes **attention** on each moment's lesson. There are no exceptions. Every aspect of your moment-by-moment experience is teaching you, guiding you and loving you back to fullness with your **allowance**; for without **allowance** of that which is brought to you, **healing** does not take place. To be more than you are, you have to **allow** it to be so, and not block it with your emotions or your neglect of the physical.

If you **allow** the energy of your being to come forth, you will be **healed**, which leads to the **balance** between your spiritual and your humanness, for they are both of great value. Your human experiences represent the expansion of what God is. When balanced, **nowness** comes forth; for in your true self, there is no living in what was or what will be, for what **is**, is all there is. There is nothing else. Being in the nowness generates **empowerment**, for there is no power that can overcome your divine intention so long as it is empowered with the **wisdom** of understanding the dangers of power without wisdom and love. Therefore, **you will not allow your empowerment until you are wise**, for you have had the experience of power without wisdom and now you know that to be wise and powerful is **balance**, so long as love is the engine of power and the crucible of wisdom. These three, in balance, in the now, create the **beingness** of being who you are: wise, powerful, loving and unique. You are a unique being in this experience, just as a wave has its unique quality as it breaks upon the shore. However, the unique wave is a part of the ocean, and you are also one with the ocean of divinity. There is nothing that is apart from your mental, emotional, physical, or spiritual grasp, because it has been **integrated** at a speed beyond measure. And it is just not the integration of your divine self, but it is the integration of all that is; for you are never apart from the ocean of divinity.

In **integration**, it is the integration of you with the ocean of your divine self that occurs; and with the integration of your divinity, all that you are comes forth. After you are integrated, you can consciously create, divinely. If it is your ascension that you wish to create at that time, it is so. It is now. It is perfect. But if it is another wave of uniqueness that has forgotten the ocean, then that also will be perfect; for you are a creator being, a divine creator being, choosing your experiences.

Ascension is the result of each of these steps integrated together. It is not something unique or different from the **nowness** of you. So, in your **healing** call forth all that you are, and as you ascend to great heights, always look to your divine state for guidance, for you will be tested at many points along this path. And, who is the tester? The tester is **you**, for in your wisdom, you know that you need the fullness of balance in order to take the next step.

You may call upon the ascension flame at any time and I, Serapis Bey, will be there. The ascension flame will help with each of the states of progress. Merely by calling upon it, there will be divine attunement of your bodies with your ascended body. With each of the steps, pay diligent attention; and call upon the ascension flame to come forth and it will heal. It will be my greatest pleasure to do so.

Kuthumi, Channeling 21 [3/15/93]

If you master the moment, you will ascend. Of this I can promise you. You are all great masters ready for divine expression at all times. However, once in a while we have to come to shake you up so that you remember, and so that you do not tend to get too comfortable in your information gathering. You have been given the keys to mastery. They are to love God, to love yourself and to love your neighbor. Further, you are to be in discernment and not in judgment. Finally, you are to heal yourself in awareness of self. Is it not simple? But it is the myriad creations of humanity that have made it difficult. Walk through your fears for they are illusions. Overcome your doubts for they are false barriers. Nothing is worth losing your Soul. And I warn you that in your energy space, the karmic result of mis-creation is great. For the one great responsibility which comes with your increased energy of divinity is the responsibility of using that energy within Divine Will.

Blend of Energies, Channeling 12 [10/5/91]

There is no limitation on who you are. There is no real separation from your divine self. You are an ascended being. I have only come to remind you of what you already are. There is no mystery of life in your heart. The mysteries are evidenced in the mind and in the emotions. There is no mystery in love, for love seeks not but itself. Love seeks no return and shines unconditionally upon all who would receive it. You are love. As you walk from your heart space you realize that you carry this energy and consciousness, wherever you go. There is never a separation unless you choose it to be so. Make your choices wisely for they determine the magnitude of your expression of your divine self. Enjoy the loving comfort of who you are.

Keeper of the Light, Channeling 10 [9/14/92]

In the perception of human consciousness, there is the sense of separation. In truth, there is no separation between your physical consciousness and that of your higher dimensional consciousnesses; or between your physical body and that of your higher dimensional bodies. It is an illusion you have created in order to experience a slowed-down reality. And so, the integration of yourself in multiple dimensions culminates in what has been termed "ascension." What has often been misunderstood is that there is more than the ascension of the physical. There is ascension beyond the ascension of the physical, for there are levels above the fifth dimension. Most who will be ascending from physicality will be going to the fifth dimension. The fourth dimension is one you are all quite familiar with already, for you visit there often; and since a part of your reality exists in the fourth dimension, there is no need to stop there. What I refer to as ascension beyond the physical is, indeed, the movement and integration of higher dimensions beyond the fifth dimension. The true knowing you have of your experiences is difficult to put into the perception of third-dimensional words, but it is real; and whatever level is experienced as you experience your energy of self, your perception may go as far as you allow it to. For above the use of words, the mind needs to walk the perception of the level which has been experienced.

Christ Consciousness, Channeling 11 [9/28/92]

Ascension is merely the walking through the doorway into divine self for all time from the physical, unless at some later moment you would choose to again return to the physical for a divine purpose of service. Many of you made that choice, for you chose to come here to be of service. Since you are ascended beings, this will not be the first time you have ascended.

It is time to recognize the scope of your dimensionality; for you came to show the way for humanity to be in consciousness of God. When you came here, you had to allow a forgetting of all that you are for the world was not yet ready for your "allness." You have all done quite well, not only in your forgetting, but in your remembering. Some have forgotten a little bit more than, perhaps, was planned; but that is OK for you can never lose what you have gained. Instead, you can only reach new experiences.

What does this mean as a divine Ascended Master hiding out in limitation? Well, you can no longer hide, for you have exposed yourself as an Ascended Master ready to step back into your ascended state. We hear the minds of many saying, "Oh, my goodness, how could I possibly ascend? I have all of these issues." Believe me, you do not realize how close you are. It is like putting on a raincoat and then when the rain stops and the sun is ready to shine, all you have to do is unzip it and take it off. That is how easy it will be at the time of your ascension. So why the struggle, the issues, and the pain before then? It is because you are learning new things. In every new experience, there is expansion which will make you a greater ascended being than you were before; for what humans do not realize is the extent of the growth that occurs upon this planet. It is easy to be divine when everything goes your way as it does in other places. How easy is it to be divine when it seems like nothing goes your way? If you can bring your divinity into the darkness that is here, then you have broken new ground in the expansion of what the divine is.

Be prepared. You do not know at what time I or another will call to you and will say "Come, dear child. It is your time." At that time you will be lifted up by the love of your own being into your self for the greater expression of who you are. Do not think that it is a long time away. Be prepared each day as if it were your day.

Do you see the ascension, in your point of view, as in waves, as some channels speak of three waves, or do you see it as more individual? There may be individual ascensions for there are those who have fulfilled such great light that it will be the honor of the divine to assist their ascension individually. There will also be waves, for the wave of ascension is a blissful energy wave that will circle the planet. It will raise up many to have the clarity of their ascension. At that time, they will make their choice to ascend or to remain.

The number of waves is not yet determined, but it will be a divine number. Three represents a probable occurrence, but let me state that this is not absolute. This has not been predestined to occur in an exact fashion. It is created anew each moment. So those who would say it would occur in this way are seeing what is currently created, and that may change in the next moment. The divine energies that determine what is to occur move in the way in which the space for that energy has been created; and, at this time, there has been enough light manifested into this dimension to allow the ascension of a great number of the population of this planet. As those who have prepared themselves begin to ascend, it will create even more light and will, again, change the number and the method of the following ascensions. So it is not absolute. It is created evermore, for the divine is ever expanding and ever changing.

Kuthumi, Channeling 38 [11/7/94]

There has been much interest of late in the physical body, for all of a sudden people have remembered that the physical body has to come along this time. How often has it been the philosophy to reach God by escaping the physical body? This is no longer allowed. Now you must take the physical with you as you ascend. In times past, the vibrational quality around the planet was such that it was extremely difficult to spiritualize the physical body. That is why so many disciplines worked so hard to move out of it. You might say it was enlightenment without ascension, for if you leave the physical body, you leave a part of you behind. The body is Divine Self. How many look upon the body in the morning and say, "Hello, Divine Self, aren't you beautiful today?" It would be advantageous to do so.

Ascension has become commonplace in thought, and you have been told that ascension is occurring, not only within mankind, but upon the planet itself. I would venture to say that the present ascension process is much more than that. There are legions of beings upon this planet not in three dimensional form who are also ascending from their dimension; for ascension is not a three dimensional experience. It is evolution. It is movement from one form to another. It is movement within the vibration of God. And so, accept the great enjoyment of caring for the physical body, the great attention to health and quality of life within this body, for it is a part of you. It is a part of you which must go along in order to have a full ascension.

St. George, Channeling 42 [2/13/95]

Tonight we have spoken of your being responsible, creative, purposeful, and of living your life fully. To live your life fully does not mean going out and doing wild and crazy things, unless that is your intention and your Divine Will to do so. It means living each moment from fullness; taking the responsibility of your creation; taking the responsibility to create fully in your body and in all else that you are.

Some of you will see the total freedom that comes with full ascension, including the ascension of the physical! But to do so, each moment is important. Each moment is your next opportunity to become fuller in life, for it will take all of you this time. You have said, "Don't let me escape any more. I do not want to leave all my consciousness in my body when I go. I don't want this painful extraction of energy from this flesh." You have said this! So now it is time to integrate it all; for you have said to God, "I only wish to ascend when I am in fullness because I do not want to be in my next stage carrying around all this energy from bodies in past lives." You said that because even though you may have ascended, that burden of carried energy is still with you.

Why do you think so many Ascended Masters are working with you? It is because they need your help to clear their remaining stuff! You put these people on a pedestal in perfection; but they have this stuff still with them, and you are clearing it for them! Why do you think they love you so much? This probably comes as a shock, but I want to tell you that you help me to clear my self. I am willing to love you fully, in all ways, because you help me; for although I have ascended, I ascended with residue that can best be balanced in physicality. It can be done otherwise, but it takes so much more energy. Here on Earth it can happen in a snap. It can be done, but since your physical body cannot withstand the total jolt now, it will happen in stages so that you can continue in your biology. We don't want you to become a little pile of ashes on the floor!

Maitreya, Channeling 41 [2/2/95]

The body is your divine creation, and you have a great vested interest in it as a part of you and as a part of your God-head. It is fully intended that as you created it, you participate with it in all dimensions. This will happen on a regular basis in the coming years, for ascension should not be looked at as a translation or removal from the three dimensional life. That has been the perception in the past because those who have ascended have not come back due to the density in consciousness that often remains upon the third-dimensional planets, particularly this one. During this transitional period, that process will continue for some who are not yet ready to fully energize their body before the body gives out.

However, that is not the path that has been chosen for the future of this planet. Instead, there will be individuals who are here at this time who will fully energize their body with their God-beingness. That means bodies that do not age; bodies that do not have maladies, dislocations, illness; bodies of total freedom; bodies that manifest with the divine imprint within them. These bodies will be what they should be, and may not necessarily be the present form. You will have the ability to create your body for whatever purpose is necessary. As an example, if you were to go forth as a teacher and your form would be better to be different than the image you presently create, you can change that form's image to be what is appropriate at that time. Remember, the body is without limitation. It is only the density of thought and of emotions and of cellular walls and energetics that keep it from being the body that will be. Through your carrying your body with you during these times of energetic awareness, it shall become enlivened to the point that it is totally without limitation. Then it will be capable of ascension in total physicality.

Maitreya, Channeling 51 [2/6/96]

Could you touch briefly on "ascension" and whether or not it is important?" It would be very difficult for me to be brief with "ascension." [Laughter]. Ascension is a subject that will take a great deal of time, and I would like to address this with you at some time; but for now, let me just say that ascension is an every-day, every-moment experience. Ascension is not a point in the future at which you will flash into a ball of light and rise to the heavens and everything will be OK. Ascension is the process of your becoming.

Ascension means, "consciousness being aware of higher realms of being." That is all that ascension is. When a being accepts this, they infuse much light into their body and lift from the planet to move to the heavens. That did not just happen because it was the right time and place. It happened because they had been infusing light into their body every moment until the point that they were done with their experience here. Then their body became lightened and became multi-dimensional, and they moved to express their consciousness in a dimension other than the third dimension. But it was not "the ascension" that is the event. That is after-the-fact. The ascension is the every-moment, every-day experience of ascending— of bringing more and more of yourself into beingness by infusing more and more of your energy into your physicality, into your intellectual being, into your emotional being.

So then our moving from third dimension to fourth dimension and then into fifth dimension, is that part of the ascension process? There is much mis-understanding about moving to dimensions. The root of the thought of mankind and the Earth moving into the fourth and fifth dimensions is the very essence of what has made man try to escape this planet ever since he got here. But you cannot escape this place until you accept it totally. And then you won't escape. You will thank it, and love it, and then move on.

Three dimensions will not cease to exist. But what happens when it becomes a multi-dimensional experience—when it becomes the dimensions of three and four and five and six and so on all blended together? Isn't that a multi-dimensional experience? There is a sixth dimensional being in this room at this time. What do you think that being sees, feels and thinks? Now, if that being is one who had integrated three dimensions in his level of experience to where he was truly a multi-dimensional being, then indeed he could see and be with you in nearly a physical sense and he could become completely physical if the energy required it. But if this being had not integrated third-dimensional experience in his experience, then he could not participate with you in full third-dimensional physicality, for he would have to enter dimensional coupling to experience you on this dimension.

That is why beings will say, "We don't see you in the same way. Your body is different." They say this because they do not have third-dimensional experience integrated into their vessel of experience; and therefore, they cannot totally be in the here and now.

Therefore, what will the Earth experience be like when it is integrated? Will it be that Earth has moved to the sixth dimension, or will it be that the third, fourth, fifth and sixth dimensions are now integrated into a new level of experience that differs because it is a new dimension of experience, multi-dimensional, fully conscious, fully expressed, and fully understood! There are unique factors to this system which have never existed before.

Kuthumi/Maitreya, Channeling 52 [2/20/96]

It is always interesting to see each one of you in this way, because I have seen you before in the way in which you are when you allow your consciousness to be conscious in other dimensions; for many, at their time of sleep, allow their consciousness to flow into a higher dimensional body, a body that is still you. They travel and communicate and go about their business during this time.

Consequently, we often find it amusing to hear so much discussion about how humanity is working so hard to ascend to these higher dimensional existences, for you already exist there. So what is so special about ascending to a place of which you are already so familiar? I say it to you in this way so that you will realize that you are multi-dimensional beings. There is nothing so special about being able to exist on what you would term a higher dimension. In fact, in some ways it would be less special for you, because you are here for a particular reason. You are here for a particular path of creation; and in other levels of dimensional experiences, those particular paths of creation cannot be fulfilled in the way that they can here. That is why you are here.

And so I would like to shake up this whole idea of the "holy-of-holy dimensions" being other than this dimension. This dimension is, in fact, the <u>culmination</u> of creation in those other dimensions! This is true because manifestation is created from God. It comes from that aspect of God that is not in motion. From that reservoir comes the divine potential and intelligence and energy that flows out for a particular probability of creation. As it moves into what you term reality, or manifestation, it takes on form and function and intent and intelligence in all of these dimensions until finally it flows forth in this dimension!

You have heard the words, "as above, so below." Is this not the description of this? It means that all which exists in third-dimensional form has to be supported throughout all dimensionality unto unmanifest God for it even to exist. And so that which exists here exists in all those places. Consequently, this third-dimensional experience is a culmination of creation throughout dimensionality!

This does not mean that all creations in all dimensions exist physically, for there are many creations on different planes that do not necessarily have a physical counter-part. This is because they are not supported in that creative vortex to be third-dimensional. But all that is third-dimensional is supported in all of those other dimensions.

One way of understanding this is to realize that God wills in generalities, and it is created beings who take those generalities and create them, specifically. Who are those God-beings that create so specifically the generalities that come from God unmanifest? It is you! You are not humanity thrown upon the planet to experience the energetic whims of creation. It is you that are the creators! That is why there is so much responsibility in being conscious; for where there is consciousness, there is responsibility. Where there is consciousness, there is creativity and there is creation.

Therefore, you are creator God-beings creating specifically that which is God-intended generally. Is this not the aspect of you that is your Divine Will, the aspect that takes in the energy of God and creates specifically based on the interpretation of your individualized, divine path? And so there is but one true responsibility for humanity, and that is to be aware of your God-intention, and then to act from that. If humanity did but that one responsibility, this would indeed be a paradise of love and light—would it not?

Lord Michael, Channeling 23 [2/22/93]

Do you realize that each and every one of you is meant to be a messiah upon this planet? Well, how far do you have left to go? Be diligent in your discernment, for although the road is sometimes difficult, the reward is great. You are who you are because you have chosen to be here at this time to create life everlasting for yourself in all dimensions.

A wave of ascension is coming. Its time frame has not been firmly established, because it depends upon the developing consciousness of those who are on the planet. This wave of ascension will be an opportunity to ride to your mastery. For some, it will be rather spontaneous because they will have earned that final infusion of consciousness. For others, it will take some time, possibly two to three years before the next wave occurs. Again, when we give references to time, they are not absolute; for time is a variable and it always depends upon creation of consciousness.

You do not have to cleanse each and every point of energy completely before ascension; for the dispensation from the World Council says that grace will lift the remaining imbalances within you at the time of your ascension if you are close enough. You have heard before that it is required that a majority of your imbalances be in balance. This is so, but the ascension will take different amounts of time based upon the percentage of completion of your work. The information you have been receiving on ascension and ascension waves is over-simplified; but if you have balanced a majority of your energy fields, you will ride that wave of ascension. When you ascend, you will carry all the energy that you are to a dimension of your choosing that you are allowed to move to. The physical, mental and emotional bodies are energy that you have created for the purpose of experience in this realm. In ascension, you take that energy with you if you so choose. It is converted to a subtler level of energy, recombined and available for re-manifestation if you so choose.

St. George, Channeling 47 [11/6/95]

Do not feel frustrated because you are not manifesting your God-self completely in your physicality. It is not what you decided to do, *yet!* I have said that you have the power to ascend now if you wish. I have said this to many, because to ascend does not require complete clarity. Ascension is very much over-billed. There are many beings who just wish to ascend. All of their life has been geared toward the wish to ascend. They are missing the point. The point is their Journey. The reason you are here is your **Journey**, not the end-point. When you read a book, do you read the last page first, or do you read the book for the enjoyment of the journey it takes you upon? You are here for the Journey!

You can ascend if you wish, because you have cleared out enough of your karma, you have cleared enough of yourself, and you have allowed enough of your God-head to be present to be able to ascend. But what would happen if you ascended now? You would still have baggage. Guess what happens? It is just like taking a train, and you have your baggage in the baggage compartment. It arrives with you, and that baggage cannot be cleared easily. That baggage is best cleared here, because it is easy, it is fast, it is efficient, and it is fun. Go ahead and clear that baggage now. You don't want to take that unbalanced energy with you. And remember, all of the baggage was not yours when you came. There was some unclaimed baggage which you claimed when you came here.

And so, in your Journey, love the Journey, for it is a great, loving act which you are performing. In the Light of this love, it is time to examine yourself. Has everything in your life been created according to what you are here to create? It is time for your journey to get focused, completely and totally in you—in what you are to create and what you are to be. And that is not easy in this world at this time. But listen within yourself for all guidance and counsel again. And if what I say to you resonates within who you are, if your being inside says **"yes, it is time"** to be completely and totally one with what I am, then do it. Because if you feel it, if you know it, and if you do not act on it, you are denying for yourself the experience you have created for yourself. And if you ascend without fully absorbing that experience, you will have short-changed your Journey!

Unidentified Energy, Channeling 4 [5/16/92]

I will be your teacher for the will of ascension, for only with great determination will the energies magnify to produce actual total physical ascension. Be at peace within yourself. Allow all current issues to be balanced with the energy of healing and transmutation.

With the movement of the ascension energy, every aspect of self that is not of divine resonance is healed, transmuting all that is not of divine idea. The physical is transformed to the divine physical body of your intention, and uplifted into light for conscious multi-dimensional experience. The emotional body is healed so that it envelopes the physical like a light blanket, being the vehicle for divine interpretation for the physical experience. The mental body rises up to the divine intellect, allowing the communication of spirit in a complete and natural way for moving with divine guidance. The lightened body rises up, not for dramatic appeal, but for the demonstration of the overcoming of physical barriers; and for the proof that the bodies of the individual have transcended the limited experience of precious physical existence.

In the transformation, the divine self becomes one with the multi-dimensional light body, allowing the complete direction from Divine Will and the greater expansion of self. As the individual evaluates the results of his creation, even greater amounts of light from the divine source are integrated into the light multi-dimensional bodies. This process continues on, and the creations become greater and greater in order to absorb more energy from the wisdom of divine creation. The ascension of the physical bodies is the first step in the process of becoming greater and greater creating God-beings under the direction of the Mother/Father God.

The energy of the ascension flame interacts with the physical in a most direct way. Each particle of physical energy is made of light. The finer the particle, the greater its resemblance to the light it is created from. The ascension flame unlocks the aspect of the coding that previously only allowed a one-way movement of the light into particles. The ascension flame allows the coding to become two-way, so that the particles can move into pure light energy or move from light energy to particles. An ascended being in physical has the physical structure in both manifestations at the same time. Each movement involves particles moving into light and back into particles. The result is the appearance of physical form, but it has the properties of light. In this way, structures can become immediately invisible, or defy the laws of gravity, or teleport on a light beam to different locations, or even manifest in multiple locations at the same time. The key is the ability of the ascension flame to heal the time-lock of the one-way coding thus permitting instantaneous transformation.

This healing is allowed where the threshold energy of the being is high enough to support the transformation. This is why ascension usually takes place in stages, for too much stress could cause a breakdown of the coding point, thus re-locking the one-way movement. In fact, individuals are constantly healing, re-locking, healing, re-locking in their everyday lives. Now is the time for humanity to understand that the ascended light body is a real possibility for everyone who will allow their energy to remain divinely directed.

As more of the cellular/particle/energy structure is re-coded into free light/physical flow, eventually the threshold is reached when the whole structure may be ascended into the light body. The grace of the divine comes in when this point is close, and reaches down to the calling vessel to aid in the final transformation to divine light energy. Let it be known that nothing is lost in this process, but the integration of divine multi-dimensional experience is gained.

Throughout the ages, divine beings have reached a threshold where Divine Will or Grace has allowed their acceptance into full conscious multi-dimensional experience. It is now time for greater numbers to gain entrance into their divine structure.

At the time that your Divine Will tells you it is time for your full ascension, bring forth the energy of ascension with the following petition:

Let it be known that I petition the Mother/Father God for acceptance of being into the family of ascended beings. With humble heart and will of divine power, I hereby bring forth the divine energy of ascension. The power of the ascension flame now encompasses my entire being, uplifting every cell, molecule, structure into divine state of light energy. The divine light holds the energy of all possibilities, and my physical structure is contained within that energy, ready for physical manifestation at the direction of Divine Will within my being. SO BE IT!

CHANNELED ANSWERS
TO SPECIFIC QUESTIONS

You have said that in previous times there were periods of numerous ascensions. Can you tell us when that was and who it was? When beings first came into form, the veil was almost non-existent and so they could create physical form and ascend at will. They could do this many times each day. They could try physicality and then go back and think about it. The physical forms were not as dense at that time, so ascension was as easy as walking from here to there. That is how physicality was first experienced. It was experienced as an experiment. It was just touched because the spiritual being was just not sure how it would be. This was not on Earth. This was in a system where the third dimension was not so dense.

Can you tell us about Earth? Spiritual beings upon this planet have ascended since the dawn of time. When Earth started into its proper time and environment, spiritual beings came down, but initially they did not create their own bodies. They inhabited physical forms that were present on the planet. Then a split occurred at about this time. Some beings would manifest themselves physically in their light bodies when they came to a physical planet; but there were some who weren't content with that. They wanted to experience physicality more fully. And so they began to inhabit the forms that had been created for the fun of creation. After they experienced that, they would leave. They would not be completely involved. They would not be incarnate. They would just be visiting. In this way they began to experience some of the physicalness of the planet. Then came the time when the beings who were upon the planet evolved to where they were more inhabitable, and the attachment to those forms became more lengthy until a few began to forget that they could leave. In fact, the grand plan did not foresee the strength of fear, and what happened is that the strength of fear overtook the dominate spiritual knowing and started the forgetting process while in physical form.

Was there any consequence to this? What was then experienced was that when they did leave that physical form out of shear fright, or death of that physical form for it could be either, they brought back the energy of that third-dimensional experience. That energy was quite heavy and quite unbalanced. There was no avenue for its balancing in the other dimensions, or at least they thought there was no avenue for balancing. This started the cycle of "we wish to return to clear this heaviness that was so uncomfortable," which became the cycle of birth/death/rebirth. Then these beings, knowing that they were going to be in it for the duration, participated consciously in that illusion of the physical form. They made some mistakes along the way which generated the myths of the part-human forms. The part-human forms were not a myth. They were the reality.

Did these beings come from assorted planets? Originally the beings that came to this planet were from one group. They were the ones that could come in and out of the physical form of their light bodies quite easily and they enjoyed creating the physical forms. Then another group came. They wished to dwell and they became more attached. These beings came from different locations. The original group came from those Lords of Creation who were creating this system. The second group came from a planet who had experienced physical form but wanted more. They wanted to delve deeper into density. They wanted to understand more fully where God could go.

Did this happen during the time before the Sirians and the Orions came? Yes.

Have there been any large number of human ascensions which are more recent than this such as the Anasazies or the Mayas? Not all of those people ascended. There have been times when there have been groups of particular spiritual families which have ascended, some whose bodies died and some who took their physical bodies with them. To take your physical body takes a tremendous amount of ascension energy, and so most ascended without the density of their human form. But in doing that, the energy still has to be reclaimed, and it creates what has been referred to as "baggage." In ascending with the body, you energize all the body, all the karma of the body, and all the experiences of the vessel of three dimensional experience. When that happens it is a grand and glorious event. It is like the birth of a star.

What is the difference between the soul and the vessel of experience? The vessel of experience is contained within the soul. The soul is the manifestation of the spirit in creation to house all the experiences of that spiritual being. It is a part of spirit. It is that part of spirit that is the experiential, that is the embodiment of the spirit in creation.

    What is the soul that the vessel of experience is not? The soul is a structure. It is a multi-dimensional structure that the spirit utilizes in creation. The soul can take that structure totally into unmanifest reality. The vessel of experience is the manifestation of that in creation. The soul can move into or out of unmanifest reality. The vessel of experience is what is created as the soul moves into creation. This is quite a complicated understanding.

    You once said that the soul understood all the experiences the personality <u>has had</u>; the spirit also understands what experiences the personality <u>will have</u>; but the personality knows only what it <u>presently has</u>. Is this an easy synopsis of how those three work together? It is fairly clear and fairly accurate because each is contained within the other. But let me say, as wholeness becomes manifest, those definitions become one. And so, the definitions themselves are a description of separation, and it is important not to dwell on energy forms that reinforce separation.

Do you feel that those of the New Age have a clarity about what ascension means? Despite all of the talk, there is still some lack of clarity on what ascension is. As we have said, ascension is indeed the movement of physical consciousness, for the physical body is physical consciousness and more. Ascension is the infusion into physical consciousness of a wider spectrum of energy and dimensional experience. And so with each healing, with each expansion, with each influx of light, the physical consciousness ascends a little because there is a fuller spectrum, a wider range of consciousness, an enlivened physicalness of that person. And so ascension is a continual process from creation of the body to the time in which full ascension occurs. For example, in one incarnation perhaps full ascension had not been reached, so the physical body dies, but then the physical consciousness is regrouped after the death of the body. This regrouping is not immediate. It is part of a transition which has not been discussed very much. The transition is to recoup consciousness after the physical death, for without full clarity and clear movement, it often takes some time for that energy to be released from the physicalness to the entity. And so ascension is not just of the physical consciousness of this incarnation, it is the ascension of all incarnations upon this physical plane.

That means that this physical incarnation is the culmination of all previous incarnations. If it is within the life purpose of this being to reach full ascension, then it will indeed be just that—full ascension of the physical incarnations of that being represented in this way by this direction of physical consciousness. However, this incarnation is not the sum totality of that being. It is only a portion of that being's energy that is focused into physical consciousness. And so ascension is often looked at as such a major accomplishment of this being, but most of that being is already in an ascended state in the sense that it is not in the physical. Instead it is in a highly energetic spiritual existence. So what is the importance of ascension if it is not such a major graduation of this being?

Is there the possibility that what many have termed "ascension" is what you are terming "full ascension?" Indeed, what has been called ascension is the culmination of ascensions! It is the final result of a continuous movement of ascension to the final act, although I truly hesitate to use the word "final." But it is the transition of the physical body truly into energetic light body in completeness. That is like saying that a long race is merely the crossing of the finish line. The race encompasses the beginning and all that occurs before the finish line. I make this distinction because in thinking of ascension as the final movement of energy, it is as though it is something that is not a part of your experience each and every day. It is something "out there" which is unreachable but which may some day happen if you are a great being. But in truth, each person is already running their race each and every day. It is not a race of competition or time as you might think, but a race according to life purpose. And many races have a different duration. Many individuals like to go around the track thousands of time and others perhaps only once. So what happens after ascension? It is part of the process. What happens after you finish the race and you cross the finish line? Well for many, they decide to run yet another race, perhaps on a different track because they already have experienced that track and know each curve and each obstacle and each movement of the surface.

Is it possible that some who have already won the race might want to go back and run another race on the same track because they know how to do it and they want to return to give additional service to others who are running their race on that track. Indeed, and perhaps they come back in a way in which they have to move quite slowly so they can communicate quite clearly with the others who are moving slowly. *When they do this, are they aware of their previous experience?* Usually they are not. How could you be truly in the role of running the race if you already knew all there was to it. What happens is that your wisdom and experience come through as needed in your running of the new race in order to support that life purpose. Usually that race is run on a different track because there is a phenomenon which occurs when you run the race again on the same track. That phenomenon is that the familiarity of the track may make it very difficult not to move into past recognition. So usually those new races are quite short when run on the same track.

Does this explanation help to clear up some of the issues of ascension? *Yes!* We would like to talk about what happens after ascension at another time, for we feel that is important information. Perhaps this is for later literature!

SUMMARY

These teachings state that **ascension** is not a quantum leap which suddenly raises an entity into the fourth or fifth dimension from third-dimensionality. Instead, it is a day-by-day, or even moment-by-moment elevation from pure third-dimensionality in which there is no awareness of consciousness in other dimensions, into pure fourth-dimensionality in which there is an awareness of consciousness in all dimensions. It is this "awareness of the awareness" which distinguishes fourth-dimensionality from the third. Therefore, the ascension from third to fourth-dimensionality is generally a growing awareness of this awareness, and not a sudden and instantaneous shift from absolutely no awareness into full consciousness in all dimensions.

These teachings also say that ascension brings about no finality. Instead, ascension is as if you were a child taking its first step. There is much to life which is beyond the first step of a child; and these teachings say that there is more to living as an Ascended Master after ascension than there is to living as a human after taking the first child-like step.

Further, these teachings state that before any thought of ascension is possible, there must be the intention to fully recognize who you are, to balance that which needs to be balanced, and to live in integrated divinity in the now. Without doing this, ascension will not occur no matter how devoted an individual has been to the service of a particular Master or to the acceptance of a specific discipline, for ascension requires mastery of the divine self in the now.

These teachings also declare that now is the time for a multitude of ascensions, and that most ascensions will occur in a wave of blissful energy which will encircle the planet. This does not rule out the ascension of individuals who have fulfilled such great light that the hierarchy will assist their ascension individually; but it does state that most entities will ascend in successive waves of mass ascension. Furthermore, these teachings state that in this ascension, the physical body is to be brought along if mass consciousness will allow it. But whether the body physically ascends or not, it is the Journey to ascension which is the most important thing; for a joyful Journey is a prelude to any ascension and it is the Journey which is to be loved, not the end-point itself.

None of this is to say that the sudden, instantaneous quantum leap through dimensionality cannot happen, for it can happen in an instance within the grace of God. However, for most individuals with Free Will, the ascension from third-dimensionality to the fourth will be a gradual, evolutionary passage, rather than a dramatic, revolutionary one. Because of this gradual ascension, most fourth-dimensional beings would appear to be just like a third-dimensional being when examined solely with the five physical senses. It is only when viewed from a different set of senses such as those possessed by a multi-sensory being that the difference can be noted. Also, because of this gradual ascension, many who are on planet Earth are not fully third-dimensional personalities. Instead, they are at some higher level, say 3.35 or 3.71, as their consciousness in all dimensions starts to progressively develop within them. [For further information, see the the definitions of "dimension" in *Appendix C.*]

Finally, when your divinity tells you that it is time to ascend, there is a petition which will bring forth the energy of ascension. This petition is repeated at the end of the channeled information. However, it should be noted that the petition will not be honored as long as there are commitments still to be fulfilled.

Dear Masters, have a great ascension!

The words to the following song were given to the editor during the night while he was attending a weekend workshop on ascension in the fall of 1995. "They" refused to let him go back to sleep until the words were written down. The workshop group sang this hymn later that afternoon. It was well-received and is presented here in a sense of sharing.

THE GROUP HYMN OF ASCENSION
[Sung to "The Battle Hymn of the Republic"]

Mine eyes have seen the Glory of the ninth dimension Ray
We ascended to that level on this great and glorious day
We give thanks to all the Masters who give guidance on the way
As we go ascending on.

Chorus Glory Glory to Ascension,
We will reach that great dimension
If we go with no dissension
As we go ascending on.

With the thought of full Ascension God created you and me
Then there was the wise decision that our Will should e'er be Free
Thus with self-determination we will live eternally
As we go ascending on.
Chorus

We give thanks to Father-Mother for the great, eternal Love
Which we feel comes to our presence from the Central Sun above
And for help in our Ascension by the descent of the Dove
As we go ascending on.
Chorus

We'll assemble all our pieces into one coherent sum
Then we'll meld them all together in a great eternal hum
And we'll shine in our enlightenment for all the time to come
As we go ascending on.
Chorus

CHAPTER TWO
CREATION

INTRODUCTION

There are many stories in the reservoir of human consciousness which tell us about the creation of humanity and the creation of the world in which humanity lives. Most of these stories have been called "myths." Myth is a term that has been greatly misunderstood, for many feel that the term means a fictitious story which has been created entirely by the mind. Some even go so far as to say that all myths are lies.

However, there is no reason to belittle myths, for they often are stories which have been able to touch our souls with truths which are every bit as valid as today's newspapers—and possibly even more so. Joseph Campbell has done a magnificent job in putting the understanding of myths in front of the American public through his famous TV interviews with Bill Moyers. Campbell has said, "A myth is a secret opening through which the inexhaustible energies of the cosmos pour into human consciousness manifestation." In other words, myths touch our deepest sense of being in order to provide answers for questions which are too profound to be answered in any other way.

Creation myths have been generated by almost every society in the history of the Earth. There are a number of excellent books which relate these stories such as the Hamilton book [*Appendix E*].

The purpose of this Introduction is not to present creation

stories. Instead, this segment is to introduce the general subject of creation, and to present the thought that creation continues today. In regard to the Creation Stories, this Introduction will merely suggest that Zoroasterism was the first major religion in recorded history to propose a God who created all things; and that the Creation Story of Zoroasterism is a precursor to the Creation Story presented in the Old Testament of the Bible. This Old Testament Story has been accepted by Judaism, Christianity and Islam as being representative of the Creator God whom they all accept. It begins in the very first chapter of the Bible by saying, "In the beginning God created...." The chapter then goes on to tell how God created heavens, earth, light, Day, Night, living creatures, etc. In other words, the God of this Creation Story created all that is.

In Christianity, the Creation Story is further refined in the New Testament. In the very first verse of The Gospel According to John, it is said, "In the beginning was the Word, and the Word was with God, and the Word was God." The English term "Word" is a translation of the Greek word "Logos," a Platonic concept which represented "the eldest and most akin to God of all the things which have come into existence." In Platonic philosophy, the Logos was used by God as his agent in the creation of the world. *The Amplified Bible* defines "beginning" as meaning "before all time" and "Word" as meaning "Christ." Although other points could be made about these verses, the major point here is that God used an agent to create manifest reality out of unmanifest reality, a point which is made often in the channelings of *Chapter Five* of this book, the chapter on Christ Consciousness.

Many of the channelings on creation received from the Ascended Masters bear a remarkable resemblance to the Creation Story in the Old Testament. However, despite the resemblance, the interpretation of the story is different, just as it differs among the three great western religions. In Judaism and Islam, God creates without an agent. In Christianity, God uses the Logos [or Word] as the agent of creation, but the only Logos which God uses is the one known as Jesus Christ.

In the channelings presented below, all who experience the Christ Consciousness in all levels from unmanifest reality to third-dimensional physicality are agents of creation; and the channelings further propose that this is how God creates today—through each and every one who embodies the Christ Consciousness. This means that each and every one of us creates a new reality for God each and every moment. Excerpts from some of the channelings which present this understanding are presented in the following section.

CHANNELED INFORMATION
Kuthumi, Channeling 46, Session 1 [10/28/95]

In your wise literature, there are statements that say the following: "In the beginning, all that there was was God, and God had the stirring to recognize Self. In recognizing Self, there was an immediate recognition that Love was the first tangible stirring into manifest reality." This is so, because in order to feel Love, there was the Creation of the space in which Love could move. In that recognition and feeling of Love, the desire was developed for it to be expressed more fully. That is when there became the Creation of what is termed the "sound of God." It is not the same as physical sound. It is the sound of God. It is the movement of God, for when God moves there is "God sound." So God, in his desire to multiply the Love that is the nature of being, gave forth the sounds of multiplicity which resulted in the Creation of space and the Creation of the energy [or Light] occupying that space.

In your literature, there also are the simplistic viewpoints which state that, "In the beginning there was God, and then there was the Word, and then began Creation." And so it is that God created Creation. But what was in God when Creation began to manifest? Were you in God? Indeed you were, for everything springs from the unmanifest energy of the God-head; and as Creation sprang, so did you.

Now God was, in a way, experimenting; for to think that God in his wisdom created a universe in perfect order and with a perfect plan would be to think that it was already totally created and experienced. If that were the case, then why create it since there would be nothing to learn from it? And so Creation is a grand experiment with Love begetting love, and experiencing love, and creating love and creating the myriad aspects of Creation that are and have been. In this way, Creation began and moved. Where were you? The answer is easy; for you were in God, unmanifest as well as manifest.

So God created company. In the desire to share Love, Creation created beings. Where were these beings? These beings already were in God, but became manifest. Does this mean that God was a multiplicity of beings before Creation? No, it means that God was, and all that was, was unmanifest. What that means is that all that is created out of the God-head, had its origins in the infinity of unmanifest reality. And so beings were created for the purpose of sharing love, and of creating love, and of expanding itself. As this experiment of Creation moved [and moves], it created [and creates] more of itself. God, in the on-going experiment of Creation, created beings to help in this process because sharing, and being in partnership with other beings, was a new phenomenon.

Beings were created in divine number to help this process of Creation. Where do you feel that you are in those beings? What is your lineage? Well, Creation unfolded in many diverse ways. At first, there were beings that were made in the image of the part of God that God reflected on, and saw, and multiplied. They were very similar to God. Then diversity began to spring forth. Although whatever is created is created in God's image, different types of beings began to be created in space; for whenever energy moves from unmanifest God to reality, it creates space, even in the finest dimensions close to where all comes from. In the finest dimensions, there is the experience of space which is not third-dimensional space, but it is space in which energy moves.

There is a part of you that exists in unmanifest God, and in the very finest aspect of reality which is closest to that unmanifest reality—the dimension where it is so fine that with your inner ear, you can hear the "sound" that a particular type of Creation makes when it comes from unmanifest reality into Creation. You have the ear to hear that. I tell you this because I wish for you to hear from that level. You are here to manifest reality. You are here to bring forth the divinity, firmly and completely, into reality. For you to perform these Creations, you must be Masters of manifestation. To clearly manifest in all dimensions, the most important linkage is that which sits directly next to unmanifest God; because when you can express your intentions from that level, Creation is instantaneous. When you create from that level, you are God! This is because in creating from that level, there is no unbalanced ego that is doing the creating, and va Creator; for only God creates from that level.

I wish for you to create from that level rather than create without it; because when you create without that finer perception, you introduce time. I wish for you to be Masters of time by creating beyond time. In this way, you become what you came to become. You become your God-being in physical form. You bring divinity into physicality. This is what is intended. It has always been intended that you be God-beings in full responsibility of your Creation. It has been very easy in past times to say, "What a mess they have made of this world. I don't like being here. I would rather be somewhere else." You have all felt that in one degree or another because this world is so foreign from where your heart dwells. Yet, you persevered and persisted because your divine purpose was to stick it out.

We are here to ease your path. We are here to assist you in such a way that the creator and the created will become one. We are here to assist you in overcoming the frustration of knowing the divinity within and knowing the physicality without, but of being unable to know the gulf between. You came in this time and in this place to clear and to be conscious of that gulf, so that you could be conscious in the continuum from divinity to physicality; for it is in the consciousness of this continuum that you become Masters of manifestation. You become Masters of all that is, and you fulfill the golden being of your purpose; for you came forth to do it all, to do it more fully than I did, to do it more fully than any Master that has walked this world. When you can create in all dimensions between unmanifest reality and physicality, you will create as none has created before you. In this action, you will have truly expanded God!

Kuthumi, Channeling 18 [2/2/93]

I have come to talk about the Science and Application of Being; for one of the most confusing aspects of being alive as a human is "What in the world am I doing here? Why am I here?" The great mystery of life is a mystery only because part of the process of the life experience is forgetting some of who you are. This forgetting will continue until the time you can come forth in human expression in total manifestation of your divine Being.

This life is lived to create experience, because experience creates space for light. Even in the forgetful state of your God-consciousness, you are God's instrument in creating God-space. Light will flow where there is space. The Divine Light will flow into your God-space as you create it; and in that creation you allow greater multitude and expression of God, for you are creating more of what God is.

For a moment, place yourself in the position of the Creator where you create Beings to help you in your creative endeavors; and you bless them with the ability to be God, to be in your image and in your application of natural law. But being a wise Creator, you have created a natural law which respects the light of divinity, and which allows that light to be used only in proportion to the maturity of the Creator. Yet, you allow those creator-beings the Free Will to choose their direction and their application of your divine law. As this creative process grows and prospers, you rejoice in the development and maturity of your created God-beings until creation becomes diverse in space, in dimensions and eventually in matter. By means of this experience of creating a variety of God-beings, you come to the realization that different systems of experience create different avenues and different time-frames of maturing in God's divine wisdom. You also see that there is a difference in the application of God's Love and power in those systems.

Within this wisdom, Earth was generated as a very special place with a divine directive. That directive was, and is, to create a garden planet in matter where the history of creative God-beings may be recorded. In addition, Earth was, and is, intended to be the accelerated God-school for those who are brave enough to enter and for those who meet the qualifications of entry. Finally, Earth was, and is, to be in dimensions other than matter form. As a result, there are many dimensions residing in this space. That is why whenever you ask for help, there is an immediate response; for there is no limitation in space for those higher dimensions.

This story of God creating God-beings to create anew in

order to expand the experience and the light of God's creations is your story. That is why you are here. As creative Light-beings, you are now realizing your God-inheritance and your creative abilities in the will of the divine.

With the knowledge of who you truly are comes the excitement and the application of that inheritance, and also the responsibility to use it wisely and divinely. As you have been told, now is the opportunity to manifest physically those divine gifts that you possess; for in the sense of three-dimensional expression, the lid has been taken off the game. Through the grace of the divine, you are now free to accelerate your development and to be creator God-beings in this realm. This is not a far-away event. It is here and now. There is not one of you who could not create a matter-form if you had the intention and the attention and the diligence to do so. There is not one of you who, within the space of one year, could not walk upon this planet as a Master, as a Bodhisattva, healing the planet, healing the people and waiting for your time of full ascension.

This is so because you have created it, and because the divine allows it. All you need is the intention of placing energy on your divine guidance and the powerful engine of the universe will respond to you. You are at the controls of the universal creative engine, but as in an automobile, it must be steered and guided wisely; for this time of accelerated evolution is, indeed, a two-edged sword. Great heights of God-manifestation are now available; but great falls are also available. Therefore, you have been warned to watch each step carefully and to discern your divine direction. This is imperative. With a heart which is in Love with the divine Creator, and in Love with Self, and in Love with your fellow Beings, you shall make no misstep.

And so, what is it you wish to be in this time and in this place? Are your goals those of your divine Self, or are they of your ego-personal self? Those steps taken in alignment with Divine Will will create majestic achievements; those taken in the name of ego will result in great falls. There is great safety in moving forward in the divine; there is a great risk to move forward in the personal. So, first discern your divine impulse; and when that discernment has taken place, allow the energy that flows through you to manifest that impulse. In the divine you can accomplish all things; but in the personal, you can truly accomplish little other than fear, failure and unhappiness. In the divine, you can live in the joy of the impulse of every breath of divine energy that pulsates into this universe.

There are no followers in divine creation, there are only Creators. You are God-created. You are God-beings. You are one with all that is and shall ever be. So the Science of Being is the application of Divine Law in each moment. The Application of Being is amplifying and allowing creative energy to flow through your divine vessel for manifestation in whatever dimension is appropriate. And thus, the Science and Application of Being is the fullness of a God-Being creating with the wisdom, and the power and the Love of the Creator-Being that has created all that is.

This is truly a simple process, for only in the personal has it been made difficult. There is no language you need understand; there is no mathematical formula that is your secret to success; and there is no philosophy or history to know. This is all very interesting knowledge, but it is not necessary for a God-Being; for as you capture the divine Self that you are at the divine core of your Being, there is no knowledge that cannot be added unto you. Those who revel in the intelligence of humanity lose the divinity of their Being. Those who revel in the material world live outside their divine Self. Those who revel in religious dogma live a false Self. But those who live the Science and Application of Being are God-creators, an extension of the Divine, creating in this universe. When you master the Science and Application of Being, then indeed, you become a Master.

Throughout the ages there have been those who have attained mastery. Many of you have already attained mastery, not only in other realms but also in this realm. You are here again with some forgetting to create new experiences to do it again. This is your wake-up call. It is not your first, for some have had thousands of wake-up calls. But this is indeed very timely. I promise you from the dimension of my experience that if you diligently apply your energy to living in God-Self, it shall be so.

The Science and Application of Being is a simple process which has been complicated by human confusion and by those who have taken the Light and called it their own. Don't let them do that, for it is yours to create!

Kuthumi, Channeling 22 [3/20/93]

The purpose of this Journey is to bring forth your divinity into your humanness rather than your humanity into divinity. Use this time of balance to call forth that which you are. You are not the personality, and you are not those emotions that you feel. In permanence, you are the divine spiritual Being that animates your life so that you can create in each and every moment. Use this creative time wisely, for you have great support in your evolvement.

You have been told that this is the time of blessings. This is the time of dawning, of new creation, of the expansion that comes after the time of contraction. Expand into new life by merely being more of who you are. Mastery is your goal and it is easily within your reach. If you are ever unsure about what you should create, ask for guidance within. Ask what your divine Self would do. If you do not immediately feel the guidance from within, stop and ask again. Do not let a precious moment go by without creating mastery. You were told there are no unimportant moments, and this is indeed true; for you do not know which moment will be the moment of your creation or of your ascension. Likewise, you do not know what could be the moment which translates your creation into the absolute divine.

Kuthumi, Channeling 46, Session 2 [10/29/95]

It is suggested that, instead of using the word "waiting," you substitute the word "creating," for we are never truly waiting—we are always creating. Each of you is a multi-dimensional being, and as a human being, the word "multidimensional" is used almost in a special context, for it means that you are a special lot—a special type of created being, a special type of consciousness, a special type of a way in which a consciousness expresses itself.

Prior to the development of the human, there were many types of created beings that did not feel in the same way that you do, for they did not understand feelings and emotions. They were, and are, almost devoid of emotions. They were created before the God-head realized that for true divinity to completely exist in manifest reality, he must have a full range of feelings. The reason for this is because it was not originally understood that when space was created, it was the nature of feelings which created that space. In other words, God could not move in a creative fashion without creating space. What created that space was the <u>feeling</u> of Creation.

God created many types of beings to exist in this manifest reality, but many of them did not have this range of feelings and emotions. Consequently, they only achieved a limited manifestation of the God-head. Without the full range of emotions, they could not truly be creator Gods; because to create, you must have the full range of feelings as well as the full range of the emanations of Light out of God. So the intention of God was to create a family of God-creators in His/Her image: friends, companions, associates. Out of God's love, S/He created to create this family of beings. But the beings who were created without feelings or emotions could only occupy the space that God had already created. Since they could not create new space, they ended up fighting over the space that was, because they knew that they were limited in that way. These are the archetypes who cause us to fight over space, even today; because captured territory is, in this archetypal essence, the same as captured God-head.

This brings us back to why humanity is so special. It is special because humanity is the synthesis of the ability to create space, and the ability to manifest Light in that space. Thus, mankind has a special role as a multidimensional creator—a special role to be God in that way. Do angelic beings have the same range of emotions that humanity does? They can, but as an angelic being, their feeling is in direct relationship to the feeling of their environment. So angelic beings feel all that is around them, and they act according to that feeling space; but they do not have the same range of feeling that a human being has. That is why many angels in their evolutionary path wish to become human. There are many angelic beings on Earth today, because the human biology, fused with consciousness, is the ideal vehicle for achieving God-head in manifestation. This is why you are pioneers. It is because this has really not been done in this way before. The Masters who preceded you have achieved degrees of God-consciousness in the past; but until the human family as a whole comes together in united, co-creation of divine intention, it will always be incomplete.

What happens when the human family comes together in this

divine Creation is awesome. Time will show what this will be. We see what it <u>can</u> be and what it <u>might</u> be; but we do not <u>know</u>; for there has not been conscious, physical God-creators in a cohesive, planetary family before. There are planets where there have been great achievements in consciousness, for Love is the dominant energy in those places. But have these been human beings? The answer is "No." Humanity has been present on several planets, but not throughout the universe. Humanity is a relatively new phenomenon. That is because God has healed enough of its Creation to allow itself to be manifest as a human; and you are His/Her grand experiment in co-creatorship!

Maitreya, Channeling 54 [3/26/96]

There is now great diversity in creation. There are things that happened in the early cycles of this creation cycle that caused aspects of the God-head to be not in synchronization. This happened because creation is a process of experimentation. There is not an absolute blueprint for creation. Instead, there is the energy that flows forth from God to create in a general probability; and the Creator-beings take this energy and bring forth the creative result. In the early stages of creation, there was conflict amongst some of the beings that were close to the God-head. What these beings were reflecting was the lack of experience within the God-head for creation. Does that surprise you? The commonly accepted principle upon the planet is that God is absolute and in perfection and all perfection flows from God; but God is ever growing and ever expanding. So, does it not follow that God is also learning about Him/Herself?

In the burst of creation that flowed in the initial stages of this creative cycle, there were aspects of the God-head that were not in synchronous motion, and this developed some deep seeded conflicts which have been reflected throughout creation. That is why you experience so much conflict between these aspects of God on this dimension. Those non-synchronous aspects are the Mother and the Father aspects of God. If you look closely at the chaos, confusion and conflict in human existence, it can nearly always be traced back to these fundamental divisions that occurred early in the creative cycle of this system.

When you look at it, it is kind of pathetic; but such is the state of humanity. Such is the state of all of creation. Otherwise, creation would be in wholeness. But those fundamental rifts throughout creation have been ignored for millennia because they were too powerful and scary to deal with. These rifts have kept humanity, as well as other races of beings, from moving into wholeness more readily. But in hindsight, have these rifts not been perfect for us?

These rifts had a grand intelligence behind them, not necessarily knowing what would happen, but knowing enough to know that God is so powerful that unless there were powerful restrictions on moving into wholeness, the experience of living as a Free Will being to find out how to go about being God would not be experienced. It would have been automatic. But the best teacher for evolving Gods is the experience of going about and finding what is in alignment with God and what isn't. If it were natural to you to be in alignment with God, there would be no issues. You would be happy, joyful, going about creating, and accomplishing everything that already existed in God in the first place! So why have creation if everything already existed?

Creation exists to expand God, and God is expanded by finding out what is in God-alignment and what isn't; for creation truly springs from the discovery of who you are. Now if who you are was automatic and never in question, would you have created exactly what you have created in your life? No! Would God be the same? No!

In other words, diversity has sprung from experimentation. It is as if God said, "Everything is like me, but I want to create beings that are different." As an example, if you were in a room of people who are you, wouldn't that be a little boring? So how do you create diversity? God could say, "I'm going to create all of this diversity," but all of it would be such a pure reflection of God that it would still be exactly like God. For diversity, God allowed the experiment to let creation go on by itself without running to completion through total alignment. And so that is what, I suspect, happened. I cannot know. I am not clear enough in those places to know exactly, but this is what I suspect for it is what I can be conscious of.

And so, in the diversity of not knowing God, creation exploded in ways that could never have been predicted. Well the danger in all of this is that God gets lost. Now God is never truly lost because nothing exists without being God; but the knowledge of alignment with God is lost. That is the danger; and that is why all that you create must be based on your total alignment, at least to the extent that you can experience it!

Blend of Melchizedek
and St. Germain, Channeling 3 [5/4/92]

Look at these times during which you are activated by energy not only as what you can do for the planet, but what can you do for yourself in concert with the planet; for one occurs in concert with the other. They work together; for within each one of you, you are your own universe. You are your own creation of life, and the creation of a planet is no different than the creation of your own being. You have the power within each one of you to create planets, and how could you create a planet without creating yourself? How could one be created without the other? You have the power within each one of you to heal planets, and how could you heal a planet without healing yourself? How could one be healed without the other? Without the creator, there would not be the created. Without the healer, there would not be the healed. So in healing the created, then you, the creator, are also healed. See in yourself that which you know needs to be healed. What part of your creative ability is ready for healing? What part of your life calls out to you for that healing? This can be healed at this time; for within each one of you is also the mother of creation, and as she is activated on this planet, your creative energy is also activated.

Maitreya, Channeling 47 [11/6/95]

All energy that moves in divine order is the energy of creation, because all energy that moves from unmanifest God is the energy of creation. It takes many forms as energies from God, but it is always that which creates anew; and in this way, each one of you is creating yourself anew. You create a new self each moment. You create how that self is manifest and how that self is to be allowed to manifest in the next moments.

You are all wise beings and there is very little that I can tell you that you have not already heard on some level of your being. There are Ascended Masters that you work with, but do not forget that when you look in the mirror, you are looking at a Master. Too often you ascribe beauty and magnificence to that which is unseen, to that which comes through with great clarity and power; but understand that the power and clarity which comes through from those unseen is clear because they are not encumbered by a physical vehicle that is not in clarity. Each of you has that same clarity and power in your non-physical consciousness. It is not that you must pass a physical test of incarnation after incarnation in order to be a powerful God. You already are, and that is the riddle of the ages in which the Master said "You already are, you just need to realize it." So when you look in the mirror, realize you already are that Master as well. You are that great being of Light that came from God for a specific purpose to explore that which has been created, and that which will be created and that which is created in a way which is unique to you and not duplicated in any other place throughout all creation. So you are indeed a pioneer of God. You are a unique aspect to explore and create and to be God in your purpose; for each experience allows you to create your unique vessel that becomes greater every moment. As God grows, God changes and is evermore again anew, and you have more to discover. God grows because you grow in experience and creation; and as you grow, so does all that is God. As pioneers of God, you are on the frontiers of consciousness in the universes. And so, in being God, you now have the opportunity to create consciousness, for there is great clarity here to be co-creators with God.

Kuthumi, Channeling 48 [11/28/95]

Make no mistake that everything you do in your life is a creative process, for you are constantly creating in every aspect of your life. Because of this, first look to see what is it that you are creating which is in alignment with your divine purpose; for everything you do is your creation. Every step you take, every motion, every look, every thought, and especially the energy you carry about yourself with your intention, is your creation.

However, without clarity of purpose it is possible that you could create in ways that are not divine. This may confuse you, for if everything is linked to that which comes from the unmanifest reality that is divinity, then how could it be not divine when it is created in the physical?

First of all is the clarity of the definition that all is divine; because <u>all</u> is, and all that <u>is</u>, is God. But let us look more closely by asking a question. What in your action is in the process of increasing divine energy, and what in your action is in the process of decreasing divine energy? For you see, all is divine, but it is not necessarily increasing that which you term "God." It is not necessarily in fulfillment of your divine purpose or of the purpose of divinity in action. If the action is done in Love, it can increase divine energy; but if done in non-Love, it can decrease divine energy even without decreasing God, for God is still the All. But in this way humanity could create that which is not divine. The responsibility to create with clarity is yours to make, and you must have the desire to have the movement from within unmanifest reality spring forth with a clear definition of what it is to be created. Make that creation in divine love!

Kuthumi, Channeling 46, Session 2 [10/28/95]

As God-creators, you are on an exploration into consciousness. You are here in a three-dimensional world in which time has meaning. But what is time? What are eons and eons to God? Within the concept of Creation, time has no meaning; for the cycle of Creation is like a giant wheel. When one Creation ends, another begins because there is always more Creation. There is always yet another cycle. It continues, because God is ever-expanding, ever-learning about Him/Herself.

You hear the term in your literature, "absolute," as in "God is absolute or all-knowing." It is time we broke some of these terms apart. God is all-knowing for that which S/He knows; but God is learning each and every moment, just as you do. God is all-powerful or omnipotent in the Creation in which the rules allow it, but some Creations have Free Will; and in those selected universes, intervention is not allowed. In other words, Free Will Creation must run its course. Does this mean that God would be powerless to change things? Not really, because if Free Will Creation gets to the point that it would destroy itself, God would probably move in and reset the rules rather than let it be destroyed; although God has already let some parts of His/Her Creation be destroyed. In other words, God is a kind conductor, but one who plays by the rules.

What this means is that there has never been anything like you before; and because of your individuality within Free Will, there will not be anyone like you again; for as God learns and grows from you, then God creates anew. But you will always be, for you are eternal. What you are is never lost, it is just built upon. As you build a brick wall, you build one layer upon another. Your soul grows in the same way, and all accomplishes divine purpose, even that which is an unloving Creation. Now, as the world moves to where it does not need these unloving Creations, then humanity will have grown to the point that it will have learned those lessons, and it will no longer need them.

So where does that put us today? Mankind has, indeed, learned a great deal, and has learned enough to move on to the next stage of evolution. That is what is occurring in this age at this time. Although there are lots of created beings who are not as yet in this space, they will be given an opportunity for rapid acceleration and growth. If they don't move with the accelerated energies that are available to them, they will have another place in which they can continue to learn, to grow, and to create.

Maitreya, Channeling 52 [2/20/96]

You are creator God-beings creating specifically that which God intended generally. The act of taking in the general energy of God and manifesting a specific act of creation is an action of interpretation upon your divine path. And so there is but truly one responsibility for humanity, and that is to be aware of your God-intention, and then to act from that. As you do this within your life, you create it for others. You do not have to shout on a street corner, for merely by creating in your life, you create what is called the archetypal experience for others who are similar in your energy stream; for you have come to bring forth this God-creation for many in addition to yourself. That is a natural consequence of your living in consciousness, creating from your individualized divinity, and acting from that knowing. In the process of that living, you create a paradise in the wake of your movement. If you could look back and see in the wake of your energy stream all that you have done, you would be well pleased, for you are creating paradise in your actions. You are creating Love in form by your actions.

Now, if you do not create in alignment with your individual-ized will of divinity, what happens? Instead of this clear direction, it tends to muddy the waters, does it not? But often this is needed to reach the level of clarity to move forward again in your particular way. It is not wrong, nor is it even inefficient. It is your particular way.

So the primary responsibility of mankind is for each to create from your individual will, to act from that knowing, and to allow this to happen only in the energy of Love; for you cannot separate Love and will and power in consciousness. It all comes together in the recognition of self. Throughout the ages there have been many path-ways for mankind to open the doorways to God-living consciously. But I say to you that there is only but one pathway needed, and that is to be aware in the way in which you are aware, because each and every individualized stream of God is a different, individualized God. Therefore, there is not one path that is going to work for each and every person, and no one can tell you how you can be you. Only you know that.

There is no guru, there is no universal path, there is just you and your desire to be God in consciousness that you are. There may be little bits of energy to help you move to the sacred space within yourself, but there is no guru for pioneers of God-creation. How could there be? Would you give your power to another being when you are as powerful and when your heritage is the same? It is a community of God-beings is it not? So how can one creator God be more important than another? They are not—believe it!

Maitreya, Channeling 51 [2/6/96]

All of the needs of humanity are important because you live in this world; but they pale in comparison to the creation of Divine Life by following your Divine Will. In other words, you create in your life according to the boundaries that you have within your creative abil-ity. If there is a need to create a lack of prosperity in order to gain spirituality, then you may generate great spiritual awareness, and be poor in self in the process.

However, such a narrow approach is no longer necessary; for at this time and in this place, there is now the opportunity for power, for love, for prosperity and for wholeness to be all achieved together. In the recent past this could not happen, and so many great spiritual leaders have come forth upon this planet only to suffer greatly in their lives. Was this because they were spiritual? Or was it because they could create only so much in the atmosphere of mass-consciousness at that time without violating the karma of the planet and of humanity?

Many of you have had great struggles in your life because you are an archetype creating a spiritual pathway. You not only created that clarity within yourself, but you were dragging much of humanity along with you in that process. Your present challenge is to listen for clarity, to have the courage to create from that clarity, and to accept the responsibility for what is created in the process.

As an example, one of the decisions that you helped to make was whether or not this planet would evolve by a huge quantum leap, or whether it would progress evolutionarily. During the last fifteen years, there have been great decisions made as to how this planet would evolve. You were part of that decision. There was the possibility of great shifts upon the planet accompanying great consciousness shifts to where humanity would be divided into those who were willing to move, and those who were not willing to move. But those of you who have been here said, "This is a good place. It is moving. There is much Love here. There is hope. It can happen. It will happen. I commit myself to creating it." This led to the decision that this planet would move gracefully on its path. You helped to create the path of smooth evolution for the Earth. You are the archetype of that pathway. You created it!

Blend of Maitreya/Buddha, Channeling 15 [11/9/92]

In this time of change there are waves of fear that are moving across this world; for each human incarnate at this time has the general knowledge of what is occurring on the planet embedded within their cellular structure. We refer to Earth changes as they are generally described, but which are rhythmic healing sessions for the Earth and its inhabitants. The waves of fear occur because of the prospect that humanity will be no more. This is the greatest fear.

On some areas of the planet, life as we know it will not be the same; but this is not an ending, it is a beginning. As more God-beings recognize the energy that they have within their own self and their ability to radiate that energy to the planet in order to create modifications in the Earth changes, then those changes will become much less dramatic; for it was not many years ago when the Earth, itself, was on a path of destruction. It now is on a path of healing. All of this is needed. Just as you go through many transformations during your growth, so too the Earth being goes through her transformations. Would you deny her this?

As you recognize those subtle changes within yourself and move with that flow, your physical body will only undergo subtle changes; but if you resist and ignore them, your body will create dramatic changes, sometimes even resulting in death. And so it is with the Earth. If the Earth is allowed to respond to the changes within her on a subtle level, then the outward manifestation will also be subtle. But what would make Earth undergo dramatic changes, possibly even leading to death? It is the consciousness that man has created around the planet. It is as if you were a growing child, and you had one of your limbs put in a strong, metal cast. That limb could not grow. And so it is with the consciousness that man has created around the Earth. The Earth struggles to heal herself, but she is restricted by this cast of human consciousness. And that is why it is so important for you to be willing to move in the vibration of peace and harmony and healing, for this movement lessens the grip of the cast which humanity has created upon the Earth.

Should the throwing off of this cast create an individual fear in you? Only if you have a lack of trust in the perfection in all things. You are a valued member of consciousness, a divine branch of the tree of life. You are most dear and most needed for your participation in what will be created in this unfoldment of Earth and all who reside upon her. You should realize that a major part of this transformation has already been created. It is already occurring, and you are creating it more peacefully than it might have been.

If you could view conscious life on this planet, you would see dramatic changes from what it was 30 years ago. If you would go back, it would almost seem to be a prison of thought. This is said to congratulate you and all who have been working with the energy of life to create peace and to create the freedom of divine expression in the fifth dimension and beyond. You have been creating well. As a result, the Earth changes will be moderate in comparison with what they could have been; and yet, the transformations will be effective. You are to be congratulated in what you are creating.

Maitreya, Channeling 14 [10/26/92]

Many of you are creating divine expression; but how much of your day is spent creating illusion rather than divine expression? In that ratio you shall see where you are placing your attention. Your bodies are being tossed about because you are in the middle of a conflict between the forces of illusion and the forces of light. Do not be afraid, for from what we see on the horizon, the forces of light are winning, if winning is the correct word to use. The nature of life is light, whereas the nature of darkness is illusion. Illusion is a part of your life because the third dimension is the battle ground of light and dark. The third dimension is the knowing of that which is not known. It is the longing for your divinity in a space that lacks divine energy.

The third dimensional form was created so that Creator-Gods would truly understand the nature of God; for to understand who God is, and what you are, is to know the void without. You have been placed on the frontier of God's expression, and cut off consciously from the memory of God, so that you could bring forth that divine light. In the demonstration of that creation, truly, a Creator-God is born.

Melchizedek, Channeling 1 [4/6/92]

It is true for all to hear that now is the time to clear that which you have created for yourself; for although there is a great movement ahead, you must remove the shackles and the baggage and the limitations that keep you from taking the first step on this new spiral. It is not to be feared. Instead it is a joy and a blessing to behold that now you can remove that which is holding you back. Behold what you are, and release everything that you are not. And as you teach the Word, you must live the Word; for although this may seem to be a two-edged sword, you created that sword. Though it may seem a trial to bear, and the fire may seem bright and deep and fearful, you will not be singed walking straight through the flames; for they are an illusion. Walk through your fears and what you have created; for great blessings, beyond your imagination, lay in waiting for you as you create divinely.

Maitreya, Channeling 30 [7/12/93]

There is no exception to mastery, except for those who destroy themselves in the process. All creation is in movement to mastery as are all dimensions, all forms, and all energies. By mastery we mean alignment with those impulses that come from the creative force that creates All That Is. You know that you are linked with that creative force. Do you realize what that truly means? It means that you are able to manifest divinity as it manifests from the absolute. It means that you exist at the point of manifestation. It means that you exist in the absolute, from whence all manifestation springs. It means that you live and dwell within what you term "God." It means that you create as a part of that God, and that you have the power of the Creator, available to be used when you allow the wisdom and the Love of the Creator to guide that energy.

Most of humanity see themselves as the tiny photon from the creating sun, because that is where their consciousness has been placed. But in reality, they are the sun. That which you identify as yourself in most moments of consciousness is but a very small facet of who you are. When you meditate and allow yourself to move within the energy, you allow an experience of different facets of yourself; and once in a while you allow yourself to travel in consciousness to other dimensions in which you exist. You are multidimensional in the sense that your being has evolved into consciousness on many dimensions.

As a human, you are a unique creation. Other parts of the creative universe move in accordance with divine impulse by their very nature. They do not have the Free Will to move according to their own desires. They know only the desire of the creative force. But as a human being you are an individualized creative God. You have been given a great responsibility; for in doing this, God has allowed you to be all that S/He is. It would be as if you shared the wealth of all that you have with your companions with only the restriction that they cannot utilize that wealth completely until they have the maturity to understand its wise distribution. In the same way, God has given you the creative wealth of All That Is; but you will not allow yourself its manifestation and distribution and conversion until you have the maturity of mastery.

There are many beings in the created universe who are quite jealous of what you have, for they do not have this freedom. It is their desire to manifest as a human soul because they see from their divine standpoint the wonderful gift of divine Free Will. But do you appreciate that gift? Do you use your Free Will wisely? Each time that you move away from what you know is your direction of mastery, you are telling God, "I do not appreciate the gift that I have been given." Some have done this because they wish to gain a small amount of Earthly wisdom and prosperity. However, you are different. You have moved beyond that element of existence. You are ready to move into complete mastery, and you are doing it publicly. Every intentional decision you make is being broadcast across the universe as if you were the star of a universal TV show!

For each of you, there is no question that will not be answered if asked sincerely within. The answer to every dilemma is within you, and the Masters will help you find its resolution each and every time. And then, when you recognize your guidance, the energy is there for you to create wisely. But you must use it. Remarkable healings, insights, powers, wisdom, are there for the asking; but you must ask and act as a creator God!

Blend of Energies, Channeling 32 [9/20/93]

Now is the time for each of you to make peace with all of the cells that you are, for creation is quite complex and each of you is a complex structure that in totality makes up your beingness. Now is the time for your beingness to come into balance and to shift from outward to inward as you balance the energy flow of the Mother and the Father. When manifesting creation, the perception is that there is a difference between the Mother and the Father, but in all manifest reality, there is only one; for the beginning point of the experience of duality is the very essence of the creation process itself.

The human soul has the unique ability to combine all rays into one creative expression in manifest reality. And thus, the human soul consciousness is the crowning achievement of the creation of life evolution, for each human being is a replication of God itself. Each human is a creator God; but this creative ability must be teamed with maturity of experience gained through evolution. This is true because all things are not created alike, and some may evolve into something else. As a few examples, individual souls are not created alike; the soul of a planet differs from that of a human consciousness; the soul of a star is an involved consciousness that at one time was a planet; and a creator God is a consciousness that at one point may have gained experience as a human consciousness.

In other systems, there have been attempts to create a soul as versatile as the human soul, but none has been as successful as this creative experiment; for the human being has been found to be capable of existing in the total spectrum from the grossest and the densest of matter to the finest energy of God. If other life forms could do this, you would see them walking on the face of the planet. The reason that you don't is because they are best suited for other dimensions. You have a vehicle and a consciousness that allows you to evolve through all time and all dimension. This is indeed a very valuable experience that you have created for yourself. It is valuable not only to yourself but to Creation.

That is why when you participate in the energy awakenings on this planet, you have a valuable contribution to make; for you have the ability to span the spectrum from matter to unmanifest reality. Therefore you can couple the energies of divinity in its most fine form into divinity which has become manifest in physical structure. You have the ability to anchor the energies of the rays onto the planet and unto your own self. This is why you work with Kuthumi and with the other Masters for the purposes of energetic activation to create that which you desire for yourself and for the planet. There is no limit to what you can accomplish with balanced will and balanced purpose, but this balanced purpose can only be accomplished when you yourself have healed; for as the healing becomes greater, the power becomes greater until your environment reflects the perfection of your being.

We would ask each of you to examine what your experience is telling you. If your body is aging, it is giving you a message. The message is that the physical body is not being nourished as it should be on all levels; for a body that is nourished and balanced with spirit and mind and emotions need not age. And what is the reflection of your work place or your home place? In this time when you can create anew and in this time of balance, you know what your experience is showing you about that which needs to be worked on or re-created. The gift of light is yours. The gift of creation is yours. As you create, fill the creation with light; for the purpose of creation is to create and to expand the manifestation of light.

St. George, Channeling 42 [2/13/95]

How often in your lives have you made decisions based on fear rather than on the excitement of the opportunities that you could create? Because of this, many feel that they have put themselves outside the realm of enjoyment, of harmony, or of prosperity. And indeed, to be in that state you must have put yourself there, because that is not the natural state of a being in humanity. The natural state of a being in humanity is to be a fully conscious creator of your universe, meaning no exceptions, no doubts, no fears left alone to multiply and grow. For you to live, you must live in freedom. Freedom is the state of being free in all areas, in all consciousness, in all space, in all time. To be free and to be alive, one must live consciously in all dimensions, from the unmanifest God-head to physical reality, for you do exist in all these realms. It could not be otherwise. For anything to exist in the physical, it must be energetically supported throughout creation to the unmanifest God-head. Otherwise, it could not exist.

You have heard that you create your reality. What does that mean? It means that every facet, every moment, every slice of time, and every experience is your creation. Do you realize the complicated energetics that are needed throughout dimensionality to support your creations? Perhaps people would not create some of the things they do if they realized how many other beings and energies are required to support what they have created. And they have quite a universal audience in their creation; for although mankind may think they create in secrecy, the universe knows every dirty little thing and experience you have created! Everything is in headlines in the universe, from the sublime to the ridiculous; from the nastiest thing you have ever done, to the most loving thing you have ever done.

It makes one think a bit, does it not? For you see, you came here with the agreement that you would be an open book for all to study as you created; because you are not here just for you, you are here for All That Is. When you came here, you not only took on the energetics of this world, you took on the energetics of this creation and of those with whom you associate on all dimensions. So, as you clear those energies within you that are not in balance, you clear energies of your personal creation, and you clear energies of the universal creations, and you clear energies of your associates who work with you although not in body. It is, indeed, always a group effort. I said you came as an open book, and indeed, that is so; for what is this reality you are living? It is an open experiment of energetics creating with the Free Will of God, and you are doing the creating!

St. George, Channeling 43 [4/5/95]

Emotions are the expression of the non-mental energy within your being. Emotions are like the substance through which life is lived; they are the fabric of experience. The mind is a linkage to your intellectual, spiritual reality; but it has no way of interacting other than in a specific way to spirit. The emotions are the fabric of your movement, because emotions bring about transformation and transmutation. In order to be transformed, there has to be movement, there has to be feedback from body to spirit in order for there to be growth in spirit. Emotions are the expression of the energy so that it can be experienced.

What is feeling? Feelings and emotions are part of the same energy. Although emotions are more manifest, and feelings are more subtle, they are based on the same energy. Some people say that the way you become enlightened is you detach yourself from your emotions or else they get you in trouble; and you detach yourself from your mind or else it will make you wander; and you detach yourself from your body or else it will make you want too much pleasure; and then you merely sit in your spirit and you will be in unity with all that is. Well, if you wanted that, you didn't need to come into a body, because you were already there!

You came here to learn from this body. The reason that so much of the spiritual evolution has involved exercises to get out of the body is because of some wise beings who remembered what it was like before they were in body. So they tried to re-create that when they were in body in order to be happy because they did not like dealing with all this stuff that the body brings up. They made their vehicle nice and shiny, and they said, "Everything is so wonderful; and I am so happy because I am not a person any more."

But you came here to be a person. You came here to be a personality of God! You are God; created by God to be God's creative co-creator; to create with God, as God, acknowledging your own God-head as part of all that is; experiencing and creating with the movement of Divine Will within your own being. And this is true for all. Why is there a push within yourself to become more? It is because you know within the beingness that you are, that you are connected from here to the God-head. There is no intermediary between you and God, because you are already there! Part of you sits in God.

Well, actually all of you sits in God. Let me explain what I meant. Part of you sits in unmanifest God. And what is unmanifest God? It is the field of all that can ever be, the field of infinite possibility. That is why you, as a creator in this body, could move a mountain if you wished to do so. It is because part of you is connected to All That Is. You are connected to all energy, to all power, and to all creativity. If you have that energetic clarity and act from Divine Will, it will be so; and the mountain will be moved. That is why every Master has said, "within you is all that is." However, it is just that some Masters forgot that it is important to become God in body. This is important because only by doing this can you become a Creator-God. Only by being in physicality can you create and support in all dimensions from the unmanifest to the manifest physicality. That is why you are in body. To be a Creator!

St. Germain, Channeling 13 [10/19/92]

How do we ask for divine creation? In prayer, one expresses self, for that Creator knows exactly everything there is to know about you and your needs, your hopes, and your dreams, your fears, and your experiences. The Creator does not need to be told what is required; but what is important is for the being to talk to the Creator to express for him/herself what God already knows in order to let self know that you know. In expressing from yourself what you desire in balance and from divine perspective, you realize more of who you are and what it is you wish to create in your divine life; for you are in control of the balance. The divine is more than willing to express and provide every need and every desire in the universe if you will open the gate for that gift. The divine will not provide that which is not of the perfection of your divine choosing because it is presently unknown to your conscious mind. But when you have balanced aspects of self to where you are in alignment with your divine purpose, there is no thing that you create that will not manifest; for you a Creator-God on this planet. That is what will be. It is the divine wish that this planet will be the home of Creator-Gods fulfilling the mission of divine manifestation and integration in the particular way that this planet has offered; for the grand experiment on Earth is not as has been done on other planets. It therefore creates a lot of attention from the God-head.

It would be my honor to lead this group of illustrious Masters in a closing prayer. I ask you to place yourself in the path of receiving.

Oh Lord that createth all that is in all dimensions and in all experiences, these Masters have come forth with open hearts and honest intention manifesting divinely in each and every moment of their lives. I vouch for their intention as a witness to their light. I ask for divine grace to come forth and wherever possible and whenever possible to provide the divine healing and energy for them and for all that they touch, experience and create for their families and their loved ones. May the divine grace flow from their hearts to encompass all peoples, all the animals, all the beings in all dimensions and the planet in her third dimension and also in her higher dimensions. In this small part that I play within your grand plan, I humbly acknowledge that I am but a part of your divine expression and that these beautiful beings who have chosen this difficult path are, too, open in their divine humility. I ask that the divine heart be open for each and every one to enter in comfort and in healing and to experience the joy that is truly their heritage. I pledge, again, to be your servant in service of your grand universal and divine plan for this planet. And to those other duties that you have assigned to me, I am most grateful and forever in your service; for your nature is my nature and in the unique expression of who I am, I rejoice in the fulfillment of who you are for there is no other. You are all that is and we are in divine balance with your manifestation, with your creation, with your Love. We ask humbly as your divine beings in service to Thee to be healed and to be full of your light expressing forevermore in loving peace. **So be it!**

CHANNELED ANSWERS
TO SPECIFIC QUESTIONS

Several times you have used the descriptive term "in this creative cycle." What does "creative cycle" mean? Creative cycle refers to the creative cycle of a particular system of creation. There is more than one system of creation in evidence at this time, with the phrase "at this time" being merely a figure of speech. Some have been present in other cycles of creation, but not all souls have been present at all of the cycles of creation.

You have stated that all are slated for mastery without exception unless we destroy ourselves in the process. How could this happen? First let me explain that nothing is lost in the "destroying" process," so it is really not destroyed. An example might help. Let us assume that a wise being decides to have many experiences and so it creates many vessels of experience which in truth are the same, but in their own knowing feel separate, distinct and different. Now if one of those vessels chooses to engage in an experience that is contrary to its energetic alignment, the creator of that experience has a choice to make. Although the creator loves it, he/she realizes what it will take to allow it to continue in its own stream. And so, the creator might bring that stream back into itself for realignment and balancing to the other streams. It is not lost, it is just re-balanced into alignment with the energy of the creator.

We know that there are first, second and third dimensions. Is there a minus 1, a minus 2, a minus 3 and so on? The answer to this is yes, but not in the sense of being an opposite reflection of what is. It is not so much opposite as it is parallel. This is a very difficult concept to grasp three-dimensionally, but it is best explained in the sense that where there is an experience that is created but not actualized, it is energetically brought to fruition in a different system. Those systems are transitory. That is why there is so much confusion in dimensional travel for the inexperienced because they see dimensional experience that is transitory and they do not realize that it is just the working out of energy at a different level than they have experienced before.

Is there a relationship to black holes? That is similar but yet different again. Black holes have to do with parallel universes that are not transitory.

Several times you have mentioned the Universal Law of Creation. Could you please define that for us? The Universal Law of Creation is quite simple. It is Love. The intent of creation is Love. That is the only intention that it truly has. It contains all that is. It contains all the possibilities and all that is desired from the heart of God, for Love is the direction; and Love is the motivator; and Love is the container of all. The Universal Law of Creation is Love. [This answer, and a personal Journey which resulted from this answer, are presented in greater detail in *Appendix D*.]

SUMMARY

These teachings state that the first step of God into **Creation** was to create the space in which Love could move. This is so because it was found that Love was, and is, the first tangible stirring of the unmanifest into manifest reality. Following that, in a desire to share Love, God created company, and those beings used the space created by God to beget love, to experience love and from that to create all that has ever existed. Because of this, each entity, whether presently incarnate or not, is a Creator-God.

Further, these teachings state that creation happens each and every moment; and that through creation, God changes by growing and learning to understand more of Him/Herself. As one aspect of understanding Him/Herself, God generated Earth as a special garden planet where the development of Creator-Gods could be accelerated and where their history could be recorded. Thus Earth was created to fulfill a number of divine purposes.

One major purpose of our Journey through the third-dimensionality of planet Earth is to bring divinity into physicality, so that divine creations may be created in all the dimensions including unmanifest God, physicality, and all dimensions between. In this way creations can exist with feelings and emotions, for they will have been created in a dimensionality in which the experience of feelings and emotions is more evident than in any other dimension.

Another major purpose of our Journey through the third-dimensionality of planet Earth is to create specifically what God has energized generally. To do this requires creating with divine purpose, for although all creations become a creation of God, those creations which are made with divine purpose increase the awareness of God within the creator and thus increase God; whereas those creations made without divine purpose only rearrange that which presently exists and thus cause competition for existing energy rather than creating from the new energy of the inexhaustible Source. In this way, creation of that which is not of divine purpose creates that which is the worst in humankind, including wars, domination of others and the like; whereas creation with divine purpose creates that which is the best in humankind, including love for all and prosperity for all.

The teachings also state that within the divine purpose, there is no "waiting," there is only "creating" for we are constantly creating in each and every moment. Further, that which we create is created in all dimensions from the physical through all dimensionality unto unmanifest God. Consequently, that which we create should be in alignment with God. An example of that which has been created with divine purpose and which required humanity's rising consciousness to create, is the fact that the transformation of the Earth has been proceeding without the mass destruction which once was felt to be necessary.

Since all were with God at the first moment of Love moving

into God-space, then all are destined for mastery unless we destroy ourselves in the process. In our Earth experiment, we are creating with emotion, and it is with that emotion that we could move into ego-dominance rather than God-dominance. In this way, our mastery would be lost, for only by losing our own ego for divine purpose can we enter into the mastery that is ours. This understanding leads to the final purpose of our Journey through the third-dimensionality of planet Earth. That is the ultimate goal of completing humanity, for until the human family as a whole comes together in united, co-Creation of divine intention, it will always be incomplete.

Finally, when there is the desire to create for divine purpose, there is a prayer which can bring forth that purpose. That prayer was given by St. Germain. It is presented at the end of the channeled information.

Dear Masters, have a great Creation!

A Story of Creation
from the Blackfoot Tribe of the Native Americans

The **Blackfoot Native Americans** tell the story of the "Old Man" who came from the south, and as he traveled north, he created the birds, the animals, the plants, the prairies, the mountains, the timber and the brushlands.

In one part of his journeys, after he had grown tired of being alone, he created a mother and her child out of clay. He buried them and returned each day to see the changes which had occurred. At the end of the fourth day, they had become people; and so the Old Man bade them to walk with him to the river. The woman asked if they would live forever; and the Old man admitted that he hadn't thought about that. And so he took a buffalo chip and said that if it floated on the river, then people would die; but they would die only for four days, and four days after they die, they would live again. However, if the buffalo chip sank, then people would live forever.

The chip floated. However, the woman was not willing to accept the decision of the Old Man, and so she suggested that a stone be used and that if it floated, people would live forever. However, if the stone sank, people would feel sorry for one another and they must die. The stone sank, and so people must die because they were not willing to accept the decisions of God in their lives.

This ends the story, but not the message. There is a lot of Judeo-Christian theology in this simple, but beautiful, story. There is the background of God's creation, followed by humankind's decision not to accept what God had offered them. As a consequence, God's vision for man has been spoiled. This story echoes the Garden of Eden story, even though it comes from an entirely different source. It also echoes the Christian belief that after three days of death and burial, a resurrection will occur on the fourth day. This belief came from people who, according to written history, could not have known of the Christian story of the Resurrection. To me, it eloquently presents the message that:

We Are One!

CHAPTER THREE
DIVINE WILL and FREE WILL

INTRODUCTION

Throughout the religious history of mankind, there have been many dogmatic belief systems which have split the established religions into conflicting sects or factions. Although such factions have happened within every established religion, possibly Christianity has generated the largest number of the most divisive sects. This is unfortunate, for the one upon whose teachings the Church is supposedly established had Unconditional Love, rather than divisive activity, as his major message.

Among the dogmatic beliefs which have split the Christian Church into competing factions, possibly one of the most divisive has been the debate between Divine Will and Free Will. This debate reached its zenith during the sixteenth and seventeenth centuries with the development of predestination as a religious concept based on the dogmatic teachings of John Calvin. This concept generated some of the more ugly activities of the period. In Switzerland, John Calvin had Michael Serventus burned at the stake because of his belief in Free Will instead of predestination; and Calvin sponsored the burning of John Legate and Edward Wightman in England for their activities in promoting Free Will instead of the type of Divine Will which was advocated by those who taught predestination.

Predestination was based on the philosophic theory of determinism, a concept which states that all events are completely determined by previously existing causes, with the Prime Cause being God. As a result of this belief, determinism completely precludes Free Will. Predestination became a serious religious concept because it was believed then, and still is believed by many today, that since God is the Prime Cause of all events, and since God is never-changing, then His Divine Will has already been determined. The extreme example of this concept was the doctrine of "double predestination" which was accepted by the Reformed Church of the Netherlands at the Synod of Dort [1618-1619]. According to this doctrine, God had determined from eternity whom He will save and whom He will damn, and nothing can be done about it, no matter what characteristics an individual personality might have. This is the complete opposite of Free Will and negates any impact which Free Will might have on the present or future events of the cosmos.

But there was much which denied Free Will in the Christian doctrines that pre-dated the formal enunciation of determinism or predestinationism in the period shortly after the Reformation. The writings of St. Augustine in the fifth century are filled with the belief that mankind had given up its Free Will in the "original sin" which caused the "fall" of Adam; and deterministic thoughts are highly represented in many of the teachings of Islam, including the poetry of Omar Khayyam, written in the eleventh century.

The question of whether mankind has a choice in what happens, or whether everything has already been determined by God, is a subject which will probably continue to generate heated debates. Those who believe in the predetermination of events will use the argument that God is omniscient [i.e. all knowing], and since God is also un-changing, then everything has already been determined because God's knowledge of all events cannot be changed. Those who believe in Free Will would have to counter many doctrines [i.e. teachings] and even much dogma [i.e. that which must be believed] in order to overcome such arguments; and those teachings and dogma are present in almost every established religion.

An understanding of Divine Will, and the necessity for Free Will as an active part of Divine Will, are in many of the channelings which have been presented by the Ascended Masters. In addition, the changing nature of God is an important understanding from these channelings. Finally, the understanding of karma and reincarnation as a function of Divine Will/Free Will also makes an important contribution. Excerpts from some of the channelings which present these understandings are presented in the following section.

CHANNELED INFORMATION
Kuthumi, Channeling 48 [11/28/95]

There is a void between the consciousness of your being divine and the consciousness of your being human, but certain steps can help to fill in this void. The first step is to be conscious of what you are doing. Most of humanity goes around in a fog without having the slightest idea of the impact of their energy on their fellow man; or the impact of their fellow man on their energy; or the impact of their manifestation on all of humanity. So you could accomplish a great deal by just being conscious. It sounds simple, and it is.

The second step is to hear that aspect of yourself that comes from Divine Will. Listen to be aware of what your energy is truly telling you; because as a conscious being, you are conscious of your interaction with your environment. In addition, you are conscious of your mental and emotional interaction with your spirit; for if you are conscious, you are aware of your spirit moving <u>through</u> you rather than having your spirit being "out there" and your humanity back here. When spirit moves through you and you react to what spirit tells you, you are on the pathway which is guided by Divine Will.

As you become aware of your direction from your spirit, you now have a new understanding of Free Will operating in your humanity. Many beings in other dimensions are always in the flow of Divine Will because of the way in which they were created. They do not have individualized Free Will in the way that humanity does. An interesting question might be that if you now are conscious of your Divine Will in your spiritual experience, are you still operating in your individualized Free Will?

An explanation is needed about how Divine Will becomes individualized divine Free Will. As Divine Will moves from unmanifest to conscious intention, God's intention moves out as an over-all energy. It then goes into its "channels" for manifestation. The word "channel" is used because it is appropriate in a three dimensional sense to think of energy moving through a channel. Those beings who are always moving within the flow of Divine Will without any effort on their part have an experience much like the sea life that floats on a wave. That is how they move. However, humanity is different; for it has a channel which gets individualized. In other words, humanity does not necessarily ride this wave of God-intention, because God-intention gets placed into all of the channels of humanity; and then it is individualized according to your experience and to your energetic makeup. Who does this individualization? You do! That is your Free Will. When it operates from the finest dimension of God that is possible, then you experience God in unmanifest reality. You experience God as the individualized aspect of yourself, individualizing the intention of God into your individualized Free Will. And so Divine Will becomes divine Free Will, or free Divine Will, because you created according to the way in which you are creating your experience. By becoming aware of Divine Will, you now begin to create in a way that is more powerful because it is supported from the finer levels of existence.

The first step of the process is God's intention. The second step is your acceptance of God's intention by having Divine Will and your Free Will coincide. The third step is when you create an alignment with your individualized divine Free Will. So many aware people know what they should be creating from their individualized divine Free Will, but they choose to do otherwise because there is energy in the way. However, by moving ever more closely to that divine intention, you clear this blocking energy a little bit more until soon, it is gone. It is an iterative process, using small steps. Humanity likes to do things in this way because it can cling more closely to the past, for humanity takes great comfort in living in the past. But that comfort is a false master. It is a bed of nails.

When you use these three steps to create, you are becoming conscious of your being on many levels because you are creating from the finer realms of energy. You are now a conscious, creating being aware of your divine Free Will and creating in alignment with that divine Free Will. By these steps, you have become a conscious being, aware of your individualized divine Free Will in intention, and creating in alignment with that.

Well, if you sit back and think about it, that is pretty

Masterful, isn't it? What is needed to move into full Mastership? It is just to clarify this whole process, to be able to discern at a finer level your individualized divine Free Will and to commune with basic self at all levels. Once you have accomplished these three steps, you are well on the way to Mastership, for the rest happens merely by living within this overall process.

Being from the North Star, Channeling 26 [5/17/93]

We talk about angels because one of the transitions that is occurring is the ability for human beings to more easily perceive beings in other dimensions. In the past, there has been a block to this perception. This block or veil was created by humans, but now it is ready to be removed. It was created so that physical life could be learned from the ground up. While you were in more lofty dimensions, you were always aware of the Divine Will, just as angels presently are; and so there was no question about what you would do. But in the physical realm, the Divine Will was not always automatically known. Instead, humanity has been given the wonderful learning experience of choosing Divine Will by the exercise of an individualized Free Will. Mankind has learned and learned well, even though it may not seem so. Because of this learning process, humanity's civilization will change greatly in the relatively near future.

Being from the Central Sun, Channeling 30 [7/12/93]

For you see, as a human, you are somewhat of a unique creation. Other parts of the creative universe move in accordance with Divine Will by their very nature. Since they do not have the Free Will to move according to their own desires, then they know only the desire of the creative force. But as a member of humanity, you have been given the opportunity to be an individualized creative God by exercising your individualized Free Will to choose to be a part of the collective Divine Will.

Kuthumi, Channeling 46, Session 2 [10/28/95]

Humanity is a relatively new phenomenon. That is because God has healed enough of Its Creation to allow Itself to be manifest as a human. But if mankind has such an important role, why is it so screwed up? You already know the answer to this. It is because for humanity to have co-creatorship with God, it must have Free Will; for only truly free beings can truly be Creators. In that desire to create a complete Creator, some very wise decisions were made. Those wise decisions created an area of learning in which the student could truly understand the nature of God. If you were created in total flow with divinity, and every aspect of your life was totally in flow with divinity as an almost automatic response, then all you would know was the Divine Will. This is the way many created beings operate. Angelic beings follow the nature of their divinity. It is the natural flow of their being. Their degrees of freedom are very slight compared with the Free Will of humanity.

Those wise decisions allowed all of creation to explore God's Creation in a way in which it has not been explored before; for we can explore it from that which is in the Light, and explore it from that which is in space which has not, as yet, been filled with Light. Such space is often called the Darkness. It is space in which the creative process has started, but has not been completed. As a result of this wise decision, humanity flew headlong into its manifestation.

You know the rest of the story, for you have lived through it or you have observed it; and you are here today. You are pioneering a way for God to learn about Him/Herself, and to learn about the creative process. You are like the tentacles of God reaching out into Creation and learning about itself in a way that has not been done before. You were told that you were a pioneer of God as a feeling mechanism to exaggerate the feeling side of Creation and to provide that feedback to God in that way. Do you remember? There are other people who are pioneers of God in shining Light into space. Each and every individual has his or her own special attribute; but all of you are a part of the grand experiment to determine if you will choose the Divine Will when you have the choice to use your own Free Will to select another pathway.

Maitreya, Channeling 47 [11/6/95]

Divine Will is a greatly misunderstood topic, for it is often perceived as directives from God. That is not so. What flows from God is support for all possibilities that are created in creation. Divine Will is the blueprint of this support as applied to the evolutionary movement in creation. Then Divine Will is individualized to each aspect of God. As it is individualized, it is interpreted according to that individual beingness and purpose.

For the individual, Divine Will is that energy which is in support of the most purposeful possibility for that individual. It emanates from the God-head within that individual. But Divine Will does not limit itself to just a limited set of possibilities. If you come into understanding with your Divine Will, you will see that it is a field of possibilities. With individualized Divine Will, there is the wisdom that comes with each possibility and the love which is the motive force behind the possibility. How could it be any other way as Free Will beings? Divine Will is divine purpose for you; but it is for you to choose possibilities within that purpose by involving your Free Will in deciding what is for you in this experience. I would suggest that instead of taking your physicality to your God-head as was previously taught, you now bring God-self into your physicality. The easiest way to manifest that is to be conscious of Divine Will; for each time Divine Will is recognized and brought forth, it becomes a greater part of your experience.

The accumulation of many creative acts performed with the highest possibility of Divine Will leads to Divine Order. Divine Order is a symphony of notes created by all creations moving as best they can according to individualized Divine Will which has been developed by the exercise of Free Will. Divine Order is a great experience. It can be beautifully harmonious in a symphony of great expansion and love and creation; or it can be not in such great harmony, and yet moving purposefully. For you see, divinity does not dictate the Order. Divinity merely allows the possibility with love, and you create the Divine Order as you make your Free Will choice to follow Divine Will. The way the symphony is played is the way in which the possibilities are actualized by you. There is great Divine Order in chaos. There is great Divine Order in the expansion of divine love. It is merely the harmony that is being provided. The symphony is the cooperative which you create. It may get out of tune once in a while, but that is also in perfection. As you go through your life, you add more instruments to your symphony. You also add more variation, more melodious opportunities, and a grander and grander hall in which the symphony is played. And then your symphony gets merged with the symphonies of others until they become harmonious together and all creation flows at the highest purposeful creation. But even a non-melodious sympathy is a learning experience on how to use Free Will to accept your Divine Will.

Melchizedek, Channeling 13 [10/19/92]

You have asked what you can do to best serve your divine self, and that is to be in the energy of that divine self. Each day ask yourself the question, "Have I devoted 100% of my attention to my Divine Will?" Each person comes into body with the goal of completely manifesting a divine-led spiritual being, rather than an ego-led physical being; for in learning the lessons of life, you manifest and express your divine soul as you follow your Divine Will. In that expression, you create the Melchizedek band of light energy, the physical manifestations of which are physical temples. But the important part of that network is the enlightened beings who create energy in that temple; for each enlightened being is a Melchizedek temple with healing powers. As you follow your Divine Will, you will be on your healing path of enlightenment; and by your very nature, you will heal all that you see.

Kuthumi, Channeling 46, Session 4 [10/29/95]

Can you tell us how ego and Divine Will work together—or do they?
Ego is an essential part of being here, for without ego, you have no tools to be here. The spiritual writings that want to kill the ego have missed the point. Ego is not to be killed at all. Ego just needs to be "ego" instead of "ownership ego." Ego encompasses all of that which allows you to exist in three dimensions.

Divine Will is forever flowing from divine source. It flows through you and through all Creation from unmanifest reality into physicality. Divine Will takes many different forms, but it is, in essence, the intention behind the energy as it moves. So as God intends, Divine Will moves. It takes Divine Will for light to move and for energy to move, for without will there is no movement.

Ego allows you to exist, to communicate, to feel, and to think in your third-dimensional consciousness. But as ego becomes "ownership ego," it takes on a life of its own, because it has navigated the third-dimensional waters so well that it begins to think that it is the owner of the being. By this ownership position, it begins to make decisions for you rather than making them by Divine Will. In this independent decision making, it begins to build up layers of ego that are not Self. It is this ego that becomes the impostor of being. Most human beings today are impostors. They are not who they are or what they seem to be. Ego, in this way, takes on a life of its own.

In the process of evolution, ego becomes balanced and begins to let go of false images, false structures and false programming. Ego is a tremendous programmer in that it wants to tell you, "This happens, that happens and when all of these things have happened, then you are done!" Ego is very presumptuous about how things are. As ego becomes balanced and the energy of divine self begins to be allowed to move in, these programs and these structures begin to fall away because it is in the best interest of the total being. Divine energy gently and lovingly coaxes ego into giving in to Self.

The consciousness is all important because there has to be recognition in order for this to happen. In other words, as the pilot of your being-ship, you recognize that there is a fault in your being, and you give permission for the divine energy to come in and remove it. In this way, ego becomes merely an operational tool without independent decision-making.

So although ego is very important, where should decisions be made? It is often thought that ego is making decisions because you need to have quick decisions in order to keep the body safe and alive; but ego requires a biological process to make decisions. This takes time. However, Divine Will happens immediately, for Divine Will is infused into the biology and is therefore immediately recognized and responded to by all aspects of the physical structure. Does this mean that you lose the ability to guide your own destiny? No, it means that you gain the infinity of who you are.

The way you practice this, and this is the crux of evolving, is that you begin to put the mind and the emotions into a state of cooperation; and you begin to create the allowance for divine guidance to be aware so that you can become aware of your Divine Will. You practice this by requiring each action to look to divine guidance and ask, "What is my divine guidance for this action?" When you create the awareness for Divine Will to be present, you are automatically balancing whatever is ready within mind and emotion to allow that to flow. Although there may be some healing which must take place for a while, the end result is that you have created a clear channel for your Divine Will; and ego has returned to its proper place as an instrument of Divine Will.

Melchizedek, Channeling 1 [4/6/92]

The physical, mental, emotional, and spiritual structures of your consciousness are changing moment by moment. Pure, crystalline energy is replacing that which was not allowing you to completely embody your unlimited self within your existing self; for you are, in truth, light beings, and you will live completely as light beings when you replace that which is unlike your true self with the pure light energy of your own being. You have learned much from your teachers about how to do this. Continue, and in this way you will bring forth your own divine self very quickly; for at this time, there is no mystery of how to be divine. All you need do is **be divine**, and all that is unlike that divine nature will come forth to be cleansed, to be balanced, and to be loved back into the light. By your willingness you allow this to happen, for nothing occurs without your permission and your desire. That desire comes from your divine self or your Divine Will, and ultimately from the Divine Will of God. So as you allow yourself to be in the flow of Divine Will, you allow the cleansing and you allow the completion of your divine purpose, a purpose for which you have been given special gifts for creation.

Maitreya, Channeling 14 [10/26/92]

Do you have fear when you face what you have created? Do you feel that the law of illusion has separated you from yet another piece of your divinity? If so, then I ask you to get in step with Divine Will and you will understand what is going on; for Divine Will will press you to face all that you have created that is not divine. In this way, fear has served a great purpose, for it has taught love. Fear is one of the greatest teachers of love; for where there is love, there is no fear. Fear is non-love, but if you love fear, it no longer is fear. It has turned to love. In this way, you use natural law to generate an experience.

Natural law is the energy behind the experience, and is the sole reality of the experience. At times, natural law may confuse you, for in that which seems good, there may be energy that you know is not appropriate for you; and in that which seems negative, there may be a doorway to more light. In this way, natural law can present an illusion of false energy; but know that there is never false energy in your divine. That is where discernment between natural law and divine intention is so important.

I can see that there is confusion. I will try to help overcome this confusion by saying that the confusion is the result of trying to see with our eyes clearly what is divine and what is not divine. There will be a time when you can do this, but at the present, we ask you to sense and feel the energy of the experience, because you cannot always tell what is a part of Divine Will merely by using the physical senses. We want you to feel or sense the energy because this fits into a part of a greater plan by which you will be guided by your Divine Will at all times; for in sensing or feeling the energy, you are sensing your own divine direction along with the energy of your environment. You will never be misled by the energy within. It is always, always true. The confusion comes from the development of discernment and building the channel of divine reception. Discernment is based on what you feel, not on what you see; and that is why you are urged to meditate and spend time within building your own channel to Self. In meditation, you allow the senses to become non-dominant, and you work to build your divine reception for understanding your Divine Will.

There will come a time when there will never be a doubt come into your mental being, or emotional being, or physical being about what is your Divine Will. The "Catch-22" is that when this time is at hand, you also may choose to ascend. It is a fact of history that even the greatest of beings have had periods of doubt before their ascension. Even the very strongest have those slight moments where mass consciousness invaded their shield. That is why you have read book after book that discusses being impeccable. What that means is that you are always listening, always diligent with your attention upon your divine direction and your Divine Will. There is no substitute for a feeling discernment about this.

Maitreya/Buddha Blend, Channeling 15 [11/9/92]

Within yourself is a feeling discernment about the being of divine energy that you are. It is a being of peace, of harmony, of prosperity, and of joy. You are the energy of peace; for the energy of the Christ Consciousness is within the divinity of each of you, and the Christ is the expression of the divine coming into manifestation. Do not despair if you are not living from that dimension of love and peace at all times; but know that by bringing forth your harmonious nature, you magnify that aspect of yourself in your life. Life was meant to be a joyous occasion of creating as a divine being moving within Divine Will. You once were that. You still are. It is only a portion of your being that is conscious of less. The divine aspect of who you are has called forth and said, "Now it is the time to come home." Going home is quite simple. Just follow your path as shown to you by your intuition, by your guidance, by your feeling discernment, and by the reflection of your everyday life as you follow your Divine Will.

Kuthumi, Channeling 21 [3/15/93]

Why, in your everyday life, do you have your physical, mental and emotional bodies in this physical dimension? You have said that it is to experience, to learn lessons, to express love and for many other reasons; but these bodies are merely tools for true Self to utilize in the physical realm. In balance, your bodies are tools of Spirit. They are magnificent creations of intricate energies for the sole purpose of allowing Spirit to exist, to express, to think, to feel, and to be in the physical. But in the process of living, these bodies become unbalanced. In some cases, you enter a particular cycle of birth with an accumulation of karmic energy in these bodies that presents an out-of-balance condition from the beginning of this life cycle. In other cases it is a manifestation of spirit to place energy within these newly created bodies in order to allow that experience which this life requires. Divine Will can balance these bodies; and as you let Divine Will become expressed through them, whatever their influx of karmic or manifested energy, then you are truly living your divinity and expressing Divine Will within your humanity.

But many times there can be an imbalance of energy which can block even that expression and manifestation of Divine Will. Fear, hate, jealousy, grievance and illusion are all imbalances in energy that you carry within your Being. In addition, there are illusions of self-importance and of self-will. All of these can block the divine state of recognition, of empowerment, of love, of power and of wisdom. But this is merely an energy imbalance which is easy to balance. Do you see why the Masters have said you are divine Beings, and that you are a step away from ascension? You know who you are, and you know what is blocking your path of following your Divine Will. You have that wisdom. It is the wisdom that you spent many, many lifetimes to understand.

Each one of you knows the truths that Jesus walked upon this planet to explain. He said to love God; to love yourself; to love your neighbor; to make no judgment of anything; to use discernment; to be humble in Spirit; to be prosperous in Spirit; and to know that you have all that the Father has. Since you know these things, then do you see the wisdom that you have? Do you see the divinity that is within your grasp? You already have the information. You already know what needs to be accomplished.

I will give you a special warning. Be aware of tricks of the mind, for your mind will tell you that in order to be a Master, you must understand all the mysticism and the history of what was. What a beautiful trap when you say, "Oh, I do not know enough to be a Master. How could I possibly heal or teach?" What a beautiful trap the mind has set to keep you in your place. If you wish to study and gain the knowledge of all of the mysteries and of all the spirituality of life, you will spent thousands of lifetimes and you will still live and you will still die each time. And why is that? Why does this keep you on the cycle of births and deaths? This happens because of the limitation you have placed upon yourself by saying to yourself that you do not know or understand. But you do know and understand. All that is needed is to follow your Divine Will, for you are divine. All that the Father has is yours, so what do you have to understand other than that there is a Divine Will which you are free to follow? Please come and join us. We are ready, and so are you!

Kuthumi, Channeling 22 [3/20/93]

You have the opportunity to run up on the hill where you can see far ahead upon your path and receive those tools of divinity which define your path. The great Masters have said, "I am the way," and what they are saying is, "I have become the path. I am the Way, I am the Light, I am the Father, I am the Mother." What they really mean is that all are the Way, all are the Light, all are the Father, all are the Mother. Become aware of this, for that is all that is necessary. Life is difficult only because we are walking upon a path, and we have created a path that is difficult. But at each moment this can be changed, for you are Grand Beings, and you create grand things. Let your friends in life be Love and Divine Will; and say good-by to old friends no longer needed, such as pain and suffering. We have done enough of that. Say good-by to old friends such as fear and doubt, for they are no longer needed. And don't take yourself too seriously; but live, instead, in joy.

Lord Michael, Channeling 23 [3/22/93]

I am here because it is time to feel the joy that will come as you embody your Divine Will; for how can you be Masters without being the embodiment of Divine Will? Would you trust yourself with the power of creation or destruction on a cosmic level guided only by your personal will? How long do you think the cosmos would last? And so, one of the requirements for greater power is the discernment and enactment of Divine Will. In mastery, your personal will and your Divine Will become one, and they will never again be separated unless you choose the separation for a special assignment. Other than that, there is no separation.

How would you know that your seat of will is changing? It is no accident that several have talked about the activity within their solar plexus, for most will feel the workings there, and even the inclination to change their physical structure in that area. How many have had the impetus to be in better physical shape and to have stronger lungs, better aerobic capacity, stronger muscles in the abdomen and solar plexus, and more willingness to challenge "what is" when it does not meet your need for creation?

How many here have the personal will to discern and to

follow your divine path? What is the experience of discernment? For many, discernment happens when they are willing to go inward to listen or to feel what is their next big step; but how many are willing to listen for discernment when they open the refrigerator door or ask for the color of their clothes? How many are willing to listen when asked to go within no matter when it occurs? Are you willing to speak your truth even though personally you would hesitate to do so? How many will accept the truth of their Divine Will in the face of emotional turmoil and in face of the personal desire for another path? Mastery is not a fifty percent job. It is a one hundred percent job to be in personal power each and every moment; for until you can live in that mastery one hundred percent of the time, you will not be allowed the empowerment of your divine Self in total.

As an experiment, when you wake up tomorrow affirm that you will listen each and every moment of that day to your divine Self, and that you will merge the will of the divine Self with your personal activities. If you reach into the refrigerator for an item and you hear, "No, not today," then put it back. If your Divine Will says you must fast, will you fast in trust that this is your divine experience? Or if you were told to eat something you would not have thought of, do you trust your divine information? Be aware of the noises of the personal that try to interfere with the wisdom and the will of the divine. If you are not clear, then stop what you are doing and be quiet and listen for the clarity. If you practice this, then soon you will be able to have that clarity no matter what level of personal or other activity you are engaged in.

Mastery is not a grandiose beam from above that all of a sudden makes you the master you know you are. Mastery is earned. Many today are waiting. They are waiting for the cosmology to generate the wave of ascension which will move them into consciousness as a creating-God, chosen because they are philosophically correct. If you are thus waiting, you will wait longer; for those who will ride this wave of ascension are those who place themselves within their Divine Will each and every moment. You have been given the tools to do so; and if you need help to adhere to Divine Will, that help is available at any time. I have offered you my sword to place within your aura in permanence, in protection and in power. In this age of relative comfort, many of you have become too comfortable in your philosophy and your correctness, but lacking in your action. And so use this time wisely, for if you were to look at linear time, as in this dimension you can, you would see progress accelerating greatly. That is why we stress the importance of making the most of each moment, for you do not have much time left.

Kuthumi, Channeling 24 [3/29/93]

At this time, there is a need to bring forth much information, and there is so much that we wish to bring forth to you; but we are not allowed to indiscriminately provide wisdom, for with wisdom is the responsibility for the consequences of your action. We have talked many times about what mastery is and how one achieves mastery. Mastery is merely the full manifestation of Self in whatever experience involves you. The road to mastery is quite simple. It is being aware of that aspect of Self that knows Divine Will, and then manifesting that Divine Will in every moment of your life. Mastery is a one hundred percent occupation. The good news is that once you have lived in mastery, it becomes easy to live harmless, joyful, wise lives in every moment; and it is easy to be in eternal freedom.

What is freedom? Freedom is living fully in all the free kingdoms of Self, living without limitation, living in whatever dimensions you have allowed yourself to create within. For you know that you are more than your minds and your bodies and your emotions. There is a part of you that is great and wise and divine. That is what has guided you to seek more out of life than what the illusion of living would appear to be. Some of you have heard this message many times, and some of you are trying diligently. Others have forgotten that this is a 100% occupation. The next time you find yourself in an experience of discomfort or anxiety of any type, allow yourself to move within that wise divine part of Self so that you can heal that imbalance by attunement with Divine Will.

Being from the North Star, Channeling 26 [5/17/93]

As you continue to act upon the information that you receive in the years to come, there will be no need for as many channels as we need today. Instead, individuals will develop the capacity to hear their guidance and their own Self from within on a more trusting and clear basis; for that is the goal of all true channelers. Our work is directed so that each one of you, and all others who would look within, would be able to have a clear communication of Divine Will and purpose, not only for those in the physical, but also for those who live on different levels of life and awareness. For you see, physical living is but a fraction of what exists in what you term "this space." In this very room at this time, there are literally hundreds of Beings who are not physical but who have the awareness to perceive that they exist in a world that is assimilated within the dimension of their perception. What this means is that each Being, no matter what dimension or level of their existence, has an awareness of his or her level as you have an awareness of your physical realm. And all are pursuing their goal of understanding their Divine Will and purpose.

To reach this goal, clear yourself of all that is not necessary and not worthy of your divine stature and of following your Divine Will. What is it in your life that does not bring harmony? Do not put off until tomorrow what you can heal today, for you do not know what tomorrow may bring. What if I were to say to you that tomorrow would be like today, except that the Earth would have transitioned and all those upon it would have reached a new dimension of understanding? To you, the perception might be that all was the same, until you realized that now men did not harm one another, and violence had vanished from the planet. If all were to follow their Divine Will, this would be possible tomorrow. But do not believe the words I speak to you. Instead, take them under consideration and balance them with the energy that is within your Self; for in the infinity of creation there is an infinity of possibilities. There is a part of each one of you that knows what tomorrow brings. It may not know how you will respond completely, but it knows the framework for the drama that you are playing; for you do understand your divinity and your Divine Will.

Lord Michael, Channeling 36 [5/5/94]

Divinity is not passive, for it is not an other-world experience. Divinity is now and forever in all experiences of you. There is no space, place or time without divinity. There is no action that proceeds from non-divine; for even Darkness is of divine origin. All that is created has its purpose and its place, and all moves towards a resolution in the Light. Those who have their attention on the Light need not necessarily experience non-light; for it is not necessarily true that in order to appreciate the Light, all must experience non-light or Darkness. This is only true for those beings who do not have that appreciation in the first place. Their learning experience is to find out what it's like to be alone.

For most, it is indeed a Golden Age that is upon us. There were many futures available for Earth; but Earth and her inhabitants have chosen a future of Light, of divine love, of wisdom, and of manifestation. Earth is in her joy of knowing her time of transformation is near. Consequently, she magnifies the energy from the Central Sun, and lets it be focused through the many cosmic computers and Masters so that it can come to you and allow you unprecedented capability and opportunity to move in your spiral of divine movement. On a practical basis, this means that the power of the Masters is indeed within your grasp. The power to change your physical body is in your power today, if it is appropriate in your divine intention. If you spend a small amount of time each day seeing your divine image and bringing it forth into your physical, your wisdom and energy will create physical results in your life. The ability to know your divine guidance is at hand. Any earnest attempt to see Divine Will will be rewarded, and all that is in the way will be removed. All it takes is constant attention and earnest appreciation of the divinity in Self and of the Divine Will.

There is no longer any excuse for wallowing in non-evolutionary action and thought and energy, for all is available. It may not seem so because it is not yet immediately manifested in your life. But do you trust yourself, and have you not already heard this message within yourself? Do you not already know that all is possible so long as it is a part of your divine intention and Divine Will? Indeed each one of you has received this message many times. Yet, how many are earnestly, each day, placing the attention and spending the time to bring forth that which you desire and which is within your grasp? Or is it that you get too busy in the things of the world and forget about the things of true Divine Will and true self reality?

Maitreya, Channeling 41 [2/2/95]

As the energy upon the planet increases, the response to your clear, divine creations also increases. This means that when you wish to create some thing in your life, it only takes time and dedication to be clear with your divine intent, and it will be created. The creation may not appear as you expected, because during the process you possibly were not completely clear of what was the best divine creation for you. As this energy increases, the time between when you initialize your creative impulse and when the creation occurs shall be much shorter. This is a two-edged gift; for if you can create this quickly, there is great responsibility to be clear with your Divine Will and with your clarity of purpose; for as I have said before, the increased energy amplifies all. So as a warning, move to clarity as quickly as you can, so that in this energy efficiency that is coming, you truly create that which flows in agreement with your Divine Will.

St. George, Channeling 43 [5/5/95]

If your intellect is tied to your spirit, and yet your body is multidimensional, and if your emotions are the fabric upon which you experience, then you can begin to see how it is all in one continuous flow. Your body is more than the physical self, for your body is infinitely tied to your emotions, your intellect, and your spirit. Your body is truly a three dimensional expression of all that you are. It is not separate, but you created it, physically, so that you could be here. Do you know that in your physical selves, you have the knowledge of your intellect and of your soul, and of the fact that it is all linked together? Do you realize the soul has a physical counterpart? The soul sits within your body as the physical manifestation of your soul; but this is not all of your soul. Although the soul has weight, it permeates the other tissues of your body, so it cannot be seen. Do you know that when someone dies, their weight changes as the soul leaves the body? That is because the soul has a physical manifestation.

I present this example only to emphasize that everything is connected. The soul is part of your body; your body is part of your soul; your emotions are part of your body; your emotions are the fabric in which you experience; and the mind is the vehicle to allow Divine Will to be expressed. The mind was developed to be a conscious co-creator with divinity that moves through it in the expression of Divine Will.

This vehicle which you call your physical body is not too hard to understand, because in reality, there is no separation. Although you often have been told about your physical body, your mental body, your emotional body, and your spiritual body, realize that it is all connected and there is no separation. It is just the way you experience; but they do all work together, especially when they work within the understanding of Divine Will.

Maitreya, Channeling 43 [5/5/95]

In your infinite intelligence, you create opportunities to expose those aspects of yourself that are not yet clear so that they can be made conscious and brought into balance. Because of this, the evolution of consciousness is a difficult task, because not only do you have things that you have created in your experiences that need balance, but you are also clearing for the world. When you balance an energy aspect of yourself and bring joy into that place, you help clear that same energetic pattern around the world. Pioneers of consciousness do grand but difficult work; for you not only clear your own "stuff," you create the energy pattern for that to be cleared throughout the world.

Because of this, the difficulties may sometimes seem overwhelming; but you are at the controls, so you can slow down a bit and rest for awhile if it becomes too much. But that is why you are here. You were told of the need for you to become conscious in all aspects of Self in order to fulfill the consciousness of all that is. Before you came here, you were told that you would do more for the world by clearing those energies within yourself than you could ever do by good deeds, for you can transform the world by becoming whole, but how many can you help through good deeds? This is not to say that good deeds are not valuable; but becoming conscious is the foundation, and the good deeds are the expression of that conscious clarity. If one being were to move into complete awareness, the effect upon the world would be dramatic. Eventually, there would be an avalanche of consciousness; for it becomes easier and easier and easier. Finally, beings will spontaneously move into awareness, because the environment in which they live is creating that spontaneity of awareness. Although that environment is quite different than the present one, it will happen!

Today, the world's environment is not creating clarity in all places at all times; but by creating that in your life, you create that for everyone else's life. Consequently, you are important to the evolution of the world. It is easy to say, "I am but one person, so what effect do I have upon the world?" The answer is easy, for by fulfilling your own pattern into consciousness, you create a great gift for the world. And then, when that consciousness is guided by your Divine Will, your gift to the world becomes even greater. Have no fear, for your Divine Will is ever present to guide you on each step of the way as you follow your path into the New Age of Being.

Maitreya, Channeling 50 [1/23/96]

In this Age of Being, many people will be rearranging their lives, because what was thought to bring happiness upon this planet clearly does not; and what will bring happiness to you will be clear to you. In your knowing, you will see what is no longer appropriate for you, and what is no longer serving you; for if your life does not serve your divine purpose, then what are you doing it for? Joy is the expression of Spirit creating in alignment with Divine Will; for there is no greater love than divinity loving itself, and it loves itself through the creation of its will and its direction.

An example of that is within each of you. How much do you love yourself when you do something which you know is not following your Divine Will? If you were to go within yourself to review the life that you have lived to this point, and really allow the process to become divine, you will find the experiences that come to the forefront are those in which you allowed you to love yourself by creating what you divinely intended within your Divine Will.

Maitreya, Channeling 51 [2/6/96]

Because of your divinity, you have within you a clear passage of Divine Will to be known by you. Divine Will is the possibilities that spring from unmanifest God through the plan of creation. It moves through all of creation like the waves upon the ocean. Within you, you receive that in the most subtle levels of creation, and it moves through your consciousness, becoming individualized. In other words, it is not necessarily individualized when it comes from unmanifest God. It is a possibility of creation. Creation is created by that which is in creation. The flow of God that comes within you is individualized according to you and to your individual landscape of being.

You become aware of this individual aspect of you that comes from God by looking, feeling and being quiet within. In reality, this is the transference of individual will from your higher dimensional bodies. As you receive this knowing and work with it, it becomes clearer until it becomes as if you were talking to another third-dimensional person. You will receive communication that is as clear as if you were hearing it over a telephone. You will know by the level of truthfulness within you that it is your guidance. As you hear this guidance, and act upon it, you are creating your Mastership. There is really no need for the great accomplishments that traditional spirituality placed upon you. In addition, you do not have to spend years of learning, because you already have the knowing. It is within you. The only requirement is that you do what is necessary to heal and to understand the guidance that is within you, and then to have the courage to move and to create from that knowing. Often this does take great courage, for this is still the world that does not accept these tenets in a conscious fashion. It is still a world in which there are many powers that wish to control you and others. But if you are a free being creating from your individual, divine Free Will, then another can have control over you only if you allow it.

The needs of this world are pressing on you each and every day. But I say unto you that these things are the by-product of creating from your individual will. If you move to achieve prosperity in your life, you accomplish a great deal; but if it was accomplished in contradiction to your Divine Will, what have you gained? Have you not been controlled by the energy of prosperity rather than the energy of self-love and of self-realization? The need for a loving relationship is great; but if the relationship is pursued in contradiction to your Divine Will, what have you gained? And what have you lost? All of the needs of humanity are important because you live in this world; but they pale in importance compared to the creation of divine life by following your Divine Will.

Kahil Gibran, Channeling 6 [8/3/92]

I would like to present an analogy about some of the difficulties which you may encounter as you pursue your Divine Will. The analogy will use a highway by saying that there is a large freeway between that part of you that resides within divine unmanifest space, and that part of you that is currently in third-dimensional body. This long freeway has many exits, and these exits correspond to the different dimensions upon which you live; for you live in many dimensions beyond the consciousness of this body. If you do not realize this, it is because your freeway has had a detour erected upon the exit ramps so that you could not travel to the other dimensions in which you exist.

From time to time, those detours have been placed for the benefit of experience; but experience is a two-edged sword. Experience within Divine Will expands the width of your travel; but experience not received within divine understanding can create additional detours. Additional detours are not necessarily bad, because they expand your experience and because there is no experience within Free Will that is not appropriate. To say that it is not appropriate would be to separate a part of you from God; for all things are of God. How could they be created if they were not? How could they be supported if they were not? They are created by beings of Free Will who, for their own understanding, have created those experiences, whether or not they were a part of Divine Will. In this endeavor, their vessel of experience has grown, and their future has been determined on a moment-by-moment basis as the freeway journey proceeds.

St. George, Channeling 42 [2/13/95]

All of you act as if your future could be read from one of your lousy history books. "Oh, I will be there, and I will be wearing my blue suit." What is going to happen tomorrow has not been created fully. You know this! And so the truth is always a probability. This is what your physics has discovered about particles. They have found that this elementary particle has a probability of being here or there! And it doesn't even have to go through here to get to there! It is probability. It is mathematical. And that's the way nature works. It is beautiful. Do you know why it is beautiful? Because it is Free Will creation! The consciousness of this particle has Free Will! The consciousness of the human being has divine Free Will to choose and create, and it has the desire to do this as it lives!

Being from the Central Sun, Channeling 25 [4/19/93]

We wish to talk about *The Science of Desire,* for this is an area that is often misunderstood. Many schools have declared war upon desire in hope that the elimination of all desires would lead to divine man. But in truth, some desires seem most appropriate, whereas others seem so inappropriate. Desires come from all levels, which makes one wonder which desire is the truthful one.

You inhabit a physical body which is conscious and has awareness and desires. Your mind or mental body is aware and has desires. Your emotional body is also a source of desire and fluctuation. And your Soul is the pathway of Divine Desire and of Divine Will; for does not any will create the impetus to move, which creates a desire within the bodies for action?

So how do we discern whether this desire that we feel is one of divine source? The easiest way is to ask it. As an example, the desire for food beyond what would seem a normal amount may be confusing because the desire can come from many directions. The physical body may need the food because it has an unbalanced cellular energy due to Soul's journeys in the physical plane; or the mind can produce the desire for food due an unbalanced perception of the personality; or the emotions can produce a desire for food because of unbalanced astral interaction. Finally, the Soul can produce this large desire for food because it knows that you will need it over the coming days. So you see, this desire can come from many sources; for each of these bodies has consciousness and they all play upon each other for the creation of movement in your life.

So we know we have desires in our life each day, and that these desires are not always what they seem. Thus you must investigate where your desires come from; for there are divine desires such as that of discerning and living Divine Will in each moment. This desire allows your Soul to fully descend into all your bodies, thus providing a divine linkage from Spirit to man and creating God-man. A very simple technique to determine where your desire comes from is to wait it out. If the desire comes from your body or your mind or your emotions, in a short time the consciousness of those bodies will be diverted to something new; whereas a divine desire persists because it is a constant message from your Soul.

Another technique is to ask your Soul for discernment. Call upon Spirit to move into your consciousness through your Soul to provide needed information about what action should be taken. Now this sounds quite simple, but how many actively use this in their lives? This activity of questioning impulsive desires is one of the greatest gifts to Mastery, because this process of discernment is what leads to the integration of Divine Will each and every moment.

A third technique is to surround the desire with White Light in order to feel within your bodies where this desire comes from. You will readily see a desire within your mental body, or feel it within your physical body; but the emotional body can be quite illusionary and will take some practice to pin it down.

But in all of this do not try to eliminate desires, for some are sent to you as a message from your Divine Will; and a life without desires would be the life of a robot. An example of a desire which is a message from your Divine Will would be a desire which states, "Let my will be made one with thy will, for in thy will is my greatest joy." That, indeed, is a desire to have!

St. George, Channeling 47 [11/6/95]

You are anything but a robot. You are God, and you have the desire to create. You are an individual aspect of God, and you create for God in your own way. When you create something new, what do you do? You examine it. You see and feel if it meets that divine perspective that you had in its creation. If it doesn't, you may modify it a little bit, because it is not all it set out to be. It is not that you have a divine imprint and then you go create exactly; for if you did that, then you would be a consciousless robot just doing what God bid you to do. That is not God's wish. God doesn't want a bunch of robots; S/He wants co-creative companionship that S/He can trust to go out and create in a way that leads to a balanced creation and to the ever-enlargement of what is in love. Many of the pioneers of God think that all they have to do is just sit back and then God will do it all for them. Well, they are abandoning their namesake. As an individual created aspect of God with Free Will, God has said "Go forth, and in love, be and create. And let us enjoy the majesty of that creation." What a magnificent gift you have been given! Much of the other parts of the cosmos are jealous of you for having been given the gift of Free Will. Use it to align yourself with Divine Will, for then you will create well!

CHANNELED ANSWERS
TO SPECIFIC QUESTIONS

Do we define our divine purpose before birth or as we develop? Purpose is a word which has many levels and possibly too many third-dimensional counterparts. A more appropriate term is Divine Will. The divine plan of your Divine Will is set into motion before the incarnation ever occurs, but it is a framework. It is a generalized understanding of the experience to be created and in the beginning, that is all it is. If the being is one that is not very open or not very likely to create consciously, then some of this framework will be more rigidly defined. For those who are more conscious, the framework is looser to allow the full freedom of Free Will to create within that framework, or even to change the framework at any time the knowing of the individual can be at the level at which the framework was first created.

Is there any other planet in the entire cosmos that has physical inhabitants that we would consider to be the same as the physical inhabitants on planet Earth? The first answer would be "No" because Earth is unique, and since Earth is unique, then the physicality that exists on Earth is unique. Now if you would ask are there places where there is physicality in three dimensions with Free Will and the ability to evolve in a manner similar to those on planet Earth, then the answer is "Yes."

Is there any place that has had physicality such as Earth has now, but they have had it in the past and they have gone on to something else? There has been similar physicality, but not identical because each system is different. Again, Earth is unique. The nurturing expression of Mother God on this planet is quite strong. It has allowed the evolution of a physical form that is unique, but is somewhat similar to other systems.

Will Earth's uniqueness be copied in other places? You wish for me to give you the secret of Earth's future, and so I will! Earth is a prototype of systems to come. The Earth experience of the integration of God in physical form creates an effect in God, because this experience will heal rifts that go completely into the God-head. When these rifts have been healed, this will allow the transformation of humanity in a way that has never been seen before. This transformation will be projected into Creation. That is one of the reasons that this is such an important time and why Earth is so important. Those beings that exist here in many, many dimensions will receive a tremendous healing due to Earth's healing and the healing of humanity.

SUMMARY

In regard to **Divine Will and Free Will**, these teachings made the definitive point that we chose to come into third-dimensionality on planet Earth to become a God-conscious being by freely choosing to do so. This differs from other beings such as the angels who are aspects of God that have no choice because in their environment, nothing else exists and so they know only that which is Divine Will.

Humanity has a more difficult time becoming God-conscious beings than those aspects who are required to live in Divine Will at all times. However, once having chosen to follow Divine Will by Free Will choice, humanity will have become more responsible God-conscious beings, for we will have been exposed to that which is not Divine Will, and will have rejected it.

In this sense, humanity has been given a great gift, for if humanity can follow Divine Will by desiring to choose it out of all which exists, then humanity can become full co-creators with God. Humanity can then be trusted to create as God would create, not because nothing else is available, but because humanity has chosen to do so by experiencing that which is not-God. In the rejection of not-God by Free Will choice, humanity has had an experience that truly helps God to define itself; for in the experience of becoming a divine being, all which is not divine comes up for healing. It is thus identified, experienced and healed; and in the healing, God indeed becomes joyful, for a new aspect of individualized God has been generated.

In this sense, humanity is somewhat of a unique creation; for humanity is the pioneer in exaggerating the feeling side of creation and is giving feedback to God about what it is like to feel. In searching for the Divine Will, humanity feels its way along not by following the directives of God, for if God knew all that was to be directed, there would be no need to feel it. It would all be already in place. But the approach of feeling the way contains a trap. If it is directed by ego-ownership rather than by Divine Will, then the feeling approach will not lead to God-consciousness. When ego starts to lead, then the being must coax the ego to give in to Self so that the feeling side will coincide with the God side.

Divine Will is a very important aspect of our Journey to fill the void between our physical consciousness and our divine consciousness. The first step to fill that void is to be conscious of what we are doing by knowing God's intention. The second step is to do only that which is in response to Divine Will by having Free Will coincide with Divine Will. The third step is to align with the Free Will that is in coincidence with Divine Will. In this way Free Will and Divine Will will coincide at all times. In fact, one can only become a God-conscious being by following Divine Will at all times.

The way to have Free Will and Divine Will coincide is rather easy, for it was explained by Jesus when he told humanity to love God; to love yourself; to love your neighbor; to make no judgment of anything; to use discernment; to be humble in Spirit; to be prosperous in Spirit; and to know that you have all that the Father has. But while doing this, humanity must always be aware of tricks of the mind, for the mind will say that you must learn new things in order to be in Mastery. That is not true, for all that is needed is to follow Divine Will. Humanity is composed of beings who are already divine. All that the Father has is yours, so what do you have to understand other than that there is a Divine Will which you are free to follow?

CHAPTER FOUR
MANIFESTATION and PROSPERITY

INTRODUCTION

It has been said that once a human being fulfills the basic physical needs of food, shelter and clothing, then his/her thoughts turn to things which are holy. In this way, the fourth aspect of the physical human could be called "religion," with the term religion being used as the acceptance of all things which are "holy." In this use of the term, religion is more than just the worship of God, whether that God is a personal or a supernatural one. In this use, religion refers to all aspects of that which is holy, including worship, moral conduct, right beliefs, participation in religious institutions, etc.

The point being made is that despite the exhortations of teachers of all religious faiths, the desire for things holy is often set aside when one is hungry, homeless or naked: the basic needs which are satisfied by "prosperity." Once the needs of food, shelter and clothing, have been satisfied, at least to a basic level, then attention often can be directed to the worship of that which is "grander" than these physical needs.

All religions have realized that these physical needs have to be satisfied for the "professionally religious" within their faith. Many religions provide manses, vicarages or monasteries for shelter, and stipends to cover the other basic needs. Other religions have established the understanding that society, in general, will provide these needs, as is the case for the monks of Burma or Tibet who are sent out to gather their daily food from the largess of the general population. But however the religions take care of the physical needs of their professional people, there is general recognition that these needs do exist for all people.

Although the writings of all established religions present the thoughts that the basic physical needs have to be satisfied, possibly one of the most definite statements on the subject is presented in the Christian New Testament. In the sixth chapter of The Gospel According to Matthew, and in the twelfth chapter of Luke's gospel there is a significant teaching by Jesus the Christ. The version in Luke says the following:

And he said to his disciples, "Therefore I tell you, do not be anxious about your life, what you shall eat, nor about your body, what you shall put on. For life is more than food, and the body more than clothing. Consider the ravens: they neither sow nor reap, they have neither storehouse nor barn, and yet God feeds them. Of how much more value are you than the birds! And which of you by being anxious can add a cubit to his span of life? If then you are not able to do as small a thing as that, why are you anxious about the rest? Consider the lilies, how they grow; they neither toil nor spin; yet I tell you, even Solomon in all his glory was not arrayed like one of these. But if God so clothes the grass which is alive in the field today and tomorrow is thrown into the oven, how much more will he clothe you, O men of little faith! And do not seek what you are to eat and what you are to drink, nor be of anxious mind. For all the nations of the world seek these things; and your Father knows that you need them. Instead, seek his kingdom, and these things shall be yours as well." [Emphasis added.]

The major point from this quotation is that God knows that humans need these things; and that if you seek his kingdom, they will be yours. Many of the New Age have taught that it is their right to manifest things such as prosperity in the physical; and many have tried to understand just how this could be done. The methodology of doing this is given in many of the channelings from the Ascended Masters; and it is strikingly similar to the teachings of Jesus the Christ presented above. Excerpts from some of the channelings which present this knowledge are presented in the next section.

CHANNELED INFORMATION
Maitreya, Channeling 51 [2/6/96]

Could you tell me more about prosperity? Prosperity is the acceptance of self in third- dimensional wholeness, for prosperity is the enjoyment of being in the third dimension with what is here for you to play with. Prosperity is a result of freedom of self. Prosperity is the ability for you to create in your life those third-dimensional aspects that serve you, be it an automobile until you can teleport, or be it a house until you create your own structure wherever you are, or be it clothing until you can fashion your own. These things are substitutes for the freedom to create anew to your divine desire. However, we are in a world in which we are not yet creating in this way; so, we create out of three dimensional stuff in the old fashioned way. We earn it. In this prosperity, we help ourselves to be comfortable in our process.

If we were to create prosperity in the new way, how would we do it? Well, we would not do it the way most of us try; for most prosperity is killed at the source by our feeling that we are not worthy. Humanity feels that they are not worthy unto God, and that they are not worthy unto themselves. If you are not worthy unto God, how could God's prosperity be worthy to you? The first step in prosperity is to realize fully that God truly is within you, and loves you, and that you are worthy of your Mastership—**now!**

One of the biggest obstacles to manifestation is the presence of the energy of lack. Getting through these energies is a multi-faceted process, because the energy of lack exists on all levels of life, especially within you. If you truly accept yourself as a child of God and as a God-creator given full license to create according to your divine intention, then you will create prosperity in your life in whatever fashion that you deem it to be so. Until you are totally clear, the prosperity which you create may not be as you thought it would be, but it will be there in a way that serves you. It may not satisfy your desire for success, but it will be enough to sustain you for the present level of creativity at which you are performing.

The first step in generating prosperity is to know that you are worthy of being God in action. As you express and acknowledge that to yourself each day, you will feel yourself becoming more comfortable with being a true part of God and worthy of all of God's prosperity. When this feeling of worthiness develops, then comes the process of being in acceptance; because even though you may now feel that you are worthy to be a part of God, have you truly taken the next step which is to accept that which comes to you?

That is really all that prosperity is. It is balancing lack and being in acceptance. After that, everything else flows from your creative input and from your creative divine intention; for as you remove lack and gain acceptance, you will create situations in your life which bring you what you need.

Often humanity thinks they have to be conscious of a grand plan about how they would, for example, create a certain house. It would be a certain color, and would be on a certain lot, and would have a certain number of rooms. Well, that is good, because it helps you to picture your creation. But that is only a part of it. Often people will do this, and then they will wonder why that house did not appear since they had pictured every room, every wallpaper, and every other nuance. Well, they will find that they were concentrating on this picture so intently that they did not address the issues of lack and acceptance that kept knocking on their door. They continued to say, "I don't have to address these issues because I have the picture!" Well, it takes more than just the picture to gain it. It takes all of the above.

Some people have much karmic energy of lack. This comes from millennia of lack. It comes from millennia of being down-trodden and killed because you were spiritual. This energy is one that is clearing rapidly now upon the planet; and if you place yourself in the stream of this clearing, you will find that your karmic energy of lack will be cleared rapidly.

But don't expect St. Germaine to come down to you and give you a pot of gold. There are some who expect that! [Laughter] And as long as they expect that, St. Germaine will keep telling them, "Yeah, I'll be down to give it to you!" [Laughter] It is your creation, but often you don't truly need to create what you think you need. In the becoming of you, you reach a knowing of what you truly need; for if you are a being in freedom with true creative ability, what do you truly need? You need **nothing** because you can create it as you need it! And then when you are done with it, you let the energy go back into God-space rather than sticking around to rot and to fall down. For when you really get creative, you create it out of material that will never disintegrate. It will repair itself. That is when you know that you are really getting good at it!

Some of us are working within the area of prosperity mani-festation and instead of looking at it on the basis of "I want this house or this thing," we look at what the house or the thing will be used for. We then hold that vision as a God-love energy related to what we really want in our lives. It seems to help bring that thing through. Is this a new way of manifesting? What you are doing is putting feeling into your creation. Rather than a sterile picture, it is a moving, feeling creation. That is what is enhancing your creative ability.

I would like to more fully address the subject of manifesta-tion, but this would take a great deal of time. I will explain this quickly by saying that for you to be conscious, you are manifesting you. For you to be conscious in all places that you are, from God to three dimensions, you are manifesting you in all of those dimensions. So if you are aware of yourself throughout creation, then manifestation is a natural by-product of your intention. In order to manifest easily, you must be whole; for manifestation and wholeness are synony-mous terms.

In other words, when you really get in touch with who you are and what you are and start expressing that, then you start mani-festing. Indeed, it is so!

St. George, Channeling 42 [2/13/95]

I am not here to tell you how to live your life, for I am only here to point out the possibilities. One possibility is never to be in poverty. But then what is poverty? Do you know what poverty is? You tell me! What is poverty? Please. Speak up! *Lack of belief in self.* Indeed! What else! *Consciousness without Light.* Indeed! What else? *You don't realize what abilities you already have.* Ah! Appreciation for what you have to make way for more. Indeed. Very good. What else? *St. Germaine once said I don't ask for enough!* Oh. Could that have something to do with creating your reality in a way that maybe you should ask for more? Or maybe is it a belief that you could not ask for more; that you're not worthy of more? *Well, why ask, if we're supposed to create?* You ask, because often in formulating the question, you've already created the answer.

So you see, poverty is exactly what it is; but it is not poverty of prosperity, of gold, silver, money, belongings, material wealth. Those are but little things. Poverty is poverty of Self. It is the decision to live in lack. Now, why would one do so? One reason is because one wanted the experience of lack; for is this not a world of duality in which one learns about abundance by experiencing the lack of abundance? But we've done that enough! We've all learned that crap! It's time to move on. There are bigger fish to fry. And so, that's why we no longer need to live in poverty; for this is the age of self-awareness in physical body. When fully aware, you will have prosperity in all forms.

What else is poverty? Poverty means being enslaved in lack, particularly in the lack of freedom. But in creating your life, you create freedom; for how would you live if you could hold out your hand and you could create the prosperity needed at any moment? You would live in complete freedom. You have the consciousness through all dimensionality to create prosperity in your hand at this moment now! You can do it! And it will begin to happen! You will go out to have good dinner; and when it comes time to pay the bill, you will know that the money needed for that bill will be available. You will trust the universe completely and totally and you will create it, because that is your divine intention as a free being. Behold, it will be there.

You have heard St. Germaine talk of this. Do you think he carried around a bunch of money? Do you think he liked to wash dishes? No! He created what he needed, quite extravagantly, I might say, and without limitation. So you see, poverty is merely a condition of living in lack. When you overcome poverty, you truly gain the freedom of life. Having money does not mean you're not in poverty; for there are many with lots of money who live in poverty. Poverty does not just mean money or belongings; but some people have both prosperity in material wealth and prosperity in Self, for these are the ones who have created it in fullness and in love. Do you see?

The process of leaving poverty is enlightenment in the process of living! Are you willing to live? Are you willing to take that body and change it, enliven it? If you start on this process, then soon you will say good-bye to poverty!

Kuthumi, Channeling 48 [11/28/95]

Up until now, humanity has not had the opportunity to be aware of its consciousness in all places. You have consciousness in all places, but as a human being, you have forgotten that. Humanity is not presently conscious in those aspects of self that sit next to unmanifest reality. To help generate this awareness, there is a very small part of created energy that springs from God for your use in creating your intention. If your intention remains divine, it is fully supported from that level. If the intention is not of divine order, then not only are you not clear at the level of unmanifest reality, your intention is not supported in those places as well.

So what happens? If the intention is divine, it is supported in those fine places and you create as you draw new energy from unmanifest God into dimensional reality. If the intention is not of divine order, then you draw energy from those dimensions that support that type of creation, and those dimensions are generally in the lower orders of dimensional experience. In this case, you are not creating new energy for its manifestation. Instead, you are now in competition for energy because you are not adding to the whole. You are taking what is and shaping it for your specific purpose. This is "not adding to that which is God." It is adding an experience, but it is not adding to that which comes from unmanifest reality into dimensional reality. Is this clear?

What it means is that you have the ability to create as God-human and to manifest anything that is of divine intention in any dimension that you wish it to exist. But in order to do this, there must be the clarity in those dimensions from unmanifest potential all the way through dimensional experience to physical reality. I have talked many times lately of manifestation, because manifestation is the essence, the living reality, of your consciousness. By the very existence of your being, you manifest. By the very movement of your bodies, you manifest. Everything in your existence is manifestation.

Therefore, to become conscious is also the process of manifesting in new and greater ways.

It is time for humanity to begin to think of living as being the ultimate in manifestation. In the past, the evolution of being has been to create a finer experience in order that mankind could move up into God and disappear from physical reality. This was because mass consciousness could not allow the experience of full divinity upon the planet. Not only would it have required tremendous energy, it would have violated the karma and the evolution of the planet at that time. But now is the time to become physically God by the very birthright that God gave you!

As God-creating beings, you move each moment in manifestation. Divinity is not just experiencing God consciousness. It is moving God consciousness through your physicality, for in doing this, you are helping this planet to evolve into divine experience. We have talked much of the effect of your healing and your manifestation of all that is upon this realm; for each time you heal yourself, you open the doorway for others to do the same. Light energy is connected in that way. If you overcome any energy within your being, you have allowed an opening within all of humanity to heal that accumulated energy within each individual that is energetically connected to that energy. It will be as if you were a vortex that just sucks in all the energy all over the place and heals it.

As you exist, you manifest. This happens even if you are in your divine meditation and your heart rate decreases, and your breathing rate decreases, and your pulse decreases, and your energy becomes settled and fine and light filters into your physical body, and you become invisible because you have become light and you have moved your physical into your divinity. Even then you are manifesting, for that is manifestation as well! The most fine creation next to unmanifest reality manifests if it even looks or intends something, for that is manifestation. Everything is manifestation.

That is why God is ever-growing. That is why a religion that creates a static and absolute God has no understanding whatsoever of life. They have no concept of what God is. They have created a God that is a dead God. God is living and growing and expanding and experiencing and creating every moment of **now**. As God's emissaries into this dimension, you are God working in myriad ways. That is why the age of religious movements of a Guru and his children is gone. This is the age of Masters, self-fulfilled in their God-beingness, creating as God-conscious beings, and recognizing that the least of you in physical evaluation terms, is equal in God to the greatest manifesting energy. As many Masters have said, the lowest beggar is the greatest Master, because everyone is the greatest Master. Relative evaluation has no meaning. Although many in the New Age are becoming quite arrogant over their clarity, that will be their downfall; for there is no relative greatness. Each being is expressing his or her God-beingness in the way which is the perfection of energy at that time.

We have talked about how each person, by virtue of experience and manifestations, has created a different vessel of God; for you may be a huge, magnificent vessel of God of experience and of manifesting ability compared to another being that may be new in these experiences. But which is greater, and which is lesser? Are they not both God, expressing in an individualized way? And who is humanity to judge the order in which creation occurs? In the next moment of **now**, what is the situation to be? In the ultimate reality of your experience when God-consciousness comes forth over your cosmic awareness, you will realize that you are all one and the same. The observer and the observed become one. Then you have the ability to observe your individualized energy from any other perspective of being.

All of this results from the Journey in which you have learned to manifest divinely, by manifesting at all levels from physicality unto unmanifest reality!

St. George, Channeling 46, Session 3 [10/29/95]

It may seem strange to hear these words, but believe me, there is nothing that is not in-between. In other words, everything is in-between. Everything. You must understand this if you are to manifest; for in order to manifest, you must be in consciousness in all dimensions and in all levels of the manifestation process. If there is one gap, it is lost. It will not be manifested. It will exist in the etheric. It will also exist in the next layer, but if there is a gap, then it will not manifest even though it will exist above that gap. This is because the energy does not flow. One gap and the energy will not flow.

That is why is it so difficult to manifest. You have to be conscious on all levels. There were Masters who could manifest, and then it would disappear. It might last for a short time, but then it disappears because the Master was not fully conscious in all dimensions. He could not maintain the manifestation. This was because not only must you be clear in order to manifest, you also must be stable in order for the manifestation to persist; because if you create it, you are now responsible for it. You cannot go wily-nilly creating and then forget about it. If you create it, you are responsible! Think about that. Think about the impact if you create something in this world out of the ether. You are totally responsible for that Creation, so it had better be divinely ordained.

Let me go over this again. If you are in your individualism of God, and you are guided to create in this world, and you create it, then <u>you</u> are the Creator; and <u>you</u> are the ultimate possibility of that Creation. This manifestation does not merely apply to grand and glorious ideas. Instead, the one who manifests a rock must consciously get involved with making sure that the rock stays manifest. This is because you are part of all that is. In your wholeness, you are a part of the Devic kingdom that keeps manifestation intact. If it weren't for the Devic kingdom, all that has been manifested would go away.

That is the practice of manifestation that all must do. You must learn to cooperate with Creation. You are a God-being. You created, and yet you cannot do it without the cooperation of the universe. You can't do it alone! Do you think when Jesus manifested loaves and fishes, he did it alone? Did Jesus know how many scales that fish had? Did he even care? No, he provided the impetus for his Creation, and he provided the support of energy from physical to Godhead for it to be created; and the whole of Creation just joyfully jumped in and said "Hallelujah" and created it. They loved it. That's their job, and they love their job! There is no greater pleasure than to create. It's fun! And it is waiting around, waiting for you to get with it! But you will not be able to get with it until you have become aware of your consciousness in all dimensions—all the way from unmanifest reality clear to third-dimensional physicality!

Adama, Channeling 20 [2/15/93]

As you know, there are some who will begin to manifest great riches in their life. This cannot be done automatically. Instead it requires the attention to your ability to manifest prosperity for yourself and for those projects in which you wish to become involved. The Masters have riches of unlimited fashion, and there is no limit to the prosperity that can be obtained on this Earth plane; but the major limit on the physical manifestation of this wealth is your ability to handle it. How many of you are now capable of receiving riches and following your Divine Will in their use? How many would be affected by wealth in a way that would be negative in their path? The questions to ask yourself are these: what part of myself is not yet ready to receive prosperity in my life; and what aspect of my energy is not balanced in the manifestation of this prosperity?

How many could receive a pot of gold and be able to place it aside for months on end until you received specific divine instruction as to its use? How many could resist the lure that riches bring in the gratification of the physical? When you are confident of your ability to listen to your divine destiny in your life and in the prosperity you receive, then there will be no limit to that prosperity. And if your Divine Will is to buy a new home and a new car, so be it. You have earned it, and earned it well.

If your Divine Will tells you to donate a percentage of that money to a cause of merit, then that too is well earned. But what if Divine Will said that you should give it all away? Could you do that? Could you take a pot of gold and hand it away knowing this was your divine direction? Do you trust God enough to realize that it could be replaced tenfold? Riches do not come from man or from the physical plane. All riches and all prosperity come from God, and you are a God-being capable of manifesting that which is in your, and the world's, best interests.

There are not yet enough individuals available to handle mani-festation for many of the projects we would like to do on Earth. It is not our intent to place a financial burden upon any light worker for that manifestation; for if life is not flowing, it is not yet ready. The development and the manifestation of these projects will not be a struggle, for the world has struggled enough. Because the number of light workers to come forth for these projects is still small, we will utilize those who are available by enlisting your help in manifesting your own personal prosperity to help in these projects. We do not ask that you give anything of what you currently have, for this is not a movement of dogma, or of rules, or of percentages, or of begging. These are projects of divine manifestation, and only in the flow of that manifestation of new prosperity will these projects be developed. So if you are ready to be an instrument of divine manifestation for you and for that which you are guided to support, ask for that manifestation and create the healing that it may come forth.

How many here know within themselves they have the power to bring forth the light of Christ Consciousness in every moment of their lives? Indeed all do or you would not be present. Do not be ashamed of riches and the mansions of God, for life need not be a struggle. And when you no longer need any personal prosperity in the physical, it can be added onto you in the spiritual. Simply put, balance those personal, egocentric, emotional needs for prosperity in the physical world, and bring it forth from that spiritual level as an instrument of the divine that you are. For if the calling comes from the personal it will be limited; but if it manifests from your divine state, your manifestations shall be unlimited.

Sananda, Channeling 2 [4/13/92]

By your desire, you are helping to bring peace to this planet; for within each of you is that link to your own Christ Consciousness which is the Christ within you. The Christ is the manifestation of God in the physical within you, and within all things that are divine; for the Christ is a part of you, and nothing is manifested into this creation without the energy and the empowerment of the Christ. The Christ is a manifestation, a vision, an aspect, a part of the God who is the energy behind all that is. Nothing manifests without the Christ energy, for the manifestation process encompasses the Christ energy.

So, indeed, because you exist, because you have consciousness in being on many dimensions, you are an embodiment of the Christ. You can never separate yourself from that which is the Christ because you are the Christ; and through this Christ, you and other divine beings manifest all that is.

Kuthumi, Channeling 24 [3/29/93]

Do you realize how many of you here have lived lives of Mastery upon this planet? Just because you are not divinely manifesting at this moment in this life does not mean that you have never manifested or uncovered the mysteries before. How many feel that they are just remembering rather than discovering something new when they come across a great truth? That is one of the benefits of reading your records. It is that you can begin to realize "Hey, I can do this. I've done it before." Or you can see the archetype of one who has accomplished such divinity in action and merely by imitating that archetypal energy pattern, you too can be swept up into the whirlwind of your divinity. That is why the great Masters have said that if you follow their steps, you will find your Self. They have created a pattern, and if it suits you to follow this pattern, I will help you in that effort. All of you have been endowed by the Creator with the ability to manifest universes; but until you allow your Self your own Mastery, you are not permitted to manifest things that could cause havoc on too large a scale.

Maitreya, Channeling 34 [12/6/93]

What has been agreed to is that the Mother and the Father will move together in balance and in creation of the next Golden Age of this planet, and all upon this planet will move in this balance as well. It will not be allowed that you will be given the use of the power that you all possess without this integration. This is why there are so many in this spiritual age who are seemingly without power, or money, or will, or support for their needs; for the power of their manifestation will not come forth until it will move in a harmless fashion, until it will move in such a balanced state that their ego, their personality, their mind, their feelings and their emotions will not be corrupted.

Absolute power does not corrupt absolutely; but imperfect expression of absolute power does corrupt. You want prosperity? Then balance yourself in all aspects, and it shall flow forth. You have asked many times why those in this movement do not manifest great riches; but what would happen to those if they would receive great wealth at this time? Would that wealth be dealt with from a level of mastery, or from a level of issues about prosperity and power?

We do not wish those who are so close to their complete expression of their divinity to fail to see those pitfalls. We want them to continue their assent. To give wealth where it is not used according to Divine Will in alignment with personal will, would create havoc; and who wants to create more energetic karma that is not balanced? But material prosperity is but one aspect of life whose manifestation requires balance in your being. Do not despair that you have not received what it is that you want. Trust that all is for your best interests, for you have created it that way.

How do you bring forth that which you truly desire? By healing the expression of who you are at this time; for there is not a group of Masters who choose either to withhold or to give you prosperity. Instead, there is a group of beings manifesting in bodies upon this planet; and when they have manifested in balance, then prosperity indeed will flow from the Universe, freely and completely. It does not matter how this prosperity appears. It could be a Master who carries this prosperity in a backpack out of the mountains, or it could be the appearance of wealth in your living room, or the opportunity to make wealth in enterprise or through your labor. Remember, there were many who waited for the Messiah, but yet failed to recognize Him when He came. So do not insist upon the form in which your prosperity will be manifested; for what is more valuable: the flow of love in your life, or always having $500 in your pocket no matter how much you spend? If you truly experience the love in your heart of who you are, and of the God that created you, of what value is the money; for by the nature of your radiance, all would come to you. So what, indeed, is prosperity? Be not so quick to judge.

In the next few years, there will come beings who shall bring forth the energy of that of which I represent. These beings will bring forth the start of the Golden Age of this time. Please understand the warning I am about to give. First, know that you are always loved and you have our deepest respect; for the love of your being has shielded you from the importance and the magnitude of your Journey. Next, please be certain to look within yourself, for your guidance must come from within. There will be many voices coming forth in the coming years who will say that they speak the truth, but the truth must be felt and known within yourself. Many will come to confuse you, and you must know within yourself what is true. You must be strong within yourselves. You are protected as long as you stay in alignment with yourself; for each one of you carries divine energy with you at all times. But you must be within your own center to hear the calling of your own knowing. When you have balanced all, when you have cleared all, when you are in a constant state of divine love, then you will manifest all that you wish. Until then, manifestation on a large scale is not permitted.

Melchizedek, Channeling 19 [2/10/93]

Those who have come into this system from different points in the galaxy and in this universe bring special attributes and energies. One of the gifts available on this planet is the ability to manifest divine energies of all points of creation. In many systems there are solar constrictions on the manifestation of balanced universal energy, but Earth is a creative balancing point. Those who manifest their divine being on Earth will manifest "holistically on a universal scale." This is one of the reasons why the Earth has attracted so many beings from so many star systems and so many cycles of evolution. As you have heard before, this planet is very special in the rapidity in which a soul may evolve. Of course, that is why you are here. You are here to learn how to manifest all things throughout all creation. There are very few places where this can be learned; and to learn it with complete Free Will is even more rare. Earth has given you a great gift. Use it wisely, and know that the truth can be known only from within!

Kuthumi, Channeling 43 [4/5/95]

The Masters can generate an amplifier of energy based on their technology and their clarity of consciousness. They can create a "projection" to help create a special effect on the planet. You remember that any physical structure has to be supported throughout the dimensions all the way to unmanifest reality in order for it to be in creation; and so for there to be a clearing, it has to be reflected throughout the dimensional chain of creation. In other words, to manifest in the physical, it must be made manifest in all dimensions. As we have talked before, if you were to create something out of the ethers, the initial creation starts from unmanifest thought and proceeds throughout all dimensional experience until it manifests physically. If you were to create an apple within your hand, that apple is the result of a chain of creation of unmanifest thought to the physical reality. It is this way with all physical reality. You have heard the expression "as above, so below." This must happen because all is supported throughout creation. As one effect from that, if negativity of love is created in the physical, it obviously exists in all dimensions from the unmanifest reality to the manifest physical. So you see, you not only have an effect upon this world with every thought and action, but you create an effect throughout all of creation. In other words, all of the energy which you generate is supported throughout the dimensions. It must be so, for manifestation can occur in no other way. That which is manifested physically must also be manifested in all dimensions, even unto unmanifest reality!

Maitreya, Channeling 29 [5/27/93]

There is a vision for a life in which you will experience the merging of the mind into spirit. This is so that you allow yourself to manifest the "inconceivable you" that you are to be. The only way the "inconceivable you" can manifest is if the mind does not try to conceive of it; for if the mind conceives of it, there is the possibility of a trap. The trap is that the manifestation could be done for intellectual reason rather than divine reason. In this manifestation, there must be the allowance of spirit so that reason is divine reason, not intellectual reason. That is the only way that you can be allowed to manifest the "inconceivable you" for if the manifestation is done by intellect rather than divine reason, the opportunity for mischief would be great. You will be permitted to undergo this manifestation only when you can handle it in a divine manner. This is true for any manifestation.

Kuthumi, Channeling 43 [4/5/95]

Can we move God-force with just intent, like healing for someone going to the hospital, or manifesting something in the physical? First, you must examine the source of the intention for although human intention is very powerful, divine intention is infinite. And so intention is, as you would say, a first step. With intention comes the attention to create the energy of the intention. With the attention comes performance, and the performance is dependent upon the availability of the energy that can flow through you to create the intention through the attention.

You all have divine intention to heal because that is your loving nature. You all have varying degrees of attention to place upon this intention, and you also have varying degrees of clarity to allow the infinite energy to flow through you to accomplish your intention. You can heal on any level given sufficient availability of your energy to accomplish that intention. As an analogy, the availability of energy is much like a physical pipe; for if you pour water through one end of a pipe and there are dislocations or leaks or blockages, not much will come out the other end; but as you heal, clear, balance and open yourself, this pipe becomes an infinite flow of energy to accomplish any specific purpose. To utilize this energy, you must increase the availability within your being of the energy to be made available. This is accomplished by balancing all of your structures.

The physical, emotional, intellectual, and spiritual bodies really function as one body. As this one body becomes balanced and clear, the energy is ever present, not only to manifest healing, but to manifest your divine intentions in the physical. An example of how this body can manifest healing is the case of Jesus. He was so clear and balanced that healing was made manifest by merely being in his presence. This was so because his condition was unconditional love and healing for all; so in merely being, and not even knowing that you were behind him, you could be healed because you created the opportunity for yourself to be there.

In a similar manner, each and every one of you has the opportunity to be complete and total healers of any and all aspects of creation merely by being clear channels for divine energy flow. Now each of you has a unique makeup, and that makeup determines the characteristics of the energy that flows through you. Some energy might be directed more toward healing than is the energy of another; whereas another may have greater energy for manifestation. Consequently, it is not everybody's intention to necessarily be a great healer, but that is why I first mentioned the intention. If the intention is there, then it is divinely ordained and it is so. It means if you have the intention to heal, then you have the ability to heal. It is just a matter of allowing it to come forth by the experience of it. As you practice the healing, or as you practice the manifest creation, then you uncover aspects of yourself that are in restriction so that that they can be balanced to where the next time they will be a bit more open. One day, this will become a clear channel which connects you in all dimensions between physicality and unmanifest reality. When this happens, then you will heal or manifestly create whenever it is your divine intention to do so.

Do not forget that you are, indeed, God-inspired, God-aware, and God-creators here upon this planet to be Creators of the New Age. In becoming God-present, you create change throughout the world and throughout all dimensions. And so each one of you, in your own way, leads this revolution in consciousness. We thank you for that.

Keeper of the Light, Channeling 10 [9/14/92]

Light is an expression of the divine into manifest reality. What does that mean? It means that the great, unmanifest, infinite potential which creates all has a desire to move into manifest reality or, as you term, creation. As that impulse of desire moves from that which is formless and becomes a very subtle aspect of form, it moves in the vibration of light and the vibration of that created light also carries a sound. The ancients knew the sounds and the frequencies of creation as creation became manifest. I know this sounds esoteric, but it is a practical application of your own abilities to manifest; for in understanding and knowing the quality in the sound and in the frequency of light as it moves into creation, you understand how to manifest yourself.

All that is in a dimension is supported by the light impulses which form that particular dimension of reality. We will talk mainly about the third dimension because that is the easiest to understand when the consciousness is in a physical body. In your space you see objects, movement, and quality of matter. All of this is built from light. When you are in an advanced state of perception in meditation or in working with the energy, you will often see light take on different forms around a body or an object. When this happens, you are seeing the light that manifests the object. This leads to the question of what is the reality? The perception is that of a body. The reality is a symphony of light that manifests the quality of a body. So, which is real? Is the light real? Is the body real? Reality is the perception of what is. When you perceive the body it is, indeed, real. When you perceive the light that manifests the body that, too, is real. It is a finer perception of the reality of what the body is.

We talk of light because as you develop your ability to see beyond the third dimension, you will begin to see the light that forms the third dimension. Beyond that light are the other dimensions of finer frequencies. These frequencies have the quality of form, but the form is not as dense as the form you are used to. Because of its density, a body in the third dimension has a quality of matter; whereas a body in the fourth dimension has a different quality and it may not always seem to be the same.

You are a multidimensional being which exists on many levels, and those levels are interconnected by the essence of your consciousness and by the nature of your being. And so, you can exist in several dimensions at one time; and as your perception of yourself grows, you will come to know yourself in many different forms.

We need to understand the existence of our light bodies in order to understand how things can be manifested. As we become conscious and balanced and integrated in all dimensions, we realize that, in truth, there is no separation between our physical body and that of our higher dimensional bodies. It is an illusion we have created in order to experience a slowed-down reality. But if you wish to manifest on any particular dimension, you must become aware of the existence of that manifestation in all dimensions; for if it is not supported in all dimensions, it will not be manifested!

St. George, Channeling 46, Session 3 [10/29/95]

If there is any conflict or discomfort in your life, it is there because it needs to be looked at. This is always the case in physical form. You would not be uncomfortable if you did not have something; and to deny it, is to deny yourself. We have had enough of that! We must realize that if there is lack of comfort, it means <u>look inside</u>, for you must find what needs to be healed.

You have a grand teacher in your life; for everything in your life that you see teaches you. You are taught by the present "now" that must be healed; for if it is not healed, then you deny the future "now," or you create the next "now" to be that which is not to your higher purpose.

The greatest teacher is every instance of your life. To learn, you have to feel what is appropriate and comfortable; and you have to feel what is uncomfortable. You have to examine yourself, to look inside and to see what needs attention. Every moment of your life is your opportunity for the next step of enlightenment, but humanity has denied their own creativity and their ability to be God. We meet again to talk about this because it is something we must always keep in front of our consciousness. As we become more and more clear, there is a greater opportunity to begin to deny that which is in front of you because of your clarity! If you become more and more clear, there is a greater ability to deny that which is in yourself. It is the opposite of what you think. That is why the greatest Masters that this planet has ever seen often <u>fail</u>! Why do they fail? They refuse to look at those parts of themselves that need attention. Because of their clarity they get immersed in the harmoniousness of their being, and attribute anything that is non-harmonious to that which is outside of themselves.

You have always thought that as it becomes clearer, it becomes so much easier to become whole. Let me warn you that as you become clearer, the final clarity becomes very difficult to ascertain. I bring this up because you are to the point where you have such great clarity that it becomes very easy to hide out in that clarity. This is what I'm saying. It is like having the job on the football field to run with the ball, and you run 80% of the way to the goal line, and then you ease up because you have it made. What usually happens? Somebody catches you from behind. In the lessons of clarity given in this life, you catch yourself from behind, because each one of you has a fail-safe mechanism. You will not allow yourself to be whole until you can handle it.

In other words, you will not let yourself manifest on the physical until you are clear enough to handle that responsibility. Manifestation is an incremental achievement. As you gain the ability to handle the responsibility with the energy of manifestation that you have been given, then you will receive the next influx of energy. And as that is allowed to be responsibly handled, you will receive the next influx until the point that you are indeed whole in the way you intended to be. That does not mean that is the end. That is only the way you are whole at this stage. There is always more.

So, what is the lesson? The lesson is to be ever diligent in the acknowledgment of yourself, in the realization of yourself, and in the examination of yourself. Do not deny that which is there for you to see, because if you deny it, you hide it; and if you hide it, you bury it; and if you bury it, you are less than you were. It is simple, but it takes great dedication and love of self, because you are not supported by this world. Those who achieve self-examination and healing are ridiculed. People who feel with abandon are ridiculed. People who love with abandon are ridiculed because they have no common sense; and people who always speak the truth create fear in the people who hear them. Those people are not in balance, and consequently, they are afraid of your truth; for somehow they know in their deepest part that your truth will allow you to manifest, and that reality becomes truly frightful to them.

Maitreya, Channeling 47 [11/6/95]

Why is it that you have not yet manifested your Mastership in the physical? We have talked many times about why this is so, and you all understand it well; for you have been incarnating through this process and you know what you are and what you have created. You see it before you each and every day, because your life is your teacher. Your environment displays before you that which you are and that which you have the opportunity to become. As Masters, you are here at the dawn of this very significant and beautiful creation. It is the time when this planetary sphere in this solar system is to become something much more manifest in its God consciousness. You are here to be aware of this process, to help create it, and also to have fun in the process. Often, fun has been left out of the equation in physical life, but that is changing now. Cannot Mastery and the Journey to Mastery be fun? Have we not had enough of the learning of "not-God, not-Light"? It is true all is God, but it is determined that the lessons of duality have often allowed humanity to experience that which is termed "not-God" because it is termed "not Light," but yet is a purposeful creation to allow vessels for greater Light. So what you are in your creation is a grand spiritual being that is indeed one with God; and in that energy, you are manifesting an Earth that is much more manifest in its consciousness. Continue this within your divine intention!

Maitreya, Kuthumi, St. George, and Sananda as a Blend of the Christ Consciousness, Channeling 44 [4/17/95]

We are here as a blend of energies so that you might experience a blended energy of the Christ Consciousness; for we often share energies to present more of a blended energy of all aspects of the Christ Consciousness.

We feel that there is an important message for all light-workers; for there is much confusion at this time upon the planet. It might seem that those who resist the evolution of consciousness are getting stronger, and those who are in the pathway of light are not gathering the momentum and the prosperity that would be duly accorded them according to the wishes of those in this movement. But I must go back to the lessons of old that again restate that all is as it should be; for there is not yet clarity and balance, even among the pioneers of this revolution in consciousness that allows such prosperity to come forth.

This may shock you, but those who are most recognized for their work in this field have much work yet to do on themselves; for you know in your heart that you are provided what is appropriate. At times, that with which you are provided is provided as a lesson; for it is not to be misused but is, instead, to be used for your greatest purpose. Today, if the prosperity were to flow forth in majestic abundance for those whom you know, how would this prosperity be utilized? Would it be used to create monuments to their contribution in consciousness, or would it be used to truly foster change in an evolutionary manner?

Today, most prosperity is created to learn that it is not the goal of consciousness. Prosperity is merely a by-product of living in consciousness so that consciousness can create according to its divine desire. Prosperity is a human condition as is poverty, for Spirit knows it is always in total prosperity. If you are supported in every way, and have the most perfect environment for each and every one of you, are you not as prosperous as it is appropriate to be?

Possibly a better question than that of material prosperity is that of evaluating what particular experience does your own situation afford you that is leading you to a new level of yourself? Oftentimes, gaining prosperity is just realizing that you already have it; for if humanity thinks that it has to generate a formula to create prosperity, then humanity will continue to struggle, for a God-being realizes that prosperity flows freely, easily, and almost unexpectedly. Who creates prosperity? Is it humanity, or is prosperity like the water behind a dam just waiting to flow as soon as the proper opening is allowed to open? There is enough potential energy available within this room to feed and to house the world, if applied according to Divine Will.

So what is preventing this prosperity from coming to those who are in balance and who have Divine Will as their intention? Let me explain it in this way. Most of humanity is in lack because it is the lessons of lack that are being learned; and it also is the mass conscious need for being in balance. It is just not the right time and place within the Divine Will of the cycle of evolution for this to occur, for all of those who are not, as yet, in balance would be affected. If any one of you who is in perfect balance as a Creator-God would like to generate prosperity across the planet, you must first understand how it would be received and how it would be used.

But you might say, "I am only creating prosperity at this time for myself because I know that the planet is not yet ready, so just allow it to come forward for me, so that I can become content." What is the answer to that? Why is this not happening? In truth, it is happening. People are being supported beautifully according to their ability to be in the balance required for it to come forth. And what of those who complain that they are not receiving? What of those who feel that the guidance from the Masters promised riches, but the largess did not appear? What of those who feel that they are ready, but they are not being supported? Are they ready? The complaining is that part of themselves that is not in balance; and so those who complain, really are saying, " I am not quite ready yet to heal that part of myself that keeps me from being in prosperity."

Everybody in this movement is supported in the way that is their perfection. For the most part, they are all eating, they all have houses, and they have modes of transportation. There is support in a way that permits them to grow in the size, scope and majesty of their consciousness. If an average light worker who is working so diligently on this path had millions of dollars placed at his or her feet, what would happen? He or she would probably say, "Oh, now I can buy this new car, or I can start this new business, or I can travel from here and go there." But what is most appropriate for their evolution? Will their mind and their being be taken away from their primary objective by having all these other opportunities that aren't necessarily in the focus of that direction?

Those who have achieved the balance and have achieved the consciousness do not want to be prospered out of divine existence. They do not want to let the riches deviate them from their divine path; for prosperity is powerful, and so is materiality. Instead, they say, "Let us gain freedom because with true freedom comes true power. Let us have the freedom to love and to be loved. Let us have freedom from the constraints of time and materiality."

We needed to talk about this, for the desire for prosperity is almost like a plague upon the light workers at this time. The plague is the creation of that which they think is their direction, but which, in truth, would be a diversion from their divine path. They want to manifest prosperity without first having manifested their presence on all those dimensions which exist from physicality to unmanifest reality. This is truly putting the "cart before the horse!"

CHANNELED ANSWERS
TO SPECIFIC QUESTIONS

Is there a difference between manifestation and creation? Creation is all that has been made manifest. Creation is also the whole principle of energy moving from unmanifest possibilities into manifest realities. So they are words that describe the same things, and as words go they have a usefulness. However, these words do not fully describe the process or the subject since although they both describe the same thing, they do so with different views. Manifestation describes the process of creation since manifest reality is creation. Creation is described by the process of manifestation, but where there is the most difference is in third-dimensional manifestation. Manifestation is most commonly understood to be the manifesting in three dimensions of a third-dimensional form. Creation is usually understood to encompass all that is. Creation is expanded by manifestation. Manifestation only exists because there is creation.

Does karma interfere with manifestation? Being here on Earth is a process of discovering and awakening you. This world is full of energy and history, and so is your being. You choose a particular pattern of life in order to most effectively bring into balance those energies that you carry within yourself that seek balance; and you create new experiences for yourself that allow you not only to balance your energies, but also to create new opportunities for yourself. This is often called "karma" meaning that you have energy that is a part of you which is creating aspects of your life because of past actions. Well, karma is often misunderstood, for it is merely a sum total of the energy that you have that is creating. If you created energies in past experiences that did not move in balance, then those energies remain with you. As a part of your energetic makeup today, they help to create your experiences so that a similar energetic experience can allow those energies to move into balance.

As an example, if in a past experience you had been self-depreciated and you had not felt worthy for whatever reason, then you would have that sense of energy lack within yourself today. That energy would create a new experience in which you would be allowed to come into knowledge of the fullness of your power. By doing this, you would be able to manifest, for then you could create from that balanced worthiness of yourself. In other words, karma which becomes balanced does not interfere in manifestation; but karma that remains unbalanced will leave you with unbalanced energy patterns that will inhibit manifestation. *Are you saying that if you balance the karmic energies, the problem that inhibits manifestation will disappear?* Indeed!

In March, 1996 you mentioned that any earnest effort to manifest today would be rewarded a hundredfold over what it was seventeen and a half years before. Does this imply that something special happened on or about September, 1978 and if so, what was that special event? What it implies is that in the beginning of the decade of the 1980s, there was a revelation of spiritual awareness upon the planet. This was slowly building in the 1980s until there was a dramatic recognition of the opening of the heart of the planet during the time of the Harmonic Convergence in 1987. The Harmonic Convergence represented a reaching of a certain level and momentum of spiritual awareness upon the planet. Subsequent to the Harmonic Convergence events happened which look like a very long Fourth of July. This is what you have termed the opening of stargates. From dimensional perspective, it is the sudden and dramatic opening of a channel of interdimension energy. It looks like an explosion of fireworks to us.

    How does this relate to the question about the seventeen and a half year interim period? When you have a piece of cloth that you start poking holes in, you soon begin to be able to see through it. That is what is happening to the veil between dimensions. If you look at this veil and see these giant explosions that are piercing this veil, you will see that the veil is becoming thinner, and that there are these big openings in it. This is happening in many dimensions. And so over the past seventeen and a half years there has been a very dramatic increase in the ability for energy to flow interdimensionally. Manifestation in three dimensions requires interdimensional energy transfer. If the resistance to that interdimensional transfer is dramatically reduced, then the manifestation process becomes easier. That is why any earnest effort to manifest today has a chance to be rewarded to a much greater extent than it would have had in the late 1970s.

You have stated that if the Devic Kingdom did not do their work, manifestation would not continue to exist. Could you please explain this? Indeed, the Devic Kingdom cannot choose *not* to participate in manifestation, for they *are* manifestation. As energy moves into third dimensional experience, it is guided by the energy of its creative pattern. This creative pattern is shepherded by the Devic Kingdom, especially on Earth. This is because the Earth is meant to be a true reflection of the fullness of God in three dimensions, and thus humanity on Earth can experience multi-dimensional consciousness. Consequently, the Devic Kingdom needs to be ever-present as a governing mechanism for how humanity manifests.

The flow of energy into manifestation may be described by using an analogy with water. Water flows, but water is channeled in its flow by the guidance of the Earth which directs its movement. The energy of manifestation is similar in that it rains fully upon this dimension, but it is guided in its manifestation by the Devic Kingdom which understands and resonates with its creative pattern.

On Earth it is not as if there is energy that comes from unmanifest God and then independently manifests through all dimensional reality. This happens in other universes where the energy from unmanifest God has a pattern as it moves into reality of its own fruition in all dimensional experience. However, you would find that to be a much more boring place than Earth, for on Earth you are allowed to participate in its manifestation, and participation is important. In this universe, and in this solar system and especially upon this Earth, there is the total ability to modify energy as it moves through dimensional experience through the interaction of divine principle and wisdom and will. The job of the Devic Kingdom is to use its wisdom in order to allow the energy that moves into manifestation upon the Earth to be guided within karmic principles and within the Divine Will of this place.

If it were not for these hands of guidance, mankind would have long ago destroyed its flow, for since mankind spans multi-dimensional awareness, in the unconscious awareness of dimensions

mankind could reek havoc until it develops its fully conscious awareness. And so the Devic Kingdom keeps the order while mankind
becomes aware of multi-dimensional consciousness. It is an important service which the Devic Kingdom performs, and humanity must
learn to honor them for this vital service.

*You have said that in order for manifestation to occur in third-
dimensional physicality, there must be no gaps all the way from physicality to unmanifest God. How do we prevent or heal these gaps or
how do we even know that they exist?* First let me clarify the term "no
gaps." What this means is that for that particular stream of manifestation there needs to be a clear path from unmanifest God to physical
reality. It does not mean that the entire beingness of the person doing
the manifestation is clear throughout all that interdimensional and
dimensional experience. For example, there are beings who create
quite easily upon the planet, but yet they might not be very spiritual
beings. In fact, those who manifest prosperity can seem to be just the
opposite. The reason is because they have a particular channel of
clear communication within their beingness, but it is not a very wide
or wise channel. It is a clear channel or else they could not create in
this way so easily. This is often set up before an incarnation in order
to have those experiences in that particular life. So, "no gaps" means
that for that particular manifestation, there is a clear channel through
dimensions. Now, a very spiritual being has what are called, in this
dimension, governors throughout their dimensional energetic flow.
Even though you may have a clear channel for a particular manifestation, if it is determined in your own development process that
it is not in your best interest to create in that particular way,
then a governor will take effect and create a little bit of a misalignment. That misalignment notifies that being that there is something
that needs attention. Why do you think that New Age people, as you
call them, have such a difficult time being prosperous? There are
governors in effect all over the place, because there is a tremendous
need for lightworkers to overcome and balance their sense of their
lack of worthiness, for how could you possibly move into the God-
head if you were not worthy? Lack of worthiness is what has created
all of these religions that have altered the truth. The lightworkers will

form a religion in the same way and it will also get off track if worthiness is not healed. That is why there is such a lack of prosperity amongst all of these beautiful, powerful, creative beings. They are wise enough to know that as soon as they overcome their lack of worthiness, then the prosperity will come. They have to do first things first.

SUMMARY

In regard to **Manifestation and Prosperity**, the major teaching was that nothing would be made manifest in physicality until it had been made manifest in all dimensions between physicality and unmanifest God; and that even then it would not be made manifest unless the creator was clear enough to use the creation for divine purpose. This means that until an entity is conscious of his/her divinity in all of those dimensions, with no gaps in the creative stream that channels through all dimensionality, then manifestation in the physical will not take place.

Prosperity, on the other hand, was stated to be the total acceptance of Self in third-dimensional wholeness, for once that acceptance is made the being lacks for nothing; and the energy of lack is the main reason for an absence of prosperity. The energy of lack exists because humanity has let itself become involved in lack over many millennia. The lack was created by a feeling of unworthiness. It was the feeling that humanity was not worthy of God. By accepting that humanity is fully God in physicality, then it will lack for nothing, a state which is that of prosperity. In other words, once the acceptance of being God-in-physicality is made, then anything can be made manifest, for the lack of manifestation is generated by a lack of belief about who you already are. When humanity can get in touch with who it really is and starts expressing that, then it will start manifesting prosperity and the generated prosperity will be used for divine purposes.

The teachings also say that until manifestation can be generated from the inexhaustible Source, then any manifestation is only a rearrangement of that which already exists. In this way, it is a redistribution of the energy "owned" by another and does not represent an increase in the amount of prosperity which is available for all. Consequently, it will manifest for only a short period of time until it is "borrowed" by another who is manifesting from a source other than the inexhaustible Source.

Further, the teachings say that no manifestation can come forth until the being doing the manifesting is balanced in all aspects. The manifestation will then flow forth in an inexhaustible stream. This is because if there is present an unbalanced karmic energy known as "enslavement to poverty," then that in itself will stop manifestation from happening. The "enslavement to poverty" is generally caused by not having a belief that the consciousness already exists in all the dimensions between physicality and the inexhaustible energy available from unmanifest God. With this, we have come a complete circle from the opening paragraph of this Summary.

Finally, it is taught that since Earth is a creative balancing point, then unlike other systems which have restrictions on what can be made manifest, Earth will manifest "holistically on a universal scale." This will happen when all of humanity becomes whole by coming together in united, co-creation of divine intention. When that happens, the presently instituted governing mechanism of the Devic Kingdom will no longer be necessary, and within our balanced energy streams, we will thank them for the service they have been so admirably performing.

CHAPTER FIVE
CHRIST CONSCIOUSNESS

INTRODUCTION

Humanity is confused by the term "Christ Consciousness." This is unfortunate, for an understanding of this term is helpful in accepting humanity's role in evolution.

Because of the similarity of names, many people think of Christianity or the Christian Church when they hear the term "Christ Consciousness." This is not only understandable, it is possibly useful; for the being claimed by the Church is one who can be described as the most radiant of all who have embodied the "Christ Consciousness." This radiant one embodied the Christ Consciousness to an extent which is possibly greater than any other being in the recorded history of Earth, or even possibly in the history of the Cosmos. In bringing his radiance to Earth, he was instrumental in absorbing and successfully clearing a tremendous amount of mass consciousness.

But the one whom we have known as Jesus Christ is not the only one who has assumed the mantle of the Christ Consciousness. There will be many from the Christian Church who will take offense at such a statement; but it is a statement which must be made if the evolution of humanity is not to be restricted by those who worship the one who sits at the hand of God, rather than God Him/Herself.

To help understand the difference between the concept of

"Christ Consciousness" and the person of Jesus Christ himself, some understanding about the reason for the similarity in names might be useful. First, let us describe how that beloved being of Palestine got the name "Jesus Christ"; and then we will describe how the term "Christ" is used in the phrase "Christ Consciousness."

It is highly unlikely that the beloved rabbi was ever known as "Jesus" or "Christ" in the Palestine of his day; for each of those names is the Latinized version of the Greek name which he was given many years after his death and resurrection. It is probable that his name during his lifetime was Yeshua [or Yehoshua] ben Yoseph; and if there had been a literal translation of his name from the Aramaic language into Greek, we would probably know him today as "Joshua" rather than "Jesus." However, it seems that the translation used was not a literal one. Instead, it was a numerical translation, as was often done in those days.

Numerical translations use the numerical equivalents of the letters in one language, and then translate them into the numerical equivalent of the letters in another language. Two thousand years ago, this was done because of the great esteem in which numbers were held as the key to understanding the order of the universe. It was a world in which numbers were held in high regard, oftentimes in a higher regard than mere words.

In the Aramaic and Hebrew alphabets, each letter had a numerical equivalent. When the numbers representing the letters found in the name "Yeshua" were combined, the total was the number 888. Every letter in the Greek alphabet also was associated with a number. When the number 888 is translated into letters of the Greek alphabet, the letters IEOUSS are found to be one result. A slight re-ordering of those letters created the name "IESOUS." Iesous became a useful name for the one who had brought forth the teachings upon which the new religion was founded; for it not only made a pleasing sound, it had a uniqueness which was much greater than the uniqueness found in the name "Joshua," a name which would have resulted in the literal translation of his Aramaic name "Yeshua."

And so, the one who had been known as Yeshua in Palestine became known as Iesous in the lands in which Greek had become accepted as the language of the literate people. These lands were the lands which had first been conquered by Alexander and assimilated into the Greek Empire; followed, after the death of Alexander, by the Roman Empire which covered much of the same territory. These also are the very lands into which Christianity was brought by the missionary journeys of Paul. Consequently, Iesous became a well-known name, better known than Yeshua. From Iesous, it was an easy step to the more Latinized form of "Jesus," a name which has persisted into the English language.

The term "Christ" followed the route of literal rather than numerical translation. For many years the Jewish people of Palestine had been looking for their "Messiah," a name which means "the anointed one" in both Hebrew and Aramaic. The term "anointed" means "to be sanctified" or "to be made holy." The Jewish people hoped for the anointed one of God to lead them out of their miseries. Some felt that the Messiah would be a military man who would conquer those who had conquered the Jews, for the Jews had been conquered by many people among whom were the Babylonians, the Persians, the Greeks, and, at the time of Jesus, the Romans. The Zealots are an example of an element in the Jewish society at the time of Jesus who wanted a military Messiah somewhat as King David had been. Others felt that the Messiah would further define God's Law by which the people would be governed. The Pharisees were such an element at the time of Jesus. Still others felt that the Messiah would be a builder who would build grand temples in which the people would worship. The Sadducees were such an element at the time of Jesus. But whatever feeling there was about what the Messiah would do, all felt that the Messiah would be "an anointed one of God," a concept which was very much in their minds at all times.

In the Greek language, the term "Kristos" means "an anointed one." As the new religion proceeded in an orderly fashion across the lands near the Mediterranean Sea, the one who had established the teachings upon which that new religion was based became known as "the anointed one of God," or as the "Kristos" in the Greek language. From Kristos, it was an easy step to the more Latinized form of "Christ," a name which has persisted into the English language.

And so, the most radiant one became known as Yeshua the Messiah, or Iesous the Kristos, or Jesus the Christ, all of which meant that this grand teacher was an anointed one of God. Later, as last names became more normal, the adjective was dropped. In English, he became known as Jesus Christ, as if his first name were Jesus and his second name were Christ. It is unlikely that the one who was called "rabbi" so often in the gospels which tell of his life would recognize himself if he were addressed by the name "Jesus Christ." Nevertheless, it is a name used by many of his followers today.

In the term "Christ Consciousness," the "Christ" part is no different than the use mentioned above. It means "the [or an] anointed one." The term "Consciousness" means "the state of being conscious," in which the term "conscious" means "having an awareness of one's own existence." Consequently, a being who embodies the "Christ Consciousness" is one who "has an awareness in the being of his/her own existence that he/she is an anointed one of God." It is not enough to be aware that there is a God, or even to be aware that God can be embodied within you. To embody the "Christ Consciousness" means that one becomes aware that he/she is one who has been anointed [or made holy] by God. When the embodiment of an anointed one happens within humanity, then the anointing is often granted to enable the Christ Consciousness to do a special service for the benefit of humanity.

Despite this definition of Christ Consciousness drawn from an analysis of its individual words, possibly the single most significant constituent factor in any functional definition of Christ Consciousness is the awareness that we are one with God. Jesus said it when he said "I and the Father are one." [John 10:30], and then a few pages later in the Fourth Gospel stated "where I am you may be also." [John 14:3]. In this understanding of Christ Consciousness, we become aware of our state of "not-two-ness" with God. It is the understanding of the full awareness of third-dimensional reality, in that "God is All, God is aware, God is here, and you are God" [see the definition of the Third Dimension in *Appendix C.*] Since the channelings present the teaching that the Christ Consciousness is that energy which flows from unmanifest God into manifestation to create all Creation, then how could any part of Creation ever not be one with God? That is the major message of the Christ Consciousness.

Consequently, each human being embodies the Christ Consciousness to a certain degree of purity and clarity, for each individualized human being represents the movement of unmanifest God into manifest reality while being at-one-ness with God. However, there are many levels of awareness of this embodiment. This is possibly best illustrated by presenting a segment from Channeling 16 as follows:

I would like to experience the Christ. Do you have a specific energy of the Christ that you wish to have present? The Christ is an energy of the divine in manifestation, and the Christ is manifested into dimensional experience through many facets, somewhat like the many facets of a crystal. These different facets of divine embodiment have been manifested by many beings throughout creation. It is manifested by every being by the very nature of the fact that they exist, but there are those who manifest further to exemplify the purity of the Christ Consciousness. *I am referring to the highest level of divine consciousness of the Christ.* You will see that communication when you are face-to-face with God, for that is the highest level of the Christ Consciousness. This group is not quite ready for this as a group experience.

And so, the Christ Consciousness exists in us all. Some, through the manifestations which have been put into their vessels of experience, have embodied the purity of the Christ Consciousness at a higher level of clarity than have others. Since one example might be that of the one known as Jesus Christ, his story has been used often in the channelings which teach us about the Christ Consciousness. Even though his embodiment of the Christ Consciousness was possibly at a level experienced by few others in third-dimensional physicality, the potential is there for each and every member of humanity to reach that level of clarity. That is the ultimate level of the Christ Consciousness—the level at which God is met face-to-face and the Christ Consciousness becomes the God Consciousness. This will happen when each has made him/herself ready for such an event.

The teaching that each of us can become the God Consciousness differs from the teachings of many of the established religions; and the teaching that our embodying God Consciousness requires an effort on our part differs from some beliefs which advocate that all the effort will be done for us. However, each is a message presented in the channelings from the Ascended Masters. Excerpts from some of those channelings are presented in the following section. In addition, major portions of this theme are repeated in the teachings of *Chapter Six*, entitled *Jesus the Christ*.

CHANNELED INFORMATION
Maitreya, Channeling 54 [3/26/96]

Good evening. I am the energy that has been called "Maitreya." Maitreya is an aspect of Christ Consciousness, and all of you are also an aspect of Christ Consciousness; for all things that exist in creation are aspects of Christ Consciousness. You are what is called the Christ, as is Maitreya. The world tends to look to religious idols and call them the Christ because they have forgotten that they, too, are the Christ; for the Christ is not an exclusive club. Christ is for all, because you cannot exist without the Christ Consciousness. The Christ Consciousness is that energy that flows from God into manifestation to create the diversity of creation.

So if the Christ Consciousness is that energy in creation, what is the Father energy and what is the Mother energy? What is that all about? When we look at God, we see aspects that can be defined in different ways. God is not split into different beings. Instead, God is expressed and explained in different ways. Throughout the ages, there have been two primary aspects of how God has been felt. In many cultures and in many languages and in many pathways, God has been felt to be the Mother and the Father. That is such a natural way to think of God in this dimension, because the Mother and the Father represent the mechanism of life. It is natural to see that reflection in God; for God is also the mechanism of all life.

To understand this, it is necessary to understand what allows creation to take place. You have heard, "as above, so below," and it is true to my knowing. The father and the mother in three dimensions create in a similar manner to the way that God creates; for the mother creates the space for creation to be in gestation, and the father infuses into that space the creative principle. In that combination, life is brought forth.

It is the same throughout creation, because the aspect of God that is termed the Mother creates the opening or creates the space;

and the aspect of God which is termed the Father fills that space with Light. Light is the symbol and is the physical reality for the energy of manifestation. In that combination, life is brought forth and creation is allowed to manifest. That is why the great mystics who have seen this process occurring have described it as the Mother and the Father God. Beyond the Mother/Father God, as you move slightly away from that God-head, you then see what has been termed the Lords of Creation or the Master-Creators. These beings are beings that were of initial creation of the God-head in this creative cycle and these great beings carried forth the plans of God to bring forth the next level of diversity of creation. Beyond that, the same process occurred time and time again until there were multitudes of beings carrying forth the process of creation.

You and I are part of this whole evolution and process of creation. The Christ Consciousness is that energy that enlivens creation to create. It is that energy that supports, that motivates, that manifests in creation. Since the Christ Consciousness reflects those qualities of the God-head from which it comes, then even within the Christ Consciousness, there are the aspects of the Mother and the Father. Just as a mother and a father on Earth create a child and that child reflects the qualities of both the mother and the father, the same is true of the energy of the Christ Consciousness. It reflects the qualities of both that aspect of God which is the Mother, and that aspect of God which is the Father.

Kuthumi, Channeling 49 [1/13/96]

The question has often been asked, "Who or what is Kuthumi?" Kuthumi represents that energy which is collectively called the "rays of Christ Consciousness that are manifest in physical phenomenon." Stated differently, the energy labeled as Kuthumi is the intelligence of Christ Consciousness in physical manifestation. His energy can seem to be solely intellectual, but it is always grounded in the Christ Consciousness which is the first reality at the mouth of God. His energy is best explained as being that movement of Christ Consciousness through the complete physical spectrum. But since after that completion the energy circuit merely begins again, a more specific definition of the energy of Kuthumi would be "that energy which helps to intellectualize the manifestation."

Quite often, Kuthumi is the energy to be called upon when wondering what is the next adventure for spiritual undertaking for Kuthumi is able to link into the personal divine energy of each individual in a way which allows the divine plan for that individual to be looked at from the perspective of an intellectual input. Kuthumi does not create the plan, for the Divine Will in the plan comes from God. God defines, in general terms, the field of possibilities upon which each individual being floats. The particular individualized creation of each individual then refines that energy by defining it in more specific terms. Kuthumi can help in understanding the movement of this energy into manifested reality. That is why the energy of Kuthumi is evidenced throughout the planetary and physical cosmos because all of physical reality has been seen by his energy as it was made manifest through intellectual activity.

As each individual divine plan occurs, it correlates with all of physical creation. The movement of the smallest physical creature is a part of the divine plan which encompasses all that is; so you cannot be involved in one aspect and not be involved in the whole. Often individuals look at their life as a compartmentalized creation, but indeed every blueprint has a relationship with the all. How could it be any other way?

With that introduction of the aspect of Kuthumi which is involved with the Christ Consciousness, I will now move into answering your questions. But I wish to answer your questions in a way which would allow you to answer it for yourself as you consciously bring yourself more and more into the clarity and the purity of your own Christ Consciousness.

Maitreya, Channeling 35 [2/21/94]

I wish to speak with each of you about what the Christ is, and about how the Christ is important to you and to the world. The Christ is divinity moving energy from the field of "no action" into the field of "action." To do this, the Christ is the sound that emanates from the silent field of the divine mouth. In making this God-sound, the Christ becomes the movement of light from the field of infinite, unmanifested energy.

Every element of creation is linked to divinity, and every being is divine. The movement, the expansion and the uniqueness of all divine creation is carried into creation from the field of the Christ for the Christ is the expression of the creation out of the dual expression of unmanifest moving into reality. The dual expression is what you have termed Mother/Father God, the creative polarity which manifests creation and which Christ carries forth from the unmanifest into what is. The Christ is the messenger of divinity to all living things. The Christ is in all things by the very nature of divinity being in all things.

The Christ occupies the Office of the Christ which encompasses the very root action of divinity into your life. It is important because who you are is carried forth from Mother-Father God by the movement of energy into your reality. The Christ Consciousness is the consciousness of allowing that movement into your life. It is the conscious perception of your own Christ nature, of your own divine nature. When there are living Masters who are called the Christ, it is meant that they are living the life expressing their linkage with their divine parents. When Jesus walked upon this plane, he lived as the Christ, for although he lived as the energy that emanated from his divine parents in quite a complete way, he also lived as a unique personality, a unique aspect of his divine parents. Each one of you is a unique aspect of your divine parents. There will come a time when you carry forth the energy of the Christ, fully, completely, and in full recognition and understanding of your divine parents. In addition, you will accept your divine nature and your complete expression in all aspects reaching all the way from unmanifest reality to physical reality.

Many grand Masters have walked upon this plane. They, too, have been the Christ and embodied the Christ Consciousness, just as you can; for the Christ does not mean an individual being. It is merely the state of being aware of the consciousness of your divinity, of your divine parents, and of Divine Will that flows forth through your unique divinity. It is the beauty of creation that you are all different, and that you all have your own unique way in which you unfold that Christ Consciousness.

How many here are willing to do whatever it takes to fulfill your divine inheritance, to express that you are a unique God and a humble, living Christ? What if whatever it takes meant changing your whole lifestyle tomorrow? Do you love yourself and your Christ Consciousness enough to do that? You have heard the stories of the disciples who walked with Jesus and how they changed their lives in order to follow him. Could you do the same? Could you follow yourself and be yourself? Most of you will not be asked to make such great changes, for you are already on quite an accelerated path. Don't be nervous! A grand being is not going to walk before you and ask you to follow him or her to the other side of the world and to forsake family and prosperity and all that you have made for yourself. I wouldn't rule it out, but most likely it will not happen.

However, something must happen, for there is still a coldness in your hearts and they are not yet complete enough to enable you, the Christ, to accomplish what you came here to accomplish. When your heart is full of the love that you are, then all else will fall before it, if you will but allow it. It is a natural law that all which comes before divine love shall fall away. Of this, I promise you. There is no power on Earth or in the heavens that shall contradict the divine love or keep you from your divine love, other than you. You are the only one strong enough to do that. For anyone to do that to you, in this time, is not allowed. If you think it could happen, then ask yourself this question: Are they doing this to you or are you doing it to yourself and they are the instrument of your will?

It is time to shake yourself from within. It is time to stop all that you are doing that is not in agreement with what you know to be the Christhood which you should wear, boldly, humbly, peacefully and lovingly in every moment. Each one of you knows there are many things that you do in your life that are not in attunement with your Christ Consciousness. How many of your actions or thoughts were guided by an unbalanced ego, or were guided by reaction rather than creation? The energies that are present are buffeting you upon your walk; and as I have said, your unique path has become very narrow. Each time you act from a place that is not of your divine love for your Christ Consciousness, it moves you closer to the edge of your path.

That is why I talk to you of being in attunement, for you are all great masters, but the world was not ready for innumerable masters prior to this time. It had not created the energy for that to be present. And so you could not unfold your wings and allow your heart to shine in a way that would attract humanity as butterflies.

But now it is time, and the divine energies are becoming greater. It is important each day to place yourself in alignment with those divine energies. Do you realize how important you are to the future of the world in its smooth transition into the new Golden Age? All of the scenarios you have read about of chaos and destruction to this Earth were indeed possibilities; but it is through beings such as yourself that the transition has been enabled to go so smoothly and without attendant chaos and destruction. There will be those who will move in opposition and continue to create chaos, but that will not last a long time for they cannot succeed when the Christ is present in great numbers.

Try an experiment in the coming days. Place your attention upon your Christ self. Try to see your divinity, and then see how long you can hold that energy before it is invaded by thoughts apart. As you are able to hold that energy for greater periods of time, more will be added on to you very quickly. It will be an avalanche of light flowing upon you in a most natural way. The changes you will see in yourself will be magnificent. They will happen as fast as you allow them to come forth.

During this time, many expect their divinity to come from above; and they think that all they must do is to mark time in waiting for this wave of a grand divinity that will sweep them up into the glory of themselves. I say unto you, that this will not happen unless you live it and manifest it.

However, there is one saving grace. It is divine grace. You don't have to do it completely. I shall give you a simple example. Imagine that you were to be given the task of swimming across a very wide river which moves rapidly, and has all sorts of obstructions. It would be risking your life to jump in, for there are many perils upon this swim. But in attunement with yourself, you can see that there might be one passageway across this river which might be more suited to your unique ability to swim. Perhaps you could float along with the current and zigzag your way through much of the peril and obstruction; but there would be many places where you would still have to swim, sometimes with great effort.

In that situation, think of grace as a very large luxury liner that can move anywhere upon the river; and all this ship of grace requires is that upon your path, you reach some point where it can pick you up. You don't even have to go clear to the other side to be in grace. And it is not the same point for all; for maybe you did three-fourths of your Journey your last time around, and so now all you have to do is a short sprint and be an example of being comfortable with your path to encourage others. Perhaps you have done only a fifth of your Journey so far, and you must thrash wildly to pass all the obstacles you have put in your way. But still, at least you have enough vision to see that there is the ship of grace waiting for you. Be thankful you have been allowed to get in the water. There are many who are so blinded that they do not even see how to get to the river.

This example is to show you that there is an opportunity for divine grace in your life. It is different for each and every one, and it is not a far-off grace that comes forth at a whim; but it is a grace that you allow yourself, for you are always at the controls. You are the master of your own Christ Consciousness.

Maitreya, Channeling 36 [5/5/94]

I wish for you to experience the energy of peace in action; for the energy of the divine is all powerful, yet it is all peaceful. It justifies the expression, "all things are accomplished from the energy of what appears as inactivity." This means that your being springs forth from the energy pool of absolute divinity and as this Christ energy generates the birth of a being from the divine, this being comes from that which has been called "nothingness." But it is truly more than nothing. It is termed this because since it is beyond differentiation of consciousness, it is <u>thought</u> to be nothingness. However, it is All That Is. Your being springs from this energy, and so does your energy to create all things within the divine plan that you created.

In the work that you do in movement of the Christ energy within you, you are bringing forth divinity into your humanity. You are fulfilling the prophecies of old. You are fulfilling the coming of the Christ within each and every one of you, for the Christ energy is indeed your divine energy linking you with Mother/Father God into the absolute of All That Is. Those beings who have come forth in different times to embody the Christ Consciousness and to manifest the Christ energy divinely, have done so to show the path for all humanity; for each and every one of them has said, "It is within each and every one of you to be as I am, and even greater shall you be."

This is evolution. The evolution of the planet and of all beings upon the planet will allow greater and greater expansion of the divine energy. And so, you shall do greater things because as the Divine Will expands, the action of the divine upon the planet increases. Your actions have showed great movement in your divine energy. Some have achieved a transformative energy stage during which your physical bodies have experienced a new dimension. This stage of transformative energy is one of the first stages of ascension. It is the stage at which you have allowed enough Light energy to be infused in your consciousness and into your physical being that your Light body begins to rapidly anchor itself. The Light body is merely the physical manifestation of your divine self being anchored in your physical being. It is the manifestation of your Christ Consciousness.

Each time you do this, you infuse more of your divine Light self in the physical, for the process of ascension is not generally a sudden transformative experience. Instead, it is a gradual moment by moment, day by day infusion of your divine self into the here and now. It is the growing clarity and purity of your Christ Consciousness. As this infusion becomes an everyday experience, increased amounts of infusion will result, for as the Light body becomes manifest, it moves out ahead of you and creates not only your present reality, but also your future experiences. All of this is predicated on how you carry yourself each and every moment.

So divine beings, you are at hand. Travel well each moment, for it is this special experience for which you came. The Masters are with you. There are many beings who bring forth the action of the peaceful, loving energy of the Christ Consciousness. You may call on any of these, be it Lord Maitreya, be it Sananda, be it Krishna, be it Kuthumi, be it St. Germain, be it whomever you feel comfortable with. Call upon the Master of your affinity, but first call upon your-self. Each day as you work with your energy, call upon your divine self to be present; for this is the most worthy companion you can have. As you love all the Masters, be certain also to love yourself; for where there is Love there is Light. And where Light is infused, the Christ Consciousness grows and all fears become dissolved in the divine light of Christ Conscious Love. In the Light of divinity, no obstacle, fear or doubt will appear, for none of these can withstand the test of time in that Light.

So, grand beings, I leave you now in the presence of your Christ Consciousness, and in that presence I am always close at heart. God blesses you always. In Light and Love and your joy, we will speak again.

Maitreya, Kuthumi, St. George, and Sananda as a Blend of the Christ Consciousness, Channeling 44 [4/17/95]

You spoke earlier of the different aspects of the Christ Consciousness and stated that St. George was an aspect of the Christ Consciousness. Did he actually hold the office of the Christ at one time, or was he a channel of the Christ? He totally mystifies us and we would like some more information on him. George is not who he appears to be. One of the favorite pastimes of great Masters is to enter into your world of illusion with an illusion of their own; for it often takes a powerful illusion to alleviate illusion, and so it is appropriate. George always speaks the truth of his being, and he presents it in a way that is effective. You can say it is an illusion because it is not the essence of St. George. It is George playing a part to be effective.

But George has never presented himself to be other than what he is. He has said that "this is a part of me that works in this way to be effective." St. George is indeed a channel of the Christ Consciousness; but then you are all channels of the Christ Consciousness. The very fact that you have spiritual existence, and that you are aware of that existence, means that you are a channel of the Christ Consciousness. The Christ Consciousness that you channel, and every aspect that you bring forth, is unique to you in the way in which you do it. That is why you are unique and special. As an aspect of this uniqueness, what is your aspect of the Christ Consciousness? It is the summation of all that is within the Christ. We come to you this evening as a blended energy of Maitreya, Kuthumi, St. George,

Sananda and others. We come forth as a blended energy to bring forth from these, and from others, and from the rays, a blended consciousness that will help to facilitate the openings in ways that are specific for the unique way you perform; for within each person is a *unique* aspect of the Christ Consciousness.

The Christ Consciousness is often misunderstood, for many believe it to be specific to a particular being or type of energy. Because the Christ Consciousness is the movement of unmanifest God into reality, it is all that is in physicality. It is the Mother, it is the Father, it is the Son, it is the Holy Ghost, it is all that has ever been described as coming into perceptible beingness. But you might say, "How can it be the Mother God, the Father God, the Son and the Holy Ghost? How can it be all of these things?" It is all of these and more, because it is the will of unmanifest God to be; and in order to be, God creates. In order to create, God is both Father and Mother; and the result of that creation manifests into reality.

There are different levels of that movement from unmanifest reality into manifest reality. At the most subtle levels, the Christ Consciousness is the feeling and the perception of Mother and Father. As the creation moves further into reality, it is the perception of the creation of Mother and Father which is the Christ Consciousness. But the Christ Consciousness is all of that together. It is merely the different ways that the religions see the reflection of God that give them their unique way of saying what the Christ Consciousness is; but it is all of what they have said, and more. Jesus brought forth the Christ Consciousness as the Christ; but yet, Sananda had a specific demonstration of the Christ. Because Jesus was Jesus, he also was Sananda in his unique manifestation of the Christ. In the same way, Maitreya has a particular assemblage of that Christ Consciousness. In exactly the same way, you have a unique interpretation and demonstration and manifestation of Christ through the Christ Consciousness.

And so, as a long answer to your question, St. George is indeed a channel of the Christ Consciousness. In this way, he is no different than any of you. However, because of his great vessel of experience, St. George is a being who, as we would say, has evolved as a father of planetary systems.

Kuthumi, Channeling 46, Session 2 [10/28/95]

What will be occurring with each of you, is an accelerated opening of yourselves so that there is a greater connection between your physical body, your feeling bodies, and your mental bodies. I use the term "bodies" because there are more than one. Finally, there will be a greater connection with your finer bodies, your interdimensional cells that operate on different dimensions. Because of separation of Self from those dimensions, these cells take on a uniqueness of their own. What we will be doing is bringing those together into a uniform self; for today when you say, "Higher Self," it is not the higher self that you call upon. Instead, it is the next higher self that you are aware of. As you integrate that, then the higher self becomes the next higher self that is to be integrated, and so forth and so on.

That is what you are doing now. You have the awareness of your divinity, and you have the awareness of your physical consciousness. Now you are ready to integrate the next level, and then the level after that, and then the level after that, and so forth until one day, the next level is your divine self that is so close to unmanifest reality that it hears the sound of God. It can actually hear the sound of Creation. That is what has been termed in your literature as "God Consciousness." As of now, you are truly on the edge of what has been termed "Cosmic Consciousness." You have the dual reality of your divinity and your physicality. When you have spanned the dimensions between full divinity and full physicality with your Christ Consciousness, then you will truly find yourself in the presence of God Consciousness. That is what you came here to achieve, because in God Consciousness, you achieve a willing co-creatorship with God. And if you have carried your Christ Consciousness into full awareness of all that exists between unmanifest reality and physical reality, you will have filled your vessel of experience to the level needed to be a willing co-creator with God.

Maitreya, Channeling 51 [2/6/96]

You are bringing multi-dimensionality into this experience. You experience what you now see and feel and know, but you do so on more and more subtle levels until there is a point at which you can hear the sounds of the creation of any object. At that point, you are in the full Christ Consciousness of all dimensions, and your Christ Consciousness becomes God Consciousness. At that point, you can participate in the sounds of that creation. At that point, you can manifest your own creations.

Manifestation is not a tricky business. It is merely being aware. Manifestation of anything is possible immediately, but it takes awareness in all those places in which it exists—from the movement of the energy from unmanifest God through all dimensionality to three dimensions. That is why manifestation is difficult in three dimensional physicality. It is because it takes consciousness in all those places; but when you have consciousness in all those places, it is easy. It is no more difficult than your thinking that it is there—and it is! Because you create, it is there in all those dimensions of experience, and it is so.

And so, to summarize this discussion, being aware of your multi-dimensionality is also being aware of your creativity and your ability to create. It all begins with the acceptance of your Christ Consciousness in this dimension, then in another dimension, and then in all places until it reaches the border of unmanifest reality. What does this mean to you now as the world changes? It means that as you are more aware of your multi-dimensionality, you begin to create more profoundly. To express that which you are moved to do in your divinity is what freedom truly is. Is that not freedom from control of you? Is not every aspect of your life that is uncomfortable made so because of some element of control—either some outside influence controlling you or your own inside influence controlling you? But all of this control is energetically within you, because no outside influence can do that without your creation, even though it may seem to be an outside force, such as the laws of prosperity, or the laws of relationships, or your own particular energy of issue of not being able to move in a particular way because of your energy within.

Freedom is the elimination of all of that. It is the freedom to be no more and no less, to express from your individual divinity, to be fully and completely in Mastery, to be fully in your Christ Consciousness. In saying this, we have come full circle.

CHANNELED ANSWERS
TO SPECIFIC QUESTIONS

Do the teachings of the Christian Church have any current purpose for humanity? The Church serves a great purpose in providing a symbol of the existence of God. The Christian religion has evolved in the way that it has because of the religions that came before it, in that one of the great doubts of humanity has been that they are not worthy of being God. And so humanity has always looked to the messengers of God to be their salvation and to go before God for them because they did not feel worthy to go before God themselves. For Christianity, Jesus fulfilled the role of devotion that is present in the religions that came before Christianity, for the Christians believed that by total devotion to Jesus, God's grace would be granted, and by opening to Jesus in this way, it eventually became an opening to God. But the truth is for the people to see and to remember within themselves that God is tangible, here and now. In holding out a symbol of the existence of God, the Church can help lead people to this greater truth.

I think you are saying that as a stepping stone the Church serves a purpose in present humanity. Is that correct? The Church serves a grand purpose. But what has been misunderstood in that Church is the role of love. The Church has placed the role of humanity before the role of love. There is but one commandment, and that is to love.

Do Gurus serve a purpose? Is it better to have the discipline of reverence for a Guru rather than being in a street gang? Street gangs have their gurus. It is just like the flip side of a coin from a spiritual guru, but the effect is the same. The disciples give up their power and they give up their identity. This is one of the problems in the Church. In the role of devotion one gives up his/her power and identity so completely that eventually they find it.

Are we not back to both Gurus and the Church being a stepping stone? What is appropriate for the Church today is to change rapidly. What I have said before is that the day of the Guru is over. What I have said is that it is time for each individual to realize his or her own God-consciousness, to realize that they are their own Guru, they are their own Christ, they are their own salvation, and to bring forth the power of their own individualized God-head into their conscious experience of the here and now. Love and devotion to Jesus is a beautiful, beautiful experience. Jesus is one of the loving beings of this system whose love flows unconditionally to all who would ask, who would notice, who would look. But the love of Jesus flows with the intention to them, "I love you with all of my heart because God flows within me as God flows within you and look to me and then look to yourself for you are me and I am you."

I do understand the goal, but I still think that what I am trying to reach for is that in getting to that goal, does the Church or a Guru or something else organized for discipline serve a purpose in getting there, or is it better to by-pass those stepping stones completely? Everything is created for a purpose. The Church exists because it has purpose, and so do Gurus. There are those who in their level of understanding of their own God-head require the services of something like a Church in order to be with God, and that serves a very good and fulfilling role for them. But at the same time they are being misled and confused. They want to be misled and confused because they do not want to accept their own personal responsibility for their life. They want to continue to exist in a system that allows for a lifetime of hypocrisy on the outside chance that they will reach salvation before it is too late. So although churches fulfill a grand purpose and are valuable, their day is over. When I say that the day of the Guru is over, it is Jesus who has said this. He has said that those churches that invoke my name shall change and transform because that is the energy of my love which goes to you when you invoke my name. So as my energy flows to you as you invoke my name, the energy is of transformation and you shall transform according to the spiritual law of creation and the balancing of karma. If you do not transform, then it is a lack of respect for my love and the love of the God that has created all that is that flows through me.

Will the transformation occur within the existing structures such as those of the Church? Yes, in some. In others, no.

And so some will transform and survive and some will collapse? Let me say it this way. Those who are presently studying for the clergy are of the knowledge of the Light. They are being trained in a structured environment that does not feel very comfortable to them, but their love for God is so great that they accept this role to fulfill their love of service to God. However, they are confused because they know that it does not match up to what is inside them. And so the embryo of knowing about the transformation is at hand and it is growing, day-by-day.

Could you define Cosmic-consciousness, Christ-consciousness, and God-consciousness, particularly as to how they differ and whether each is a stepping stone between humanity and divinity which will become one at some point? Do not think of these as being separate, for humanity is divinity. Divinity is merely the expression of the knowing that God is all and that all is divine. Divinity is all that there is.

It would still help me to understand the differences between Cosmic-consciousness, Christ-consciousness, and God-consciousness. Cosmic-consciousness is the conscious understanding and acknowledgment that while there is physical consciousness, there is also the consciousness of the Christ. The consciousness of the Christ can be aware on many different levels, and therefore Cosmic-consciousness is not a static description, but an initial step could be when one realizes that they are Christ-consciousness in physical form and they accept both their humanity and their divinity. Christ-consciousness is the energy of God moving into manifestation. Within the Christ-consciousness is the consciousness of the Mother/Father God. The Christ-consciousness is like the child of the two. It is like the creative movement out of the womb of unmanifest reality. As the Cosmic-consciousness expands to at least the fifth dimension, then in the silent witness of physical activity you sit in your Christ-aware self, and the Cosmic-consciousness expands throughout all of the dimensional consciousness of creation as an increasing awareness of your Christ-self. When there is conscious attunement, recognition and Christ-aware of your beingness in all dimensions, then you have mastered relativity. You have mastered creation. Then what is missing? What is missing is consciousness in the heart of God, in unmanifest reality or at least as close as you can come to that and be conscious. So here is what often happens. God-consciousness starts by the recognition of physical consciousness and of the spiritual consciousness within as we have described in Cosmic-consciousness. But there are gaps. What then happens is an awakening not only that God is active and alive and creating in the physical realm, but that the awakening spirit of Self can become evermore subtle, evermore dimensionally fine, evermore closer to the God-head. What you experience is that part of yourself that sits reasonably close to God and you are aware of your physical self and you are aware of a lot of travels between the two, but you are not yet fully conscious between those two, shall we say, extremes. So the evolution of God-consciousness is the awakening in the movement of conscious beingness in all the places between the physical and that place most close to God. But just as I said when you asked about the definitions of spirit, soul and personality, as wholeness becomes manifest, those definitions become one. And so, just as it may be worthwhile to understand the definitions of Cosmic-consciousness, Christ-consciousness, and God-consciousness as it was to understand the definitions of spirit, soul and personality, these definitions themselves are also a description of separation, and it is important not to dwell on energy forms that reinforce separation.

SUMMARY

The major message about **Christ Consciousness** is that each and every one of us is an individualized aspect of Christ Consciousness because all things which exist in creation are aspects of Christ Consciousness. This is true because the Christ Consciousness is that energy which flows from unmanifest God into manifestation to create all Creation. Therefore, all aspects of God have the Christ Consciousness as a part of their very Being.

Another major point of the teachings is that as one becomes aware of his/her Christ Consciousness in this dimension, that then allows the recognition and acceptance of the Christ Consciousness in the next dimension, and then the one beyond that, and then the one beyond that all the way to the "sound of God" which emanates from the inexhaustible Source of unmanifest God. In other words, the awareness of the Christ Consciousness that is at the very center of

You is the first step into the awareness of the full divinity that is You.

Despite these major points about the Christ Consciousness, possibly the most significant message among all the significant messages, almost the "first among equals," is the awareness that because of the Christ Consciousness, *We Are One* with God. We do not exist in a state of "two-ness" with God and we never have. If all are of the Christ Consciousness, and therefore are part of the energy which has flowed from unmanifest God into manifestation to create all Creation, then how could we ever not be in "one-ness" with God?

CHAPTER SIX
JESUS THE CHRIST

INTRODUCTION

Jesus the Christ is arguably the most influential individualized energy that has ever walked on the face of this Earth. The background on his name has been presented in the Introduction to *Chapter Five* and will not be repeated here other than to say that by his very name he was, and is, a sanctified one of God.

It is highly likely that Jesus had no intention of founding a new religion, but through the efforts of Paul during the middle part of the first century, followed by the sacrifices of the early Christian martyrs during the next two hundred years, and followed further by the organization and teachings of the Early Church Fathers over the next three hundred years, a religion was established and a Church was organized. This Church was manned solely by those who accepted a set of doctrines and dogma established by the Church, for those who did not accept these teachings were declared to be heretics and were banished from participation in the Church. During the first five hundred years of the Church's existence, numerous teachings were established which differed from the teachings of the Christ. This development was thoroughly documented in *The Christian Conspiracy* and will not be repeated here except to say that as a consequence, the teachings of the sixth century religion differed greatly from the teachings of Jesus of Nazareth. That sixth century religion is similar to the Christian religion of today, at least in its doctrines [i.e. that which is taught] and its dogma [i.e. a series of doctrines which have been declared to be the truth and which, therefore, must be followed.]

It is not my intent to bash the resulting Christianity, for I believe it to have been a powerful force for humanity's pathway, and I found myself resonating positively with its teachings for over fifty years. However, I believe that certain elements of Christian doctrine have restricted the spiritual growth of its members. I feel that happened to me during my time as an active member of the Church, and I feel it happens to anyone who expects his or her spiritual growth to be enhanced by following the restrictive teachings of any dogmatic religion.

One of the restrictive dogmas of the Christina Church is that Jesus is the *only* Son of God, a belief which is not stated in any of the Gospels of the Bible in their original language. The earliest correctly translated use of the term "only Son" which I can find is presented in the Rules of Faith developed by Irenaeus in about 190 CE, almost 160 years after the Crucifixion. The earliest reference to the term "only begotten Son" seems to be in a Creed presented by Eusebius of Caesarea in about 300 CE, over 250 years after the Crucifixion. Most of the elements of that Creed were incorporated in the Creed of Nicaea which was accepted at the First Ecumenical Council in 325 CE. The original Gospels say nothing about this dogma. Instead, they use the Greek term *monogenes* to describe the Christ as a Son of God. *Monogenes* means "unique" and has never been translated as "only" except in the English translation of the New Testament. This fact has been adequately documented in all three of the previous books of this series, especially in *Christianity and the New Age Religion*. Consequently, the justification for this position will not be presented here other than to say that any religion which proposes a "greater than" position for their leader is not subscribing to the equanimity of all within the grace of God.

There is much that could be said about why the Early Church Fathers acted as they did, but that has been presented in the previous books and is not the major subject of this book. Suffice it to say that the channelings below present a different picture of Jesus the Christ than does the Church of today. The Ascended Masters who channeled the information for this book sincerely love the Christ who is presented below, and so do I. Those in physicality who prefer this Christ to the Christ of the Church are growing in number. Their voice is being heard more and more.

CHANNELED INFORMATION
Maitreya, Channeling 56 [5/28/96]

Christians look to Jesus as their agent for salvation and forgiveness. Could you please comment on that? What happens when you do something which is not in your best interest or the interest of others? You feel badly, but yet you have an opportunity at that point to balance the energy you created. That is one of the gifts of the grace of God. As long as you are aware of that energy within your human experience, you have the ability to balance it, to clear it, to become whole with that experience, and to allow that experience to come within your integrity. The Bible clearly states that if you ask God for forgiveness, you will be forgiven. There is no "agent" needed for this. When you ask God, what that truly means is that if you are aware of the unbalanced energy of your creations, and you move into your divinity with God and ask for forgiveness, you open a channel within yourself to your divine self which allows energy to flow into your experience and to heal or balance the energy you feel. The trivial interpretation is that you merely ask God for forgiveness, but it takes more energy than that. What if you don't mean it? Then how much forgiveness are you going to generate for yourself?

Perhaps another way to say this would be to say, "Be in God, and forgive yourself," for are you not a divine being who is one with God? How could you be separate from God and still exist? So in your God-head, in your association with God in asking God for forgiveness, truly what you are doing is being in God and healing not only that energy within yourself, but all the streams of energy that move from that creation. And so God has given you the gift of allowing yourself to be healed each and every moment that you are willing to move into your divinity and forgive. Each time you do it you get a little better at it. Perhaps the first few times you may not feel all the energy. Maybe there will be just a little bit. But if you are willing, you will feel that energy again and you will do it again. And soon, you will be able to heal all that your vessel of experience allows.

Let me present an analogy. If you needed a gallon of water, you might go to a well with a one gallon bucket. But if you were not very good at dipping that bucket into the well, the first time you tried you would bring up only a small amount of water. You would pour that water into your vessel and then you would dip the bucket with more experience. This time you would bring up a bit more. This would continue until you had filled your vessel. And so it is with the infusion of Godliness into your consciousness. With each dipping of your consciousness into the well of God, you are able to receive what is your divine allotment according to the size of your vessel. The size of your vessel is determined by the soul experience and all the associated energetic creations which you have accumulated during all your Journeys. The more experience you gain, and the clearer you make your vessel through the movement of energy from absolute God-head through all dimensions of reality, the more energy that can flow within that vessel. And so I say that as you have increased your ability to be in your Godliness, you increase the vessel of God that can be present here and now, demonstrably, completely, divinely.

Jesus can be a great help in your learning how to do this, and I can state with great clarity that if you call on him, he will help. However, it is not his job to do it for you. Instead, Jesus learned to do it for himself, and so must you. How is it that Jesus was able to perform the miracles that indeed he did perform? It was because Jesus had developed the ability to bring forth enough energy through the vessel of his divinity to create whatever was his divine intention. His association with God was so close that his divine intention was very close to God's divine intention. They were nearly one and the same. In addition to his association with God, Jesus worked with other non-physical energies during his life who cooperated to expand the vessel of Godliness that could be expressed within the physical life of Jesus.

You can do the same. You can grow beyond your limited three-dimensional existence by living within your integrity and listening for all of your love so that your life is lived as a movement of love meeting love. Every experience that you have created has its perfection. Has God learned from all of the foibles of humanity which were deemed as not-God? Of course God has! How is it that joy be joyful without knowing what is not-joy? In the same way, how is it that God can be known without knowing what is not-God? The trick in learning from that which is not-God is to be worthy of all that God has for you and to reflect that worthiness as an expression of your experience. How many people truly feel worthy unto God? When you do an action or thought that is inappropriate in your knowing of loving space, how do you feel about God? Do you feel worthy of God, or are you angry at yourself?

In truth, every action is worthy no matter what it is because it has its perfection in the working out of the energy of this experience. It may not be loving, but it has its overall cosmic perspective as energy which has become balanced. Even though it may seem that it is not good or perfect, there is a level of experience in which the energy becomes balanced and has its purpose within God so long as that experience is gained without judgment.

But what happens to humanity's ability to live within their integrity if they are constantly judging the experience of humanity? How can humanity be in flow with Divine Will if it is constantly judging Divine Will and constantly judging the actions of others who are learning and experiencing in a balancing act of their own choosing? The gift of divinity for this planet is Free Will, the Free Will to choose and decide for yourself what is the time and place of your experience and what that experience will be. It is not to trust your salvation or forgiveness to another, for you must do it yourself and you must do it without judgment. What did Jesus say when those were brought to him for judgment? Those of his day dragged the "sinners" to him so that they could hear Jesus pass judgment upon these sinning souls. What did Jesus say? He said, "I love you. You and I are one. The Father is within you and is within me. Go, and in your Father's name, sin no more. And in your name, rejoice in the opportunity that you create for yourself each and every moment of your life." I cannot remember Jesus passing judgment, except on a couple of occasions when he slipped. [Laughter]

So what does the life of Jesus represent to you? Jesus was a very evolved soul experience that came to this planet. Through tremendous energy, he came to a place of consciousness within himself that he could bring forth his life purpose. What is your life purpose? What is it that you have come to give to this world ? Each of you has a unique gift, a unique ability, and a unique aspect of your divinity to give to the planet in service of yourself and God. What is your gift to give? What is your purpose, and how does this fit into living within your integrity? If you are living your life consciously outside of alignment with your life purpose, is that living within integrity? Living within your integrity is also living in alignment with your overall purposes in life just as Jesus did during his time here on this planet. As you are in your integrity with the small aspects of your life, your ability to discern what is your individualized Divine Will will grow. In addition, your ability to live within that part of yourself that is pro-actively balancing your energies rather than creating additional unbalanced energies will allow you the clarity to know what your life purpose is. With that clarity you will move more into a life path that will maximize your divine growth, your divine opportunity.

So how do you know you are making progress? Oftentimes you know within your heart that you are moving in the right direction for you because you know it within yourself. There is always that clarity available if you spend time and are observant. This is how Jesus discovered his life purpose and followed it. This is what you should also do. And never believe that Jesus will do it for you. He will help with all the love and peace that he can send, but it would be denying the divinity that is you if he were to do it for you, for is Jesus the agent of your salvation and forgiveness, or are you?

Maitreya, Channeling 56 [5/28/96]

It has been said that Jesus worked with a number of non-physical beings, one of whom was Lord Maitreya. How did Jesus use this help for his evolvement? This happened in several ways. First, the energy of Jesus, a great being of light, had great opportunity by virtue of Jesus' own vessel of experience. Although this light was great, the mass consciousness at that time was so thick and so dense that it was decided cooperatively to make it a magnified experience. And so in this way, the energy that you call Maitreya aided Jesus in a joint effort. There were many others from time to time who also participated. Generally there is a primary spiritual identity, but others also participate in order to maximize the possibilities when it is appropriate.

Jesus had a very definitive life purpose. Because the Earth is immersed in a lot of energy that tends to shield one from his or her life purpose, it was decided to insure that there was plenty of energy and plenty of support available to help Jesus identify and understand his life purpose at an early age. At that time, he came to understand the clear connection between his conscious experience and his divine experience. This is what has been called "Cosmic Consciousness." It is when there is the duality of experience of the divine nature and the human nature. This experience is often so strong that it almost seems as if there are two separate parts. Jesus began his incarnation in a very close experience of Cosmic Consciousness, and it became fully identified to him at a very young age.

However, Jesus had not as yet achieved the age of spiritual maturity. There were many times during the formative years when Jesus flowed from clear recognition to being not so clear, because to be able to live at that time with others, he had to have some degree of shielding in order to be in concert with his family. But after the age of spiritual maturity, a clearer perspective of his Cosmic Consciousness became manifest. Because of this, Jesus could speak clearly about his Father's business, for Jesus understood the divine being to be his Father God. In his early years he did not yet understand that it was Jesus in cooperation with Father God, one and the same from that level, which represented the divine being. And so, although at an early age Jesus said, "about my Father's business," he later knew that what he truly meant was "about my life purpose." He knew that he was to be about his business, about his service to humanity, about what he came to express, about what was within his life experience, and about the energy that flowed through him as he served humanity.

At his age of spiritual maturity, Jesus began to be more descriptive of his realization of life upon Earth, but he still had to play the game in order to grow up and accomplish his life purpose. But at a relatively early age, he could no longer remain as a young person in that energy. And so at that time he left to travel, often more in a spiritual way than in a physical one. He was able to travel spiritually to many Masters upon the planet and to work in non-physical ways. He also traveled physically to be able to gain the experience he needed to develop his ability to be Jesus. The fruition of these experiences was to allow the channel between his human consciousness and his divine self to be open to the point that there was great clarity. This did not mean that Jesus was the total expression of divinity in humanity. It meant that Jesus had cleared enough energy within himself to begin his divine purpose in a way that was to be.

This is only a cursory explanation of the evolution of Jesus. How Maitreya interacted with Jesus is not really important. What is important is that Jesus had the courage within himself to live within his integrity. Every time in his evolvement that Jesus acted apart from his integrity, he became ill. He had to learn to heal that energy. In this process, Jesus healed a great deal of mass consciousness, because for him to be in his life purpose there had to be a great clearing of energy upon the planet. This was the major accomplishment of many energies that worked with Jesus, working on many levels, because without Jesus being here to anchor that energy into the physical, the great work on the energy fields of various dimensional levels could not be accomplished.

During the time of Jesus there were others who were also great, divine incarnations. You do not hear about them because it was not their life purpose, but they grounded tremendous energy in concert with Jesus for this whole life purpose to be accomplished. Jesus was not born in full knowledge of his divinity; but with help, he came to his Cosmic Consciousness at a relatively early age, and he evolved from there to become the great Master that he truly was and is. The message that has been forgotten is that you can do this also!

Maitreya Channeling 57 [5/30/96]

Christianity talks often about the death and the ascension of Jesus Christ. Is there something unusual in this experience? The death and ascension of Jesus is often misunderstood. Jesus had the desire to show the ability of all of mankind to transcend death and indeed to show by his example the truth of his words during his teaching. The truth of his words were that he and his Father were one, and that all mankind and the Father are one, and that all that is, is of the Father.

In order to show this in a dramatic way, it was decided by the spirit of Jesus even before his birth that the most effective manner would be to show clearly that there is life after death. To do this, it was necessary for Jesus to "suffer" a physical death and then to show that he had overcome that death. Indeed, there was much suffering of the physical body of Jesus in this process of dying. Many people think that because of his divinity, Jesus did not participate in this physical event; but the truth is that Jesus, by his very nature and the divinity of his physicality, was indeed present during this physical event. The way in which pain is dealt with is different when your consciousness spans beyond the physical, but nonetheless the physical reality is quite traumatic to the consciousness.

And so Jesus' body died by his design. After being moved according to the story, which is somewhat accurate, the body was raised up. Jesus not only "ascended," he raised his body from the dead and enlivened it again. When Jesus came back to Earth, he came back in different ways, for at that time to be in total physicality required tremendous energy. For Jesus to come back "nearly physical" required much less energy. By this I mean that the form of Jesus was there, but the form required a consciousness shift on the part of those with him before they could clearly perceive his presence. Although Jesus was in "near physicality" when he came back, because of the integration of Jesus' other cells in the process of bringing up his body into life and into his light being, the "near physical body" no longer reflected only the characteristics of his last incarnation. Instead, his "body" took on the characteristics of all of Jesus' experiences in the physical. If you think about this, you will understand that the physical presence or likeness of a great being such as Jesus would reflect more of him than had been present in his latest incarnation, for why should such a presence reflect only one of his travels? Would not that physical presence more clearly reflect the spiritual energy that is Jesus reflected wholly into physicality?

Is this why some did not recognize him? In a being with as great a vessel of experience as Jesus, there is always the ability to transform any presence into the likeness which existed in any physical reality in which he was present. Consequently, Jesus moved and transformed that physical aspect of his being more toward the likeness of the Jesus that they knew for the purpose of being recognized. However, because of all of the energy present, the way that the physical form was seen depended on the spectrum of consciousness of those who viewed the form and on their ability to see. Therefore, Jesus was recognized by some and not by others. In addition, as Jesus created his physical embodiment from pure energy, he became an even clearer reflection for those who gazed upon him. In this way Jesus not only reflected his own being, but he reflected a being that took on the energy of reflection of those who viewed him. He did this for the purposes of education and enlightenment. This explains the difficulty on the part of some to clearly know that it was Jesus they were seeing.

There is another energy at play as well, and that is that many people could not believe. Doubt always creates a distortion, especially when that which they see is not completely brought into full physical form but into an energetic form that merely takes on the appearance of physicality. In this case doubt becomes more of a factor in the ability to view and to see clearly. Jesus came back in nearly full physical form during the first few times he appeared after his rising up. As he moved to many more places and made many more appearances than have been described or documented, he often moved in a more energetic form than a physical one. By doing this he demonstrated the ascension more than once in order to remove doubt from those who had witnessed his ascension into what was called "heaven."

Some have said that Jesus came back as Appollonius in another life. Would you comment on that? Appollonius is an energy of the same "group," but Appollonius was in physicality at the same time as Jesus. Not all of the dates of your history are accurate. Appollonius performed miracles at the same time of Jesus' miracles. Appolonius and Jesus are not of the same individualized energy stream, but each is of the same energy of creation.

It has also been said that there have been some who have ascended and then came back as the same individualized energy stream but in a different physicality as method of additional service for humanity. Did Jesus do this? Beings do this all the time, but usually not as a full incarnation. More often it is the taking on of a physical form for a specific purpose. Many beings, however, have ascended in a different system and then have come here to take on the responsibilities of this physicality. They do this to increase their vessel of experience and to increase who they are. Some have done this to become a prime investigator as to the viability of the Godhead in physicality.

Now did Jesus come back in a full physical incarnation after his ascension? The answer to this is, "No, he did not." The reason is more due to what was done with the energy of Jesus after his ascension. There was so much misunderstanding and so much abuse of the power that was graced to the planet by his presence that it would not have been fruitful for his energy to come and re-energize in that way. Has Jesus come in physical form for a short-time specific purpose? The answer is to this is, "Yes, he has occasionally done this." But more often he has impressed his energy into what appears to be physical rather than coming in complete physicality. Before you think that this is what is meant by the term "overshadowing," let me state that overshadowing is a major mis-conception. Overshadowing implies a "lesser than" and a "greater than" relationship. That is not the case. It is more a partnership [see page 264].

Let me describe the term "partnership" more fully. There are beings on this planet who are being aided in their life purpose by non-physical beings. In this way, the non-physical beings participate in that physical incarnation, but mostly in cooperation and in concert with it to increase the available opportunity for energy, experience and education. These partnerships are important because they allow the opportunity for beings who are not directly in physical incarnation to participate physically, and by that association they are not so restricted in their ability to act, to energize, and to awaken. And so when a being such as Maitreya is in partnership, it is not done because the being with whom Maitreya works is ineffective on its own. Instead, it is a partnership relationship in which more can be experienced and accomplished. Or when Kuthumi works in this way, it is not because there is the need to bolster or to make something happen that otherwise could not happen, but merely to increase the probability and to increase the energy flow that is available.

To relate this more specifically to the experience of Jesus, and to clear up some confusion, although it has been said that during Jesus' incarnation he was overshadowed by the Christ Consciousness, this would imply that the Christ Consciousness would be separate from Jesus. How could this be when in reality the Christ Consciousness is the movement of divinity into reality, and different beings reflect different aspects of that Christ Consciousness? And so, when Maitreya and Jesus interacted in partnership, it was not that Maitreya was the grand being who provided Jesus with the energy to do miracles. Instead, Maitreya participated in partnership in the life experience that was Jesus in order to bring forth a more full aspect of the Christ Consciousness at an earlier time in the lifetime of Jesus, and to do so with a greater probability that the life purpose would be fully understood.

There is so much thought and structure in "lesser than" and "greater than," and there has been so much energy put into that misconception that it is my great hope that humanity can realize that the Ascended Masters are no greater nor lesser. Instead they may, in some cases, have more experience or possibly the ability to focus their consciousness in a way that allows information to flow which otherwise would not be directly available. It is not "greater than." How could any point or any substance or any organism or any part of humanity be "lesser than" or "greater than" if all is of God? That would be denying God!

Often the energy of a Master with whom you work will not be present all of the time. Instead, it will come as it is appropriate and needed. Although you could say that that being is in partnership with you, a true incarnational partnership is of a higher degree, almost to the point of being raised to a new level. It is a bonding of energies that allows a wide spectrum of divinity to be available. But the difference is only one of degree, and it would be rare for there to be any being upon this planet who was not in partnership with some nonphysical being at least to some degree.

Getting back to the term "overshadowing," we feel it implies something which is not accurate, and Maitreya did not "overshadow" Jesus in the sense of controlling him. Instead there was a partnership formed. Energy in partnership to some level or degree is quite common. Now what is often unique is when there is an accommodation within an individual in incarnation to be flexible and clear enough to allow multiple energy streams to be in partnership of great intensity at the same time. That is unusual enough that it has been experienced by only a few. It was experienced by Jesus the Christ.

Maitreya, Channeling 14 [10/26/92]

Each of you carries, in varying amounts, the energy of the Christ. The Christ is that energy which is the creative manifestation of God. There are many unique varieties of that Christ energy. There was a being who was known as the Christ long before the creation of this universe. Jesus is known as the Christ, and so is Maitreya. You also are a Christ, because you have energy of the Christ. By expressing your enlightenment, you bring forth the Christ light, for the destiny of each individualized soul is to be the Christed one. You already are in your creation, but as your soul matures it expands the vessel of the Christ that you are, for although you were created as God, you have not yet generated the vessel of experience and knowledge that would allow you to be as Jesus the Christ was. This vessel of experience is the uniqueness that you are. The purpose of your path in this incarnation, and all the other experiences of you as a unique spirit, are for the purpose of expanding the unique vessel of divinity that you are. In this way, the divine grows as you grow because each of your experiences is different than the experience of another. Many of you have expressed wonder that if you were created divine, why would you ever live outside of that divinity in conscious expression? The reason is to create more of what God is, by creating more of what you are. In participating in this plan of God's, you are enlightening the world, just as the one known as Jesus the Christ did.

Sananda, Channeling 5, [6/8/92]

The mission of the creation of your experience is a great expansion of God. It is the divine purpose, indeed. And the respect of your own divine self and the great life you live is honoring the purpose for which you were created. There is no limitation to the Mother/Father God that flows through you. None. As it is in all things, it is in you. As you expand your vessel, you expand that which the divine can move through you. As Jesus touched others to heal them, so can you; for Jesus realized that there is no limitation from the Father and that no task was insurmountable. The same is true for you. Jesus found that as soon as he would release any limitation from his personality and give it to God, then whatever divine purpose he sought would come forth and be manifested; for only in our personal limitation do we limit that which we are. We are, indeed, divine. Let it flow. It is that unlimited nature and energy and power and love that you are, and it is your purpose to allow it to flow in the way which your vessel of experience allows, for each of you is different, yet the same. You are magnificent beings of light grouped together for a magnificent purpose. It is only limited thought and limited action that places a limit on the reality of your being. Know that the flow is eternal and it is infinite. If you could see the frequency of your energy you would know the truth of what I say. Each one of you is the bringer of the gift of spirit to humanity. Each one of you is a Jesus of this time, and you do it in your own way. He came to show the way. In doing so he created a pattern in which you now can move. Know that Jesus charted the way. He lived the truth, and so can you.

St. George, Channeling 43 [3/22/93]

Within my hand is the energy to create whatever I wish. Within this room is enough energy to create a world because whenever this energy is used, God fills it with more. There is no lack, for lack is only created by lack of consciousness. However, people have become addicted to lack, and they say, "Oh, I believe I can create, but I can't actually do it, and I don't know anybody who can. Yeah, it may be so, but it isn't real." And that is the trap humanity has been in for thousands of years. But what happened when one person demonstrated it? Jesus the Christ demonstrated that there is no lack. He showed that there is only the expression of love, and that this creates all that is needed. Soon, the people around Jesus realized they could do it too; and there were many, many beings in body who had powers similar to those of Jesus. This is not mentioned much in your books, but how do you think the disciples could do their work as well as they did? They were very powerful beings, and when they believed, then miracles happened. Jesus had a brother in spirit who was in body in Greece at the same time as Jesus. He raised the dead, he healed the sick, and he created prosperity where there was lack. It has happened many times upon this planet, though recorded history does not show it. Whenever it happened, other people believed because they saw it. But if you believe it only because you have seen it, and if you have not done the work to become conscious, then you will lose it because the foundations were not laid. This has happened in the past, so now we are laying the foundations for clarity and consciousness, and we are doing it in this physical vehicle. This gets us back to making the vehicle more clear so that we can have greater clarity in consciousness.

Blend of Kuthumi and St. George,
Channeling 52 [2/20/96]

Recognition is the key, for in recognizing that there is something, you have gone over half of the way in the battle for clarity. As an example, it is not wrong to be in the anger, but in that anger realize that it is your energy that is coming up to be felt, to be loved, and to be emoted. It is often thought in New Age circles that if you are in anger, you are a bad person and you must be tranquil and holy all the time. But there are energies within you that have to be addressed and if you have to be angry, then be angry! Jesus was probably angry in the Temple, but it was an anger which was recognized as having originated in love. You may accept this or not, and I would say that it is for each of you to commune with Jesus in your own way, but I would say that not only did Jesus display the Christ Consciousness of his own being at all times, but Jesus also healed a great deal of mass consciousness and changed the world. The world created the readiness for change, and Jesus responded to that creation.

So what I am saying is to be careful in assuming that you are automatically in-love. Be angry if you are angry and if it is a non-loving anger, then recognize it and let it go by releasing the energy. There are beings who can see the energy within themselves and can transmute it without re-experiencing it, but there are others who must re-experience it. This is because they have a linkage to many, many other beings and in their physical demonstration of the emotion and the healing with love, they do much more than just heal themselves.

Many of you are like that, and as you flow in your particular way in the stream of this creation and you create in your own particular way, let everything else **be**! **LET IT BE!** This is how Jesus the Christ was so effective in transforming mass consciousness.

In addition, Jesus spoke some of the most important words ever offered upon this planet; for when Jesus spoke to those who felt his energy, he said, "You are as I am." What did he mean by that? He meant that, "You all are God-beings as I am a God-being. I have merely come forth in this way to show you what you are." He did not come forth to be worshipped. He came forth to show humanity what humanity is. That is all. But by his great God-presence, he attracted a whole lot of mass consciousness and he healed a great deal of the planet in his lifetime here. The life of Jesus is important. He is a great God-being who came forth in clarity to help transform a planet because that planet and human family had created the opportunity to transform. But yet, do not ascribe to Jesus that which is apart from yourself. Religion is a subject that is very near and dear to many people, and many people have very specific ideas of how life works. But I would say unto you that Jesus came to demonstrate who you are. This is what I have attempted to say to you this evening: *this is who you are!* This is who you are, **so be it**.

Your life is your teacher. It lays before you each moment in time. If you wish to be God-being in clarity and love and power and freedom, then follow your life as your teacher. And each moment, look to it as to what is to be addressed, and have the courage and conviction to do it! It takes great courage to look at each moment in your life as your teacher. Great courage! Great conviction! Great integrity! Great integrity of being. And so you have it all. You do not need anyone else, you have it all. Just go **be it**. It will happen much quicker than you realize.

Maitreya, Channeling 54 [3/26/96]

When Jesus walked upon this planet in an embodiment which is documented, he could do great things; he could do great healings; and he could do great manifestations. But his words were, "You will do these and more." The reason for this is because Jesus was only allowed to do so much. This was because of the consciousness of what was here at that time. The collective mass consciousness and the karma of each and every being that was either in physicality or waiting to be in physicality creates a karmic mass consciousness that only allows so much. If Jesus were to heal the planet, would that have been in alignment with what creation had allowed? Did the people upon the planet at that time create the opportunity for mass healing of the planet and of the people upon it? The answer to both questions is "No!" That is why Jesus could do only what he did, because he operated within the universal laws of creation. He was a universal law of creation, and in his embodiment, he functioned within the covenants of the universal law. Despite those restrictions, today mass consciousness has had tremendous healing from the time of Jesus.

St. George, Channeling 47 [11/6/95]

It is important to realize that you are here at this time to be complete, feeling beings. That will expand the vessel of **you**. Intellect is like a narrow band of energy between your God-self and your physicality, and on this band of energy is the ability to know God. It is like a telephone line over which you can communicate. It is like a laser beam. It is like a hologram where you can intellectually see and experience the totality of what God allows you to see. But there is more. The feeling of consciousness allows that band of energy to expand and to become in wholeness of what God intended for humanity. Why was it that Jesus the Christ was able to affect the world so profoundly during his physical visitation? It was because Jesus allowed great feeling in his life and great compassion. With great feeling and great compassion for life, love is allowed to flow, and it is **love** that expands the vessel of your consciousness. There are many great Masters that ascended upon this planet that were not exactly very loving beings, for they ascended on a narrow band of the total energy. But you are not here to do that. You are here to expand this energy that you are, to be in wholeness, and to be as big as you can be. And if you can be as big as the universe, then **so be it!** You would be creating universes anew, and you would be doing it with the love which Jesus so admirably expressed.

Maitreya, Channeling 51 [2/6/96]

Let me explain something that may help. Many of you think of past Masters upon this planet as being clear. I say to you that they are not. Past Masters who were on this planet and achieved great enlightenment did so oftentimes in narrower bands of energy than they would have liked because this was what they had sufficient energy to achieve at the time of their presence upon the planet. They could not, within their wholeness of being, take all of themselves with this energy and so they accomplished on "narrower bands" of accomplishment.

That is why I have said that you should not think of Ascended Masters as greater than yourself. It is a community of God. All are divine. The only difference is that each element of God has chosen different paths of experience and so they have different qualities of their consciousness. Some have chosen great experiences and they are huge in their energy of experience. They are massive beings and they seem to be so great because of their energy. It is just that oftentimes they did something so many times that they gained a lot of experience in the process. They are not greater than you. You are divine beings. You are God-creators. You have been told this many times. Jesus came to this planet and told everyone that they are God, that they are divine. He said, "As I am, so are you! And as God speaks through me, then you must come to me." He was not speaking of Jesus, the man. He was speaking of God. You cannot be who you are without becoming the Christ. Christ Consciousness is God in action; and all that the Christ is, is God in action. Without coming through the Christ, you cannot come to God.

In other words, without being conscious in Christ, you cannot be conscious totally in God. Jesus came to herald to humanity that the bonds of ignorance about the origins of life have been lifted! He came and gave the full program of Mastership. It was as clear then as it is today. And Jesus, in his own special way, made it even clearer because of his ability to love with his words; for when Jesus spoke, not only did the ears hear, so did the heart. Therefore, it was knowing on many levels. He gave the program of Mastership to all who would hear. That Mastership program is still available today. It is not written in the books very clearly, but it is still there for those who would see it.

Master DK, Channeling 24, [3/29/93]

Sometimes when no answers seem to come during your meditations, the lesson is to learn patience and to wait for the answer to come. In the beginning stages of Spirit or Self communication there may be times when the answers are not perceived quickly. This is not because they are not there, but it is because you are building the road to Self. As an example, until the telephone wires have been connected from one point to another the communication between them cannot take place. This is also true in meditation and in spiritual communication, for until you build the freeway of your Soul communication, the answers will not come easily. But the answers are always there and their clarity will increase with use and with practice as long as you are patient. As a test, do you have the trust in God to wait for the answer to come in divine time rather than personal time? Many of the greatest Masters that have walked upon this planet have looked to God and have said, "Why are you not communicating with me? What have I done wrong?" This often happens because with the last seeds of doubt, they did not trust completely. But by the burning off of the last aspects of personal control they were infused with the Christ Consciousness so strongly that their personal will became infused with Divine Will and there was no separation. And thus Jesus became Jesus the Christ. And thus Buddha became Buddha the Enlightened. And thus you can become the divine you.

SUMMARY

In these channelings, Jesus the Christ is seen as a great teacher who showed the individualized beings of humanity how each could become one with God. In fact, these teachings state that it is the destiny of each soul is to be the Christed one. However, they also state that to date few, if any, have carried the vessel of experience which has allowed them to enlighten the world as Jesus Christ did. He so admirably expressed love that he taught the world that there is only the expression of love, and that through this all that is ever needed is created. Others had the power that Jesus had, but their effects were localized rather than universal. Jesus taught a universal and unconditional love, and also taught that all are divine. He said that through this divinity and through the love in the heart, all would be with God just as he was and is. In addition, these teachings state that all who came to Earth after the time of Jesus have the ability to do more than he did if they would just do it. This is so because mass consciousness has become enlightened enough to permit deeds which are greater than the world would allow for Jesus.

In his work, Jesus received a great deal of help from the non-physical ones who cooperated with him. However, the channelings make the point often and strongly that the non-physical ones did not do the work for Jesus. Instead, after he understood and accepted the divine purpose for his life, he did the work by giving his limitations to God whenever they tended to prevent his accomplishing his divine purpose. By showing humanity that this was possible, Jesus cleared a great deal of mass consciousness and permitted great spiritual growth on the part of those who would understand and accept his example. In this way, Jesus reflected God to humanity. He is one of those who still reflects God to humanity.

One of the finest books to describe Jesus without the Church is entitled *Jesus Before Christianity* by Albert Nolan, a Roman Catholic priest. In this book Father Nolan proposes that even if the present Christian Church turns you off, if you were to look at Jesus without the Church you would still accept him as the one who reflected God to you. Both *The Christian Conspiracy* and *A Personal Pathway to God*, relate how Father Nolan's thoughts are a constant reminder of the God who calls to me. There is absolutely no dislocation between the points that Father Nolan makes and the points which are made in the channelings presented above.

One of the major messages in these channelings is that although Jesus the Christ can give help on the pathway to being God, in no way can he do it for you. However, his help and the help of the other loving, non-physical beings can certainly be a powerful boost along the way!

CHAPTER SEVEN
PHYSICALITY

INTRODUCTION

Humanity's religions have spread confusion about the human body. This is not to say that each individual religion has been confused, for each has tended to have clear teachings about the role of the body. However, if one were to place all of humanity's religious teachings about physicality in one container and look at them, there would be every conceivable teaching. In other words, the great thinkers, teachers and philosophers of humanity's religious history have tended to teach all things about the human body, and in so doing have spread confusion amongst the physical beings of humanity.

As one example, in the first century of the common era Gnosticism taught that the human body was evil. This teaching was echoed by the Docetists in the second century, the Manichaeists in the third century, the Cathars in the twelfth century and many other religions during the past two millennia. The Docetists believed in the evil of the human body to such an extent that they proposed that Jesus Christ did not really have a human body, but only appeared to have one.

As a different example, some religions have taught that the human body, while not actually evil, was at least undesirable. They have further taught that the body is something to "grow beyond." The Essenes of the time of Jesus and the Hindus of today would be two examples of many religions which have had this belief, and many sects of Islam, Judaism and Christianity would present similar teachings. Most Christianity, however, subscribes to the holiness of the physical body and teaches that the resurrection of the physical body will occur at the "second coming of the Christ," at which time the grave will give up its bodies to ascension in a burst of glory as all become one with the Divine.

As still another example, some of the more "spiritual religions" such as those of the early Egyptians, the Mayas and the Native Americans have tended to pay homage to the physical body by regarding it as a structure of a somewhat divine nature.

Although these limited examples present an incomplete picture, they do demonstrate that within the religions of humanity almost every variation on the worthiness of the human body can be found. This worthiness extends from being a thing of evil, to being a thing of present or eventual divinity.

As has already been stated in some of the channelings previously presented, the Ascended Masters view the human body as a grand experiment. They state that physical embodiment on planet Earth not only gives the ultimate ability to address that which needs to be brought into clarity, but also generates the end of a chain of manifestation which proceeds from unmanifest reality through all dimensionality unto physicality. With this teaching, the human body becomes extremely holy, not in the distant future as viewed by the Christian community, but in the existing **now**.

This chapter will present a variety of thoughts about physicality and related subjects as presented in the channelings. The organization of the chapter will be slightly different than that used in the previous six chapters. Instead of being a presentation of large segments of channelings on one subject, this chapter will present a number of separate subjects with short comments by several Ascended Masters. The source of the channeling will be presented at the end of each short paragraph.

The list of subjects covered is presented in the Table of Contents.

CHANNELED INFORMATION
The Physical Body

During the last few thousand years, you have known me as the immortal one in body; and the message that I bring to you is that your body is a part of your spirit. Often the body has been looked at as an inconvenience that can be discarded at the time of proper spiritual evolution so that you are then freed from the confines of this "three dimensional prison," but the true nature of the physical body is the expression of yourself in this dimension of experience. Every aspect of your physical body resonates with the spiritual aspect of you. If there is a sickness or malady in your physical body, it is a reflection of an energy within yourself. Limitations or lack of limitations in your physical structure represent the experiences that your spirit has chosen in physical form at this time.

[Babaji, Channeling 37, 9/21/ 94]

I have a little bit of inside information to share with you. You intended to come here to live an immortal life in the physical body, if you so choose. But after some time you may choose other avenues that are more exciting or more creative than this physical one! And then you can move on and do what you choose to do within your divine expression. But your physicality was never meant to experience death. I know that history reminds you on every page that life is death; but I will tell you that if you live, you will find that your physicality remains. We are entering a realm of consciousness that will allow people to live as long as they choose, for there is a coming time when the body will be as changeable as your mood of divine expression. You can be big, small, fat, thin, black, white, pink, green or whatever else you might choose as your creation. In the past, the body has been looked upon as something you have to put up with. It has been thought that through lots of hard work and self-denial, you can make the body live just a little bit longer. But then there is Harry. He lived a good life. Never touched a drop of liquor! Hardly ever had sex! Died when he was forty! Well, why not just go for it then? As long as you are going to live, why don't you LIVE!?

[St. George, Channeling 42, 2/13/95]

Why did you choose this time and this space to be in you? I say "in you" because your body is you. Your body is not a vehicle that you jump into and jump out of. It is you, so forget the notion that it is a disposable item which can readily be discarded. There has been too much energy left on the planet by leaving bodies laying around everywhere. It is time to take those bodies unto yourself when you ascend. No longer can you let parts of your energy be wasted to linger somewhere for a long time, because then you will have to go back to collect it.

Because of the lessening of mass consciousness, and because of the change in the karma of humanity, you have a grand opportunity to move very quickly into your wholeness. But what does wholeness mean? It does not mean being a powerful God-being running amuck and not being able to express God-consciousness in the purely created God-body which you have. Instead, wholeness means being in alignment with God, all the way from physicality unto God-space itself.

But how do you go about getting in alignment with your total Self and then in alignment with God? How does this take place? There have been many systems developed on the planet over the ages to work on this. I use the word "work" because most of them were very much work, especially in physicality. There were things such as getting awakened at 2:00 AM and being marched out across the desert on rocks with bare feet to learn the value of being not in pain; and such as not being allowed to eat; and such as being required to physically abuse yourself in an attitude of self-deprecation. All of these systems were evolved to try to find God by eliminating the body and by eliminating the here and now. What did that accomplish? If you wanted to be happy without a body, you already did that before you got one!

So it is not to do it without a body, and it is not necessarily to silence the body in the sense that it becomes so still that you become one with God, because eventually you will have to come back and be in the body again. So what is it? It is coming into alignment with God within the physicality which you presently have.

[Maitreya, Channeling 54, 3/26/96]

There are no limits in your life or in your physical form. Do you wish your physical form to be immortal or to be eternally youthful? It is within each of your powers at this time that it be so. If you wish your physical body to be a different shape, that, too, is within your power for as your intellect grows by the creation of opportunity for expansion, so your physical body can change by the opportunity of your knowledge that it can be changed. You can begin to manifest these changes in your physical system. You would not know or hear of these things if it were not possible for you, for knowing does not come accidentally. It comes as the opportunity is available if you so choose it. Many of you have heard this before, but how many have truly believed it? Now upon the planet it will be demonstrated for you, for there are those here in this room who are changing their physical form dramatically. It may not yet be fully evident on the surface, but in the energetic level needed to create such change, it is being made manifest. [**Babaji, Channeling 37, 9/21/94**]

Since so much of you resides in the physical, you have got to take care of the physical. With enough light and consciousness you can transform your physical immediately; but you're not yet there, and so in the meantime you must take care of the physical because it supports the process. It supports allowing you to be conscious. It will not be allowed, except with rare exceptions, to sit and meditate and become full of light and then let that light transform the physical. You came here to do it all. You came here to take care of all aspects of Self, and the aspect of Self that has been so neglected on this planet is the physical body. Why are you not allowed to let your light transform your physical body? Because you came here to create the pathway to heal the body so that others can do it as well. In what society is the body not abused? <u>Tell</u> me! You can take the greatest monastery, and they abuse the body tremendously because they deny it. You can take the greatest technological country and they abuse the body with technology. They irradiate it. They electromagnetize it. They pollute it, and they deny it. And they call that fun!
[**St. George, Channeling 46, Session 3, 10/29/95**]

There is an interesting "Catch-22" to the process of physical change. To change your physical form you must have attained the clarity within all of your bodies for it to become manifest; for since the physical form is the outermost structural evidence of being in this dimension, it is often the last to change based on the energetic changes within. So if one were to say, "I wish to be seven feet tall, and I wish to make this happen as rapidly as possible," you may find that within yourself there are many other energetic issues to be dealt with first. If it is your intention to welcome, receive, love, balance and heal these issues, then you would soon transform your cells so that you would be seven feet tall. Such energetic changes in the physical have actually occurred in history, often to change the appearance of an individual in order to keep him or her from being burned at the stake or imprisoned. [**Babaji, Channeling 37, 9/21/94**]

This is unknown to science, but the transformation of the cells happens only when they are infused with light, and light will go only where it is intended and where it is allowed. If the shade is pulled, light does not enter the room. If the shade is lifted, light enters the room. When you lift the shades on yourself, you are filled with light. The way you lift the shade is to remove all unbalanced energy, and then the light will flow because it is intended to do this. You can fly, you can be invisible, you can change your appearance, and you can go from one physical location to another if that is the intention of your physical cells. Your cells can transport you because they are so infused with light that the mere intention creates the change in your special location, because space is not what it seems to be in this dimension. Since you are so used to going from here to there, you think the only way to get from here to there is to do that; but in reality there is here, and here is there if you intend it. However, nothing happens without feeling intent. In other words, since the very first creative principle of God, was to look upon Himself and to feel Himself, then without that feeling, there would have been no creativity because without that feeling, there is no consciousness. Feeling is the way consciousness is understood in physical form. Well then, what is the intellect? As a ruler, the intellect is an impostor. It is only a tool of consciousness, and as such, it spans the realm of spiritual awareness. The intellect is the consciousness of being; but without feeling your environment, intelligence has nowhere to go. It has no direction. It then becomes merely wisdom, with no movement. All movement is created by feeling. It always has been. That is why the Earth hasn't moved much. It has been stuck in emotion. It hasn't felt God. [**St. George, Channeling 46, Session 3, 10/29/95**]

The Light of Shamballa comes forth most dramatically at the time of the Wesak when Shamballa comes closest to being in physicality. At this time, the Light of Shamballa indicates that the finer dimension is more present. Because of this, God can more nearly be felt, for Shamballa represents the essence of physicality in its perfected form, and the Light of Shamballa means physicality moving more into its perfected physicality. It is not that the physical moves into another dimension as some have said, for why would physicality go away? Why would the physical go away when the purpose is to be divine in the physical? So the Earth is not going away into a new dimension, is it? That sounds more like trying to escape physicality rather than being divine in physicality. It just means that physicality now can not only be physical, but can also be much, much more. Physicality can express not only dense third-dimensional physicality, but it can express the fourth dimension as well. And soon it will express the fifth dimension as clearly as you express your physicality today. Our physicality is not going anywhere, it is just becoming more conscious. We are not escaping into the fourth dimension, we are merely expressing that dimension in our physicality by being sensitive to our environment. Then when the fifth dimensional experience becomes manifest, it becomes Light. You could hold up your arm and see that it is Light and you could see through your arm. You could do that with your arm now if you would wish to do so, but you would not do that because it would not be a true expression of your physicality. The fourth dimension brings wholeness of experience in your immediate bodies; the fifth dimension brings experience of your Light, all done within the presence of physicality.

[**Kuthumi, Channeling 48, 11/28/95**] [Editor's Note: There are many spellings of Shamballa including the Sanskrit-derived Shambhala. I have chosen to use the spelling presented by Alice Bailey in her in her classical works of some 60 years ago, for those works started the awakening or awareness process in many of us.]

In the third dimension, energy works in many diverse ways. Magnetics is one aspect of the way energy works in this realm and electrics is another. Electromagnetics is the way in which they couple together in a higher level. Magnetics is considered the feminine principle and electrics the male. You cannot have one without the other because whenever electrics becomes manifest, it creates magnetism and, conversely, magnetism is used to create electrics. Whenever magnetism becomes manifest, it allows that creation. That is why the mother is the allowance of creation and the father fills that creation with light. Man's activity would not have been possible until woman created the space.

You always know when electromagnetism is present, because there is an electromagnetic field. Well, gravity works in the same way. That is why Einstein figured out there were gravity waves. So, how do you work with gravity? You don't want it to quit, because it sustains life upon this planet and is part of the master plan that creates density. But if you would couple your energies with gravity waves to create a specific intention, you could fly! Actually, there are two ways of flying. One is a cooperative coupling with gravity waves. The other is to be weightless. The way man may be perceived to fly is the cooperative coupling method; but the way the Ascended Masters fly is to be weightless, and that is the easiest way for you to fly. How do you become weightless? As you become conscious to infuse your body with light, you transform your cells with light until they become enlivened, full of light, energetic, and fully infused with your being. When the consciousness in every cell cooperates in light and love, then you have the ability to transform those cells, and you transform those cells by infusing them with so much light they become weightless. It does not mean that you lose your physicality. It merely means you have transformed the properties of that physical structure.

[St. George, Channeling 46, Session 3, 10/29/95]

The body will support true life only when it has been healed. To heal your body, nutrition is extremely important, and so are proper care, love, acceptance, honor, and integrity for the body is no different than consciousness. In fact, bodies are manifested consciousness, so if you deny any aspect of your body, you are denying yourself, and you short-circuit your evolution. When people die and they don't take their bodies with them, they leave a part of themselves behind. In leaving a part of themselves, they fail the process and it takes great energy to call that together again. Even when the body is completely decayed, there is consciousness that remains. It is stuck in many places. The answer to this problem is that you don't die at all. You already know how to ascend, for you have done it in a system where physicality was not so dense. But you came into this system with the desire to honor the physicality; for in honoring the body, you honor yourself. As a part of such honoring, it is important to create an energetic haven in which you are protected from that which is all around you and in which you can infuse yourself with light so that the unwanted "stuff" can't get in. In this haven, you will be protected from mass consciousness that is not in your best interest. It is also important to use proper nutritional aspects to clean the body, for bodies today are very polluted and congested. The body is not meant to age and wither and die. That is an abnormal response. The body ages because there is an acceptance of aging which has become locked into the cellular structure of physicality. But each one of you came into this physical life with cells that are different, and you do not have to accept aging. You came from a different system and brought in a different energy in the cells of your body. You are not of the Earth only. If science could measure it, they would know that you are different than the indigent souls of this planet. You have the ability to break the aging lock on cellular life. You do that in a two-fold manner: [1] by cleansing the body, by cleaning the organs, by being very careful of what enters your body, by being very careful what the body breathes; and [2] by energizing the cells that you have in a way which cleans and clarifies your energy. All of this is needed to support your physicality, for it is your physicality that supports you! **[St. George, Channeling 46, Session 3, 10/29/95]**

Rejuvenation of the Physical Body

Cells are naturally rejuvenated. Within the body, cells are created at a rate much greater than science currently estimates and your body has the ability to create a rejuvenated cell if that is your intention. You can create a completely rejuvenated body, for the energy that supports life on this planet will support divine, youthful bodies. If it is your divine intention, ask your body to create youthful cells rather than creating cells that have the same characteristics as the aging cells they replace. To do this, each day as you awaken, affirm that your body is recreating divine, youthful, rejuvenated cells each and every moment. In this way, your body is creating itself anew. Also affirm that you are worthy and it is your birthright to occupy and create an eternally youthful body.

Within each of you is the image of your divine, youthful body. See it and create it. It is yours. It is your right. You don't have to wait until you ascend to do this. You can do it now each and every moment. You can live in a body and create the body that never ages even without ascending. But most of you already know this. Many of you are already youthing from the inside out; so when you see the signs outwardly, there are miracles that have occurred inwardly. Many are already showing the signs of youthing outwardly.
[Blend of Maitreya/Buddha, Channeling 15, 11/9/92]

You have the power within yourselves to do majestic healing, for you have energetic connections to the God-head as your birthright. By bringing forth that energy for healing, you can heal everything until you have perfect balance of dynamic energy. With balanced energies, you can prevent the process of aging. Know that within your being is the total energy of rejuvenation. If there is the belief within you that you cannot do it, or that you don't want to do it, it is just the resignation that "I can't do it so I might as well accept it." Acceptance of the "now" is important, but it doesn't mean that you have to accept the now for tomorrow as well. In order to change any energetic pattern, it must be accepted as it is, for that allows movement; and in the movement, you can use the energy to rejuvenate whatever it is that you divinely intend to rejuvenate.
[Maitreya, Channeling 44, 5/5/95]

As you look at a reflection of your divine Self in the physical body, you see a body that is youthful, rejuvenated, and surrounded with a light as bright as the sunshine that bathes your heart. You realize that this light is the spirit of your divinity; and as your body becomes one with the light, you become this beautiful, placid sea of consciousness, of light, of harmony, and of continuous connection with all that is around you.

As you look back to see the physical body that occupies this life experience, you see this magnificent physical temple that you have created to house and manifest your experiences in this life; and you see that this body has performed exactly to your commands. Whatever state that body is in age, in strength or in frailty, in size, or in health, it has responded exactly to that which you have created.

You can also see the energy that surrounds it. This energy comprises the experiences of this life and the valuable lessons you have learned. The energy imbalances are evident to your eyes from the level of this consciousness of Self, and they are valuable learning tools that you have used for experience, but you realize that you have been living in a limited fashion because your body was not prepared to contain all the experiences you have encountered. Now your being is ready to be brought into the energy of your divine Self so that you can heal all aspects of your energetic bodies with unconditional love. To do this, you bring this physical vehicle completely into your heart and rejuvenate it by healing all that was out of balance.

In this way, the physical body is rejuvenated to reflect the beauty of your divine Self, for there is nothing in your physical body that cannot be healed and rejuvenated with the embrace of your divine being. As you become whole and complete, a continuous connection forms between your divine Self and your physical expression. There is no separation. You recognize this as you continuously immerse yourself within your own divinity and carry that divinity into your physical expression for you have been the keeper of the light of physical rejuvenation, and you are now bringing that light to humanity. **[Blend of Energies, Channeling 12, 10/5/92]**

There is no limitation to the energy that you can bring into your physical body. As you bring your Self within your physical body, changes will begin to occur physically. While much has been spoken of your light body manifesting physically, it is an integration of your dimensionality that is experienced. The physical body will begin to take on the appearance that is integrated with your other dimensional bodies and you will have the choice of how much of those bodies you wish to manifest into the physical. It is indeed possible to completely rejuvenate your body, and it is indeed possible to completely change the size and the shape of your body. These things will come in time, but you will soon begin to notice how the body feels different. As you integrate your Self over time, you will begin to realize that you really do look different. This happens because the physical body is the expression of Self, physically. As you created it, you can change it. In time, this will become easier to accomplish; but even now, you could have a much more youthful body if that is your divine intention. [**Kuthumi, Channeling 50, 1/23/96**]

The body is You. You provided the energy for it to exist, and it is manifested upon your life stream. The supporting energy for your body is in all dimensions from unmanifest reality to physicality and this supporting energy is your life stream. It is You. You are obviously much more than your body, but if your body is ignored and abused, it is like abusing your Self. The body is a holy place. It is holy for you because it is your temple of life upon this planet and your body is the physical manifestation of you in this dimension. Everything that goes into your body should be sanctified by your love and by your energy and it should be that which you know to be energetically the best for you. The air you breath and the decision of where you breath air is of paramount importance as well as how you breath it. If you allow the air to come into your body, it is life energy and if you see that life energy and know it is there and feel it throughout your body and visualize it healing you with every breath, it will do so. Air breathed in this way will rejuvenate every cell of your body, and will greatly reduce the amount of food that your body needs. There are some beings who have lived upon this planet and lived off air. Those beings came to exemplify the fact that the body is magical, as it is. It is the temple of you in this dimension. Take care of it! [**Maitreya, Channeling 54, 3/26/96**]

Other Aspects of the Physical Body

Try this on for size. There are no limits to who you are physically or sexually. You could be male today, and you could be female tomorrow. You can be large today and small tomorrow. You could be beautiful in many different ways for within each is a divine impression of your spiritual physical body. Look at it, and if you choose to look different from that, it will only be for a specific purpose. If your body today does not look like your divine physical body, then today's body has been for you to learn and grow so that you can create the body that you were truly meant to have in this dimension. How many of you in these energy sessions have actually seen the body disappear, or change shape, faces or color? How could you doubt the variability of the body? [**Babaji, Channeling 37, 9/21/94**]

The physical body is more than mere physicality. Many yogis have great talent in the physical body because they have loosened the tissues. However, although they have allowed the energy to flow clearly within the physical part, the body is more than just the physical body. The body is tied up in many dimensions, and in general, they have only dealt with the lower dimensions of the physical body. By their work, they create great clarity in the physical body; but it is not connected throughout all the levels. The true yogi connects through all levels, and the physical body movement is merely the mechanism that allows that movement to take place. In other words, the true yogis are not afraid to deal with their emotions or their experiences of life for they are open, and they accept themselves on all levels. [**St. George, Channeling 43, 5/5/95**]

It is possible to have third-dimensional physicality without duality, but to do so would short-circuit some of the grand experiment which is now happening on planet Earth. The reason for duality is a purposeful creation of space; for duality allows space to be occupied with energy of loving balance in physicality. To do otherwise would remove Free Will. There are systems which have no Free Will, and the beings in those systems are totally in balance with divinity, but this is the robot which you chose not to be when you decided to come to Earth. They are in third-dimensional physicality in the absence of duality because they have no Free Will. Free Will created duality for the purposeful filling of space with Light. In those other systems, third-dimensional physicality is not the same as it is here, for there are many degrees of third-dimensional physicality. In some, you could hold up your arm, and look through it. It is still physical, but it is just infused with Light. Where there is infusion of Light through divine purpose of creation without Free Will, third-dimensional physicality is not as dense as it is here. But that dimensionality does allow time; and manifest reality in three dimensions is a sequence of time. Those other worlds were created solely for the sequence of time, for awareness needs time in order to be understood. In leaving the third dimension, you gain experiences in dimensions which do not have time; and where there has been full Free Will experience in three dimensions, there is the awareness of awareness in those other dimensions. This is so because if you carry with you the awareness of awareness, you do so because you created it, from the basement up. To do that requires being in full third-dimensional physicality with the availability of Free Will. When all of that is present, then duality exists in order to allow space to be occupied with the loving balance in physicality. [**Maitreya, Channeling 47, 11/6/95**]

To heal the physical or to alter its form, you must provide true healing on all energetic levels, not just the physical. One way to do this is to look within yourself and see the divine image of your true spirit Self. What is that divine image of you, and is it the physical being that you wish to create each day? If it is, start creating it. Allow yourself the spiritual, emotional, intellectual and physical flexibility to create. You have been given the power of a God-being. Creation of a physical body is a minor thing. If you would be co-creators of all that is, how significant is one physical body? It is not much, but humanity has made it into the end-all and be-all of life. So become alive, my friends, and achieve Mastery in all bodies, and the physical body shall be as you wish. It is even OK to start with only the desire for changing the physical body, because it will inevitably lead you to address all other energies as well since all is linked and all is one. So wherever you start, eventually you will see all the divine aspects of yourself. [**Babaji, Channeling 37, 9/21/94**]

So what are these physical bodies and these mental bodies and these emotional bodies you have heard so much about? They are intricate, intelligent machines. They are biological in nature, but without the animation of your Soul and the enlightenment of your Spirit, you would not exist. It is only the infusion of your Soul that allows the animation of your humanness. You have heard of the chakras as vortexes of energy, and you have heard of the intellectual highway between Soul and physical. Since this is so, if you do not honor the physical temple in which you live during this experience, you do not honor your higher Self. Those who live in an addiction of any type dishonor their Soul by dishonoring that creation of your Soul that is meant for divine manifestation. In order to live in Mastery, you must honor and maintain your physical machinery. As you've cleaned up the toxic waste dump which you call your body, it will become easier to move into Mastery. And as you move into divine manifestation, the body will be kept tuned up automatically. So you just have a short while longer to do it from the level of the physical body, but it must be done. [**Kuthumi, Channeling 24, 3/29/93**]

Multi-body Experiences

The term "etheric embodiment" is confusing, for there are at least four types of etheric embodiment. The first type is a coupling with a physical incarnation that is also manifest in the etheric, as all must be for in the etheric there is a complete representation of what is in the physical realm. In this type of etheric embodiment, you do not have your energy embodied in the physical. Instead, you couple in an etheric sense with the etheric representation of a human being and you share in the human experiences and the overall evolution of that being. The second type of etheric embodiment is one in which you concentrate your energies in the etheric realm. In concentrating your energy in this realm, you are embodied in that realm as an etheric being and there is no human interaction. The third type of etheric embodiment is when there is one soul in more than one physical body. This is often the case when beings who have great energy and clarity come into the physical and they wish to utilize the maximum efficiency of that Journey and so they manifest in several bodies in order to be able to gain multiple experiences at the same time. The fourth type of

etheric embodiment is when a part of an entity goes into another body as a shared experience. Oftentimes the part will depart when it has learned what needed to be learned and taught what needed to be taught. Then the entity can call that part of itself back. This is done with a completion of the energy exchange and with a loving and honest fulfillment of the agreement to share experiences.
[St. George, Channeling 46, Session 3, 10/29/95]

Since you have said that some of us are present in more than one body at a time, is an out-of-physical being sometimes used to clear other physical bodies? Indeed, you do this all the time, especially in your sleep state. But when you are in more than one body, you generally are not there alone. When the point comes that you have provided that which you were there to provide, you will release yourself from those incarnations to come more fully and wholly into one physical presence. In all of this, you are in complete synchronicity. In other words, if you provide some of your energy to another incarnation in concert with other energies, you do it in synchronicity with those energies to provide guidance and wisdom as well as experience. This is also how you expand this vessel of who you are. You do this by sharing those other experiences, and you do this by plan. In all of this, just know that as a pioneer of consciousness, you are here to be whole. You are here to collect all parts of you into wholeness and to become greater magnifications and manifestations of who you are. And so you will not be leaving this body. Instead, you will be calling in aspects of yourself that are participating with others for clarification. You will bring all aspects of your essence into one vehicle in order to fulfill the purpose for which you came.
[Maitreya, Channeling 47, 11/6/95]

As an example, there could be an individual who was simultaneously existing in five different bodies because this was a grand being who just didn't like to do only one thing at a time but liked to spread him-or herself around. Let us suppose that one aspect of this being truly created from conscious divinity. What would then happen is that the vortex of that energy would be so strong that it would carry the other aspects of that being into clarity as well, and that being would move into wholeness. Rarely is an individual in many bodies, singularly. In other words, if there is a part of you now experiencing another life, there is most likely another soul in that body as well. And so if you were to call a part of yourself back into your conscious awareness, you would not think of it as leaving the other body without a soul or as killing that body in any way. Even when in another body, you have not left the essence of your spirit or your individualized soul. At higher levels, you may have split into soul groups but at this level you came to become clear as an individualized soul and to create God here and now. And so you wanted to bring all of the forces to bear. Often there are fragments of an individual in other experiences, not because you are resident in that experience, but because you gave up part of yourself to that energy and other life experiences. That has been called the process of soul recovery or returning the fragments of becoming whole. What that means is those aspects of yourself that you spread around because you couldn't deal with them need to be called back to home and become part of your conscious whole. You can do this quite easily just by asking for it to be so. There may be some work to do before it can be transferred, but it will come to you. The beautiful thing about living in the physical at the present time is that everything you need to do is placed before you. There is no mystery. Your life is your teacher. It is all before you. **[Kuthumi, Channeling 51, 2/6/96]**

Love

When two people fall in love, do they resonate to the same higher energy; or is their love just on a physical level? Love can take many forms. It can extend from the personal to the divine and it can represent many types of attractions from the emotional to the divine for all is energy. Divine love is a love which is a totally unconditional love. Emotional love is a conditional love, and in those relationships there is an attraction of energy for healing, and for balancing the energy relationship with the other being. Most of the people with whom you come in contact already have an energy relationship with you and for those with whom you enter a physical relationship, there is generally a working out of your karmic energies between you. In unconditional love, there is the ability to be in an unconditional love relationship

with all beings but there is an extra-special quality with those you choose to have a physical relationship with while in a state of unconditional love, for in this process you carry forth unconditional love from the heights of the heavens into the physical. In that condition there is no filling required, for in unconditional love beings are filled and overflowing with that love at all times. In coming together with another, there is a magnification of that river of love that flows through at all times. In emotional, physical love, there generally is a need to be filled, or an energy to be balanced, or a cup that is looking to be filled. Quite often we enter into an emotional relationship with another hoping and seeking that the filling would come from them when in truth, it can only come from within you.
  [**Maitreya, Channeling 20, 2/15/93**]

For what is love? Love is but an energy of life that flows throughout the dimensions. The energy of life is to create, to love and to be joyful. How can those things be possible within a cocoon of irrational, unbalanced energy? Would it not be loving to help remove the cocoon, even if doing so exposes that which is within? Sometimes it takes a great force to move and to shake these energy barriers. Sometimes this is the best approach, but not always; for there are the kind, quiet, peaceful Ascended Masters who will let you float in the loving energy of their beings, and all will be OK. That is good, too. But sometimes there needs to be some Ascended Master who will shake you up. There needs to be me because sometimes the most loving thing you can do is to break apart things and then rebuild them! Is that not what we're doing upon this planet right now? We are breaking apart all of the structures and all of the ideologies. Then we are rebuilding in consciousness. Every system upon this planet is bogus! They need to be restructured and that is what you are doing with your knowledge, with your consciousness, and with your purposeful creation. You are building a new planet with the energy of love. God blesses you for this! [**St. George, Channeling 42, 2/13/95**]

Love is not always as it would seem to be. Karma is love. Karma is not always pleasant, but it is love, for it is the love of the creator to move always into balance. There are all kinds of love. Although I do not propose to speak for Jesus, I believe that he was in total love even though he was angry at those who were prostituting the Temple. Anger is often misunderstood. It is what creates the energy or the emotion which is important. If someone is angry because of their own issue and it comes from not-love, then anger creates karma. When anger comes from love to display energy, it is love. You bet Jesus was angry when he walked into the Temple and saw how his Father's house was being treated, but his anger did not come from not-love. Anger can come from love; emotion can come from love; energy can come from love. You must look at where the energy begins and understand what is the impetus of that energy. Anger in its definition usually implies that it comes from not-love, but if we define anger as an amplified expression of emotion to clarify intention and discussion, that can come from love as well. Instead of overturning the tables in the Temple to bring attention to a point, if Jesus were to walk up to a drug dealer and overturn his transaction, how would that be? And please do not think that he would be violating the Free Will of that drug dealer, for when there is divine guidance it means that there is permission, for everything is connected. You see, it was the Free Will of those people in the Temple which allowed him to become involved. Otherwise, there would not have been divine guidance to be involved. That is why if you have true divine intention, you have permission. Now what gets difficult is when there is lack of clarity. In this case, ego intention is substituted for divine intention and then there is not permission. I only bring this up because Mastery is not a pre-defined experience. It is what you define it to be for you. We are here to become Masters. I talk in this way so that you understand that you are a Master who is unique. There is nobody like you and never will be. You are a unique Master and that is why God created you in this way because uniqueness creates anew. And so in checking with divine guidance, you create the divine Mastership that you are. And if you always walk in the love that Jesus walked in even when he showed his emotions, then you are walking in your divine Mastership. [**Kuthumi, Channeling 46, Session 4, 10/29/95**]

Earlier, you discussed actions which humans do which increase divinity and other actions which decrease divinity. When describing increased divinity, were you talking about manifestation with love; and when describing decreased divinity, were you talking about manifestation with non-love? Indeed, this is an excellent way of describing this. It is very difficult to describe this experience within the terminology of language, because all is divine, and every experience increases divinity; but from an individualized perspective there is action that is non-loving, there is action that is non-light, and there is action that decreases the awareness of your divine beingness. Possibly another way to describe this would be to say that you are not increasing <u>your</u> God, meaning that you are actually decreasing your <u>awareness</u> of the God that you are or of your God-being; whereas by increasing God, you are increasing your awareness and your vessel of God experience in consciousness. The word "love" does not do justice to the conveyance of this experience, because love cannot be defined, but instead must be experienced. Indeed, any definition of love is limited, but love is unlimited. Love can be looked at as the motivating force behind the movement of energy from God into manifest reality. Even when an action is unloving, it is love that is behind the movement of energy, because love knows from a cosmic perspective that the experience is appropriate for the eventual increase of awareness. [**Kuthumi, Channeling 48, 8/13/95**]

Abortion

Today, one of the most divisive subjects about physicality is abortion. What are the effects of human abortion on the spirit and soul of those involved? The creation of human life is a cooperative process. It is the culmination of the energies of the mother and of the father and of the entity to be born. In many cases it is known that that entity would not come into full expression in physical form. In those cases it is an educational experience for those involved who are already in the physical, *viz.* the mother and the father and any other siblings. This can happen because there is not complete movement into the physical at the instance of conception. In other words, the spiritual energy moves more into the physical as the maturity of the child in the womb increases. There is not the full integration of spiritual energy into the physical form until the time of birth.

So what is abortion and what is its effect? Truly, all events are created by the participants. Abortion is an event of dramatic upheaval, especially in this country, because there is the knowingness that life is sacred and that all life is God. And because all life is God, it is to be honored and respected and loved. But yet, each person in the family of humanity creates and destroys creations that are a part of God during each and every day. Thoughts are created and thoughts are destroyed. Energies of love are created and are destroyed as they are rejected. Physical manifestations can come close to physical reality, and then are destroyed as they are discarded. Creations, and movement of those creations back into the energetic womb before they are complete, happen all the time.

In the case of abortion, it is a learning experience primarily for the mother and secondarily for the father. It is also a learning experience for the entity to be incarnated, who usually knows quite well what the result will be before it occurs. Does this hurt this being who is present for the creation of this fetus? It can create physical pain, but in general it does not hurt from the sense of creating unbalanced energy within the spiritual realm of any who are involved because the result is generally known before the fact. As a consequence, this creation is often a cooperative creation between three mature, spiritual beings for the purposes of education not only of the mother and the father, but for all of humanity.

Is there a being that comes into every fetus or are there some empty fetuses that are going to be born where no soul is present during the creation? What you suggest is possible. There are cases where the mother and the father create the physical form without the cooperation of a third being, but usually this is a fast miscarriage because there is no energy of sustenance for the fetus. It is the energy of the third participating being that allows the energy of the mother and the father to flow into sustenance for the fetus; and so usually there is a being involved besides the mother and the father. This is generally true because whenever life is created, there is consciousness. So if there is not a participating being involved in that consciousness, then where does that consciousness come from? In the absence of a third being, it can come only from the mother and/or the father. When that consciousness is aborted, there is a more dramatic impact on the mother and/or the father because their choice to abort is interpreted as killing part of themselves!

So in abortion do you kill? Is abortion a part of energetic killing? *It must be a part of the plan in which the soul is involved.* The whole concept of abortion was created for a purpose, and it is not a recent phenomena. It has been going on throughout time. The purpose of the concept of abortion is to teach humanity the sanctity of life and the responsibility to have clarity in consciousness when creating. There is a tremendous amount of irresponsible creation, and when that irresponsible creation extends to human form, the consequences are dramatic. The creation of a human form is a cosmic event. When it is done without consciousness and in irresponsibility and in lack of agreement to be in loving partnership during the life of the created human, then there is an energetic dislocation created in the life of that new human being, whether it is aborted or not. It is left alone in the world, even though the mother and father may be present, for there is the energetic dislocation that there is not a true agreement to be family in partnership. This dislocation can be healed, but it takes a great deal of energy to heal that rift. That is truly what is the tremendous breakdown of what has been termed "family." It is due to the initiation of irresponsible creation and the lack of creating responsibly in agreement and in contract to be a family.

The situation seems to be getting worse. Is there any hope that it might switch around? It already has switched around. The continuing attention in your awareness of the event of abortion throughout this country has caused each and every mature being to evaluate how they feel about it and to examine what it is that they wish to create. And so, in this recognition it is generating the understanding that when there is responsible creation, there is no need for abortion. Those pregnancies that are not meant to be full term will go through the natural process of dissolution without the need for humanity to be involved in the sense of terminating through medical or physical means.

This understanding also applies to the subject of birth control. Birth control is needed only because there is a lack of consciousness in the coming together of man and woman. When there is consciousness, there will be no pregnancy unless it is understood that that is what is to be created. It is not an event of probabilities!

Husband and wife can agree on both conscious and non-conscious levels, and so what looks like a roll of probabilities can also be an agreement which allows the probabilities to create at the right time for the creation. When it is the right time for that creation, it is created; but if there is consciousness that it is not the time for that creation, then no pregnancy will result even if the man and woman come together without the use of birth control devices. Those devices are needed only because of the lack of consciousness. **[Maitreya, Channeling 57, 5/30/96]**

Sexuality

Sexuality is one of the most powerful energies upon the planet, for in the practice of sexuality by sexual union, mankind is able to experience a brief moment of divine energy. But even more important is the fact that in that recognition of divine energy is the recognition that there is more. As a consequence, some often mistakenly believe that divine energy can only be achieved by sexual means.

Sexuality goes very deep into the heart of God, because in the creation process, sexuality began in the heart of God. There was the creation of the aspects of God to create, and that indeed was the first aspect of sexuality—the creation of space and the creation of manifestation in that space. Sexuality is the movement of God. The rifts in sexuality, the dislocations in sexuality and the lack of understanding of sexuality go way beyond humanity. These exist through all dimensional existence to the very heart of God!

So what is sexuality? True sexuality is the recognition of the aspects of your own divine nature that are the creative energies of life, for within yourself is the totality of sexuality. In physical form it is demonstrated so clearly by the union of two people, and in this way it symbolizes what is within each. In a spiritual sexual experience, there are two beings who are whole and in their wholeness they share that wholeness and they overflow with their wholeness into all that is. They create divine energy.

How does this apply to homosexuality? Homosexuality is looked upon in such a limited way, for humanity tends to look only at the instance of participation without giving recognition to the energy streams involved. Sexuality goes beyond the participation and even beyond the aspects of a particular physical incarnation. It is the sexuality of the totality of the being, only a part of which is evidenced in this physical incarnation. As an example, there may be a man who is demonstrating and manifesting the masculine sexuality of his being while attempting to balance the femininity of that being even though he is in a male physical incarnation. In other words, the predominate sexuality of that being may indeed be much more manifest in the feminine aspects of its divinity and in the mother aspects of the God that it is, even though it is presently in a male incarnational form. As is often the case, during their energy association another being will recognize the overwhelmingly feminine aspect of that being which overwhelms the male incarnational form that is present.

Whenever two beings of whatever incarnational sexual identity come together, it is for the purpose of energy movement. It is for the purpose of sharing experiences with one another, of allowing the interaction to create the opportunity of balancing experiences for healing and growth, and of creating experiences which may be unbalanced in order to lead to further healing and growth. And so, in this coming together of any two beings, it is for the purposes of a loving relationship. What does it matter what the incarnational sexual identity is? It is deemed to be acceptable for man and woman to be together because man and woman symbolize the very nature of creation. When two members of the same sex come together, it is not for the creation of physical form, but it is for the creation of their desired experiences.

The recent demonstration of outward homosexuality by so many has a purpose which is similar to the outward demonstration about abortion. The outward demonstration about abortion allows each person in the human family to evaluate what is life, what is responsibility, what is the responsibility of creation, and what does the sanctity of a human life mean to them. The outward demonstration of homosexuality allows each person to evaluate what is love, what is relationship, and what is the responsibility of commitment to another person? The outward publicity of homosexuality allows each person to come to the conscious realization that love is love and that two beings who love each other for the purposes of shared experience make their own creation. That creation is to be honored as their decision. The actions which two people take in their life, be they man and woman or be they of the same sex, carry the responsibility of their actions; but the mere fact of two beings of any sex being together in this way is not something that creates unbalanced energy. Indeed, it can be quite the opposite. It can be quite a healing experience.

What is often misunderstood by those in same sex relationships is that the purpose of their relationship is for consciousness expansion and for the coming together to be whole. Homosexuality is a way to dramatize the energy of sexuality within their being because it is so focused upon, but the energy of sexuality exists whether demonstrated by an active act of participation or not. As an example, there could be two friends who are male and female and who have only a close friendship. There are energies of sexuality that move between those individuals. Perhaps this energy does not move consciously or pro-actively in the sense of sex, but it does move for the purposes of full energy experience. The same is true between people of the same incarnational sexual form. For a conscious person, the energy of sexuality moves in all of their actions because it is a necessary part of their energy integration. You cannot be whole in physical form without balanced sexuality in that physical form, because only when balancing your sexuality can you allow the life energy to fully flow through the body. And if that energy in flowing through the body is not balanced, then how can the body be fully enlivened?

In the past, there have been ascensions where the being ascended without full completion in balance of sexuality. That creates what we have termed the act of "ascending with your baggage." The baggage of sexuality is the very hardest to clear outside of physicality. That is why sexuality is so prevalent, so predominant, and so important within physicality. In addition, that is why the total energy picture of sexuality is so important, for it is much more than merely the act of participation in a sexual act.

[Maitreya, Channeling 57, 5/30/96]

Suffering

Suffering has value in showing that there is something of more value than suffering. In addition, it has allowed many to realize that there is great value in experiencing life through your feelings. But suffering is a cruel teacher and it became a belief system that was iron-clad. It became so strong that Earth became the "suffering planet" with only pockets of life that were not suffering in their mass consciousness. In the United States, there is suffering all over the place because people are not living lives like those they see on TV. They have no hope to attain what they want and so they suffer; but the cruelest suffering of all is the lack of freedom to be conscious as a God-conscious being. What would happen today if you were to create instantaneously whatever was your Divine Will with total disregard for the systems of the planet and the systems of society? That might shake things up quite a bit, and so there is the belief system that you cannot "have the freedom to be you." What tremendous suffering in your soul that creates!
[Maitreya, Channeling 53, 3/5/96]

This is a message of hope, a message of the ability to overcome aging, death, disease and physical suffering. To overcome suffering, you must realize that the body does not need to be constrained by civilization's viewpoint of the body, for the body is a beautiful manifestation of your spiritual being and the energy of your spiritual being can create the body in whatever form is desired. For this to be so, you must break out of humanity's solidified ideas about what the body truly is. The body is not a vessel for suffering. Instead, the true nature of the body is as a vessel which can heal itself by clearing the energy that is moving through it. When we treat a problem in the physical body, we ignore the energies that lie below it; but these energies are what have truly caused the manifestation in the physical form. To remove physical suffering from the human body you must realize that just as the physical body resides in the energy of your spiritual Self, all the imperfections, maladies and sufferings of that body also reside in the energy of your spiritual Self. If you allow the Self to move this energy through into the physical, then it will be cleansed and purified. In this way, all physical suffering will cease.
[Babaji, Channeling 37, 9/21/94]

There is suffering all over this planet. The best way to stop suffering is to decide that you have had enough of it. All suffering and pain come from a belief system, for suffering is a belief system of what pain is. People create pain so that they can suffer. They create this pain because of belief in karma as a suffering system which dictated that for every transgression against your individual Divine Will you will feel retribution which will make you suffer so that you can have pay-back. That is very silly. The only requirement for overcoming karma is that you forgive yourself. Karma is just energy looking for forgiveness. So how do individuals ever forgive themselves? Not by suffering, for it is not necessary. That is why I said that the only way to get over suffering is to say, "I have had enough of it," and to realize that it is not necessary any more. But when you do find yourself suffering, then that is a message to you. Ask yourself, "Why do I suffer? What do I believe in? How is suffering serving me?" You see, suffering serves people in many ways and in many dimensions. It can generate attention, or sympathy, or whatever. That is why this is the suffering planet, but it is not necessary. The way to end suffering is to look it square in the eye and say, "Thank you. You have been a great teacher. You have been harsh and cruel, but then I created you, and I respect you and I thank you. But now I am going to go about creating my life from those aspects that truly serve my conscious, divine Self. So thank you—and good-bye."
[Maitreya, Channeling 53, 3/5/96]

Tonight, we wish to work with the energy to help create those energy pathways within yourself which support you in your role here. You will find that when you are living yourself fully, Earth will be a glorious place, even if all of Earth is not yet where you are. That is why Masters who have been here before, could be so happy in the midst of all the suffering which the people of this planet have always seemed to sponsor. They were not happy in the sense of going around laughing while there was suffering, but happy with themselves, joyful at their opportunity to be conscious, joyful in the consciousness that flowed and flows through them.
[St. George, Channeling 53, 3/5/96]

You transcend suffering by leaving it behind you. Until an individual is ready to do that, it is their own personal creation. You cannot end suffering for others. You can only create joy in your own life. But what happens when you create joy in your life in this way? You create the energy pattern for millions to follow because once you have opened that door, the others do not have to grope around to find the door, to find the key, to turn the knob and to push the door. It is already opened for them. All they must do is merely to look up and see the light. And they will be drawn by the attraction and the love of the light, and their clearing will be so easy because you have done what you have done. In this way they will no longer be a slave to suffering. That is the value of your work here.
[Maitreya, Channeling 53, 3/5/96]

So can you be happy upon this planet of suffering? Can you be in your God-joy with all that occurs around you without letting the world offend you? I can tell you that it is possible to have great compassion for the world, but to be entirely blissful within yourself. If you believe that this is possible, then look to see if you know it. If you know it, then you can create it, because you create your wholeness and you create your beingness, here and now. Jesus is not going to come and walk upon the planet and do it for you. Neither is Maitreya, or Buddha, or any other great Master, because that is not your karma. That is not what you came for. That is not what it is all about. So many are still desperate for God to come down and take them up without having to do the work themselves. It sounds very nice when that is promised, and it makes for a very comforting story to believe that you can just hang around and sooner or later, it will all be perfect. But, I am sorry, for it is not going to work that way. You have to do it yourself. You have to find the way to be happy and to spread that happiness around you, even in the midst of all the suffering that exists on this planet of suffering. **[Maitreya, Channeling 54, 3/26/96]**

Evil

It all comes from God, and we have chosen to live on this experimental planet of contrasts so that we can find our way into oneness with God. Would you speak to the evilness that is all around this planet and is the opposite of God's grace? Evil is a misunderstood energy. Many of you have played with the word "evil" and found that it is "live" spelled backwards. That is quite symbolic, is it not? Let me ask you a question. If a being were pure in heart and had no judgment, or no feelings of doubt, or of guilt, or of being "less than," and had no feelings of the lack of being worthy of God, then do you think that "evil" would have any place to go within that person? *Absolutely not!*

So who has created evil? God did not create evil, although since God does allow humanity to create, S/He did provide the energy which humanity used to create evil through Free Will. Humanity is the prime creator of evil because humanity needs to have that reflection in order to understand what is in alignment with God and what is not. Evil is serving a great purpose for humanity by showing humanity what sickness is within itself that has to be healed.

In addition, evil does not express itself upon humanity without its being created. There are no victims, and evil does not accidentally apply itself to poor victims. Humanity creates their own victimness where evil flows. This is done because evil is a great teacher. Evil comes from a great Master who has taken on that role out of love for God's creation. Do not worry about evil. Evil will disappear when it is no longer needed for humanity's reflection. It will be gone in a snap. It can be gone from your life in a snap when you accept that evil is only an energy that has been created to show you a reflection when it is necessary. If you heal that within yourself, then that reflection will no longer be necessary in your life.

In their homes, people lock every door, and they have burglar alarms and they have guns or baseball bats at the ready. Why is that? Is it because we live in a dangerous world, or is it because there is the feeling that they are a victim of their own environment? Most probably there is a deep fear that they will be mistreated and that they are not worthy of love; but when those issues and energies are balanced, those same beings will sleep very soundly even if the door is not locked. It is all a reflection.

Look at your life and realize that if you take such precautions, it is merely living reasonably while creating anew. An interesting experiment would be to get in your car and go within yourself and say, " Do I need to wear my seat-belt on this journey?" If you had complete, and I emphasize <u>complete</u>, knowing within yourself that you did not need to wear a seat-belt, then you would not need to wear one. But until such time that you have that absolute knowing, then go ahead and wear one! That is reasonable. You do not have to be stupid to be brave. Bravery resides in facing your issues and facing yourself each and every moment. Bravery does not mean falsely creating a situation that you are not ready yet to handle.

But when evil does enter an individual's life, how do you explain it? Evil probably enters because of the energy which is associated with that particular individual. Each person's life is a complex combination of energies of creation that stem from a number of sources. An example of one source is your karma, or the energy that you carry with you, for karma is merely energy seeking to move into balance. It is nothing more and nothing less. Another source is from creations amongst groups of beings that need resolution, or from deep commitments within Self as to what one will experience in order to come to grips with oneself. But know that in these creations, there are no victims.

When you are involved in an evil situation, it is very appropriate to feel yourself completely, for it is this feeling of Self that will often lead to a dramatic healing. Traumatic situations present the opportunity for magnificent healing, for when one experiences trauma there is an opening that occurs within yourself which says, "I have created a dramatic opportunity for healing." If you think back to the traumatic experiences in your lives, you felt as if you had been laid bare. Being laid bare is merely a reflection of the fact that you have opened yourself up for dramatic healing. In these situations, it is very important to be in your feelings and not to ignore them. Oftentimes an individual will try to ignore those feelings but what happens is that they just get put into a suitcase that you carry around with you until it gets opened again. But if the feelings are explored and lived, then you allow the coupling of all the other energies within yourself also to come into resolution.

A beautiful experience can take place even though the circumstances have been traumatic, but it is not evil that creates this experience. Evil is merely the energy that moves in response to

creation. Traumatic events are usually an agreement that has taken place about what will occur, and the energies merely move to allow the creation to be made manifest. In this way, evil energetics become a superb teacher by introducing us to that which needs to be healed.
[Maitreya, Channeling 54, 3/26/96]

Chakras

Tonight, there is a white funnel of energy above the crown chakra of each one of you. If you would but allow the opening of the higher self to enter and go through you by way of this chakra, you will experience more of Self. As you are doing this, be alert to any fears that arise from old beliefs. If they are there, then love them until they come into balance; and know the truth of your experience is how you feel in your heart, and not how you think in your mind.
[Sananda, Channeling 8, 8/24/92]

New volumes of wisdom are coming to those on this planet. The ability to open those volumes is based on the opening of the sight to images not of this world. The opening of that sight is more than merely the opening of the third-eye chakra, for the third eye works in concert with other energies. In order to open the third eye, one must balance the energies within the second chakra which is the typical throttle on the third eye; but after that is done other energies must be balanced for full vision. These other energies are the energies above the seventh chakra for the third-eye chakra can be open to vision, but if the highway is not built for the vision to arrive, it will not be seen. There are many other chakras above the seventh chakra. What is commonly known at this time is the eighth chakra which is a gateway to spiritual integration. It lies beyond the direct experience of the soul. It is the Christic gateway into the soul's realm of experience. That is why the Masters have taught meditation for eons; for unknown to the meditator, the Christic energy comes forth and opens those chakras that were unknown even to most Masters. In the case of some who walk this planet, it is the opening of the eighth and the ninth chakras. A technique for accelerating the opening of these chakras is to constantly call forth new Christic energy through the voice daily, as many times as you remember. The activation through the voice manifests the vacuum for its arrival. Then in meditation, feel your spiritual energy connect between your heart chakra and that universal fatherhood around the planet. As you see your energy within the heart shoot upward to meet the energy of the Father, let the energy of the Father return down through those chakra systems into the heart. This process opens and expands all the gateways from the Father energy to the heart. Finally, use this Christic energy in manifestation, for by its use it will grow stronger. The three-step unfoldment of the Christ in action involves the calling forth and the creating of a vacuum to accept its arrival; the ongoing practice of moving the energy into the heart; and the allowance of that energy to move from the heart to manifest the third-dimensional experience. In this experience, chakras beyond those of the physical body get involved. [**Melchizedek, Channeling 19, 2/10/93**]

The fifth chakra is directly connected to the third chakra. This coupling is because the will of your divine manifestation in physical form resides in the third chakra and the expression of the performance and the announcement and the creation of that will resides in the fifth chakra. And so, although some people will fight their Divine Will by doubling up in pain from the abdomen, others choose to express it as limitation in the throat. Either will block the empowerment of Self. When the fifth chakra is involved in the blocking, and when the spirit cries out for empowerment in the physical to a greater degree than is present, then spirit will cause a coughing to show where the empowerment is being blocked. When the third and the fifth chakras work together as a team, the fifth allows you creativity from spirit and the third provides the machinery for physically manifesting that creation into the world. This is so because the lower three chakras have to do with physical and with manifestation in the physical; whereas the upper three chakras bring forth the spirit to allow such to take place. The heart chakra is the balance between the upper and the lower chakras. That is why we have spoken of bringing forth the Christic energy of your spirit Self into the heart, for the balance between spirit and physical resides in the fourth chakra which is the heart chakra. To become divine Masters expressing your divinity in your humanity, you express your divinity in your spirit, and your humanity in your physical. You are here to show others how to make the two be at one by using the heart chakra. One who has done so in the past has been called a Messiah. Now it is your turn for that role. **[Melchizedek, Channeling 19, 2/10/93]**

Doing and Being

In the present physical world, is there a difference between "being" and "doing" and if so, when do we "do" and when do we just "be"?
"Doing" is "being" in action. Just by being, you know what it is to do, and the doing becomes the movement, effortlessly, of being. Although doing without being is busy work, I would say there is always some being in doing, for there can be no being without doing, just as there can be no doing without being. By the very nature of God moving into reality there is doing, because since the movement of being is doing, then it is creation. So when the Masters have said, " Go within and, effortlessly, all will be accomplished," what they mean is, in the state of beingness, all is possible effortlessly, because when you move with action from being in freedom, there is not effort. The effort is the feeling of stress in the doing. "Effortless" means doing without stress, doing without resistance, doing without buying into the process. As a healer working with another, if you buy into their state it becomes effort, it becomes stressful, and it is with all action in this way. But if you become the detached "being," you can heal effortlessly. It is often the principle of "Let Go and Let God." But you cannot do the letting go without "being." And so you cannot just be a "be" without doing a "do"; for even the activity of letting go is creating a space in which the energy of God can heal. In this way, you are "doing." Again, "doing" is "being in action" and if you are "being," then you are "doing." **[Maitreya, Channeling 44, 4/17/95]**

AIDS

For anyone who has become infected with AIDS, breathing is very important, for it is the breath which moves the life force though various parts of the physical body. In addition, it is important for the individual to know that the condition is not irreversible. In other words, many can be healed if they wish. The most important method of healing is the response to the energetic message of the life force. That is why I discuss using the breath to move a life force back into the healing, and then to allow this life force the love that is necessary for healing.

But there is not one way of healing AIDS, for AIDS is not what it is thought to be. AIDS is not a disease of HIV positive. AIDS is the refusal to be whole. It is the way in which those who have chosen to accept this disease have given an illustration of the hatred of human turned upon itself. Thus, on a cosmic level of understanding, people contract AIDS to illustrate man's inhumanity to man. They illustrate this by being looked upon with fright. But they should realize that they do not need to stay around as a demonstration of that inhumanity. They do not have to place themselves as the great example for mankind. If they leave now, then that is perfectly acceptable. But if they choose to go through a healing process, then that also is perfectly acceptable because they would demonstrate that humanity needs to be healed.

Why is it that there are so many who have HIV and are not even conscious of it? There are millions with HIV who do not even know it! It has no effect whatsoever because they are being healed by taking it within themselves so that it does not manifest and go out. The most important thing for those with AIDS is to energetically realize that they are demonstrating to the world that which mankind is doing to itself. But if they wish, they have the opportunity to take this within their bodies, not only for themselves but for the world. If they heal their energetic body by placing the energy in those areas that are without energy, this will make humanity aware of what it is doing to itself. When they do this, the right method for each individual will come to them; and when they heal the energetics, they will open the healing floodgates for God and for everybody else, and not just for themselves. [**Kuthumi, Channeling 49, 1/13/96**]

CHANNELED ANSWERS TO SPECIFIC QUESTIONS

Is euthanasia ever appropriate or is the suffering experience necessary for the being? What is not appropriate is for a mental decision to be made, and that is the misunderstanding. The decisions are made on an economic or a social basis rather than a spiritual basis. The spiritual basis is the primary concern and many people can touch into that spiritual basis to see what is appropriate.

Then at some times it could be appropriate to end the suffering? Indeed. The situation would not have been created if it had not been appropriate, and the opportunity for shortening that suffering would not be appropriate if there had not been created the opportunity for that to happen as well. In those cases where there is not the opportunity to shorten the cycle of suffering, then it is appropriate for it to continue, for that is what has been created. There are, of course, no victims, so extended, long suffering is what that soul has needed for a particular karmatic experience. It all works in balance, and that is why in those cases where it is outside of the suffering person's physical capability to modify their environment, those who would enter into that environment to modify it need to be very clear about what is needed.

Who is capable of doing that? That is the role for true healers to take—people who have the ability to communicate at the spiritual level. People of the Temple filled that role in the times past when they could come and communicate clearly with the spirit of that person to know what is desired and with love, to know what is appropriate—either no action at all or to know what is clearly required. The level at which one needs to communicate and the circumstances are usually at the fifth-dimensional level, because the fourth is completely overshadowed by the physical suffering and the emotional suffering and so there is not clarity there. At the fifth-dimensional level and above there is clarity, although even the fifth can sometimes be affected by these situations, most obviously if there is third-dimensional physical problem which is reflected in the fifth-dimensional structure.

As pets suffer in their old age, is euthanasia or "putting to sleep" appropriate for them? It is the same situation. With animals there is an ease of communication because there is not the attachment to the physical that exists in humans. In addition, in pets there is the trusting of unconditional love and there is also the group animal soul that is very close at hand in these times of suffering to allow for clearer communication. *So in determining what to do you would still communicate with the soul of the animal?* Yes. Always.

In human organ transplants, does the physical body that receives the organ transplant receive the energy of the one from whom the organ was taken? Yes. *Is there any memory that comes with it?* Yes. That is the short answer. Do you want more?

Yes. Is it appropriate to do it? We would much rather see people regenerate their organs. *Does the fact that a body needs a transplant in its third-dimension physical body mean that the higher self has wanted to pass over and the transplant is a method of preventing that?* If the transplant is successfully accomplished, it means that there is a lesson to be learned from that transplant and it does not prevent the timely death of that person. What is being symbolically displayed in organ transplant is the rudiments of understanding how the physicality is the spirituality of the person. When a physical organ is transplanted into another, it causes a reaction within the physical system. That reaction is to not accept it because that transplant is not of the same energy. Only in those cases where the energy of the higher dimensional context of that structure is so close can there be an inkling of acceptance. This is what your doctors call "tissue matching." Even in those cases, tremendous drugs are needed to keep it from being rejected by the physical body.

Is it a rejection of energies or is it a desire not to have different energies come in that causes the rejection of the organ? It is a lack of match-up of the energies of the new organ with what exists in the physical body. The physical body is a continuous stream and movement of energy; and when there is a new organ which is not of the same energy flow, energy type, energy frequency and of higher dimensional integration, then there is a mismatch. What modern science has so misunderstood is that acceptance should be completed in a higher dimension. In other words, rejection should be healed in a higher dimensional experience and then it flows down into the physical and changes the energy makeup of the organ. But if they could do that, then they could also regenerate the organ in the first place! There is much, much more on this subject that doctors need to know and we can talk at length about this at a different time.

Many spiritual people seem to get physically larger as they go deeper into spirituality. What is happening? What is happening is that the physical body expands in an effort to achieve more energy in the physical. It is the result of energy pouring into the physical and not yet having a way to move out as easily as it comes in. In addition, as the inner person grows, the physical reflects more of that solidity of beingness being anchored in the here and now.

Is there any way to moderate this? Yes, by not being afraid to allow that energy to flow through. In the presence of fearing what would become of the body, the energy becomes locked in and growing and bulging and looking for release in its intent to travel. Many beings who channel energy become quite massive. They become quite big in their mass and they realize that they need that mass to hold the energy of which they bring forth. But that is only because that energy is not allowed to flow through their body. The intention should be to allow the energy to permeate and move through all of the body. This can be done by an exercise of having the feet on the Mother and letting the energy stream through the body and radiate into the Mother and then letting the energy radiate from the Mother through all of the physicality and not just the chakras which are generally understood to be the energy centers, for all of the body is a chakra. It is a physical manifestation of God. The energy should flow through the legs because the legs have a great role to play in anchoring God-consciousness in humanity. The legs are neglected. It is as if the root chakra is the end of the physical stream of energy, but to anchor completely the energy must flow through the legs. When it is flowing through the legs as easily as the upper body especially from the heart above, then the circuit becomes complete. Then the body can be big or small as anyone wishes it to be. If people need to have things reflected in the body, the body cooperates magnificently.

In physicality, is it particularly important to always be in clarity? There is a warning which I wish to repeat. The danger comes when you become so clear in your consciousness that you begin to move into denial of those pockets of yourself that are not yet in clarity or in balance. It is this denial that will keep you from your goal of bringing divinity into physicality. You will receive a clue when the outside world tells you, "We see this within you." Maybe you also feel it, but you move into this program of your clarity and deny it. I say that clarity is a "program" because clarity is a box just like anything else. If you create a box that you are clear, you do not allow your movement. If you hear yourself denying anything that is brought to your attention by saying, "I don't do that," or "I am not like that," take a closer look, because it may be the signal that there is something that needs attention. As you become clearer and clearer, it actually becomes more difficult to accept your unbalanced energies. This is the opposite of what you would expect. The reason is because as you achieve greater and greater clarity, then clarity becomes so wonderfully attractive that it is where you want to hang out. You want all of your physical bodies to be there. But you must wake up to this warning and don't be afraid to be "you." If "you" comes out as unbalanced, let it flow; but let it flow in a way that is conducive to its resolution rather than creating a turbulence of new, unbalanced energy. That is the only way that you can bring divinity into your physicality!

SUMMARY

These channelings present a tremendous amount of information about our existence in the physical, or our **Physicality**. This is probably surprising to the people of most established religions, for the physical body and all aspects of physicality have generally been considered to be of lesser importance than the study of theological doctrines and dogmas. However, the teachings from these channelings consistently repeat the importance of the physical body and of bringing divinity into the physical.

In addition to the importance of the physical body to God's plans for the evolution of humanity and, in essence, the expansion of God as S/He continues to learn about Him/Herself, this particular chapter had a significant amount of information about the physical vehicle itself. As one example, it was emphasized that the physical body is a part of the spirit and not merely something which is to be discarded as spirituality grows. In addition, the teachings emphasize that when the physical body is discarded as it always has been in the past, a part of the energy which inhabited that body remains behind with it. Because of this, the entity is never completely whole and will not become completely whole until all parts of its energy are reassembled into oneness. This takes a tremendous effort. For this reason, and because of the desire to bring divinity into the physical, then as soon as mass consciousness will allow it, we will no longer leave our physical body when we enter into other dimensions.

Another major teaching was that the physical body can be changed, rejuvenated, and made to last forever in whatever form the higher Self wishes the body to have. However, since the physical body is the final manifestation of all bodies in all dimensions, there must be complete clarity in all dimensions before the manifestation of the desired physical change can take place. In this way, the manifestation of the desired physical body has the same requirement as that of any physical manifestation, i.e. it must be done on all levels of dimensionality. In addition, since the physical form is the outermost structural evidence of being in this dimension, then any changes in the outside appearance must first be generated as energetic changes on the inside. To enter into this more nearly true form, physical attributes such as nutrition, proper care, love, acceptance, honor and integrity are important, for the body is no different that any other form of consciousness. Thus, to truly heal the body requires a true healing on all energetic levels as well as the clarity to accept all that needs to be healed.

The channelings also present the teaching that one soul may inhabit more than one body in order to gain a variety of experiences, and that there are several types of etheric embodiment. In addition, the teachings say that there are several types of love and that all energies of emotion, even anger, can come from love as the impetus for that energy.

In addition, the channelings present the teaching that although suffering has been of value by showing that there is something of more value than suffering, there is no longer any need to learn the lessons of suffering. The teachings indicate that suffering could be eliminated solely by deciding that we have had enough of it. Of even more importance may be the effort which those who are enlightened can put forth by being in God-joy even though others may be suffering all around them.

Further, the channelings present the teaching that abortion exists to allow each being to understand not only the sanctity of life, but also the unbalanced energy of irresponsible creation; and that sexuality exists as one of the most powerful energies on this planet, primarily because unbalanced sexual energy is so difficult to clear when the being is not in physicality.

Also, the channelings present the teaching that evil has a purpose, and that humanity has created evil for the express purpose of teaching and balancing. In this sense, even a non-God evil such as AIDS has a purpose and a meaning for those who choose to walk that difficult pathway.

Finally, the channelings address the issues of euthanasia, both for humans and for pets, and the issue of organ transplants for humans. All of these issues are ones which must address aspects of the soul rather than merely being limited to addressing aspects or issues of a physical nature.

CHAPTER EIGHT
MISCELLANEOUS INFORMATION

INTRODUCTION

In the fifty-eight channelings covering the almost 600 pages transcribed to date, some channelings have presented relatively short, intriguing insights which were presented only a few times. Some of that miscellaneous information is presented in the paragraphs of this chapter. The source of the channeling will be presented at the end of each paragraph. The list of subjects covered is presented in the Table of Contents.

CHANNELED INFORMATION
Spirit and Soul

What is spirit? Spirit is merely the finer aspects of yourself. It is conscious in those dimensions that lead from unmanifest God. It is that individualized, creative process that came from God as **you**. When you are conscious of spirit, there is a whole new phenomenon which occurs, for you are also conscious of soul. What is soul? Soul is the accumulation of spiritual experience in all dimensions. Spirit moves. It is connected from God through all dimensions, and spirit manifests in different ways in the different dimensions that are **you**. In the physicality, spirit is manifested as body, as feelings, as mind and as intellect. It is all a manifestation of spirit; but the accumulation of those manifestations of spirit in all dimensions and at all times comes together in what is called "soul." And so indeed, every spirit has a soul because every spirit has experience. Ah, but I spoke of the vessel of your experience, and what is that? The soul, as the accumulation of the spiritual experience would, in best terms, be said to be a body, and the body of the soul is what I term as the vessel of your experience, the vessel of God.

As you become aware of your direction from your spirit, you now have a new aspect of Free Will operating in your humanity. That operation of Free Will is now one that makes decisions from a finer dimensional perspective. In other words, instead of your emotion, or your mental reasoning, or your physical desire, it is direction from your spirit or your spiritual existence that makes the decision. **[Kuthumi, Channeling 48, 11/28/95]**

Angels

The advantage of being in the physical is that you have the mechanism to perceive not only in this physical level but also in non-physical levels, for the machinery that allows that human body to be animated also allows you to perceive on many dimensions. The clarity of the communication between you and your guidance is dependent upon your ability to perceive in those dimensions. To give an example, each one of you has guidance from the Angelic Realm. The Angelic Realm is a realm of beings who are non-physical, but who have shape, characteristics, and a defined purpose of their existence. One of those defined purposes is to help those who have taken the dramatic step to move into a physical body even though they truly exist in a dimension that is different from the physical. Angels typically do not manifest in human bodies to communicate with you, but rather they communicate with you through the perception of their emanations to the extent that you permit it.

If you are clear in your communications in other dimensions, you will clearly receive the answer to any question that you have. There are other interesting features of perceiving in other dimensions for you can look upon the Earth plane and see the past, the present, and the most probable future at that time. We are talking about these other dimensions because one of the transitions that is occurring is the ability for human beings to more easily perceive in other dimensions by removing the veil. What is the veil? The veil is a block to perception that humans have created and are now ready to remove. The reason it was created was so that physical life could be learned from the ground up. When you were in more lofty dimensions, you were always aware of the Divine Will because you had no Free Will of your own, just as those beings in the Angelic Realm presently have no Free Will of their own. And so, there was no question that you would follow the Divine Will at all times, just as the Angels do now. But in this physical realm the choice is not automatic because you have Free Will. That is the major difference between you and those who are in the Angelic Realm, for they are in a structure which knows nothing but God's Will at all times. In the physical, you have had to search for the Divine Will because Free Will has been magnified to its maximum. Mankind is learning, and it is learning well, even though it may not seem so for we are soon to come to what has been termed the end of a civilization. It is the end of what has been, and the beginning of what will be.

[Being from the North Star, Channeling 26, 5/17/93]

Eternal Damnation

Matthew wrote a gospel in the Bible that differs from the other gospels in its emphasis on Hell and eternal damnation. What purpose did such a concept serve, and does it still serve any purpose today? The concept of eternal damnation is born two-fold. The first creation was an effort to control those who showed defiance to the authority of the religion. The survival of one's being was a way to control those who would not listen for if there was one thing that all men feared, it was the survival of their existence in some fashion in the unknown void after death. Consequently, the fear of eternal pain in damnation and of eternal suffering would turn the head of even the most defiant one. The second creation of eternal damnation came from those who feared that they would not be successful in their mission of bringing the Christ light to the masses. Consequently, the concept was created from their own fear and their own doubt, for if one truly understands the nature of consciousness, one understands that there is always eternal forgiveness. The concept of eternal damnation was the elimination of forgiveness in spiritual energy.

Did Matthew give us a cosmic test to see if we could

overcome this fear? Does eternal damnation serve a cosmic purpose by giving us this test? Matthew, himself, was not that wise; however, the energy within Matthew was that wise. As every unbelief serves a purpose so this, too, served the purpose of the unscalable wall, the unpenetrable belief. For those who had the eyes to see, it gave the understanding that all was not as it appeared within these writings, for those who have touched the energy of God know that if there is but one thing that is true, it is the peace and love of the forgiveness of that which created All That Is. A doctrine that did not have that as its core could not be the truth of God. *Thank you!*
[Maitreya, Channeling 16, 11/30/92]

Gurus

There is a case which St. George would call "a classic case of Guru following." This is a situation in which beings of very great light gathered together to create divine purpose and in the creation of that divine purpose allowed for the substitution of outside will to dictate their actions rather than their own Divine Will. How could this happen? Well, the Ascended Masters who work with you are there for your highest and greatest good. If your highest and greatest good is to subject yourself to a Guru, they will happily provide one for you even if it means giving up your self-determination, for that is a lesson which you have to learn. In this particular case, there is a situation where these blessed light beings so gave themselves to their Guru that they lost their self-determination. And so, this great Master with whom they worked was more than happy to provide them with the lesson to learn from this, even though it looked like entrapment. If powerful God-beings, which these people are, need to learn an important lesson, the Masters will line up to help, because that is love. In this particular case, the lesson to be learned is that you always, always should be in alignment with your own, individual Divine Will and not to give away your will to a Guru.

It was the way of old that a human would give his/her will to a Guru, but it was never a way that was direct. As an example, Gurus had disciples in India. Those disciples were so devoted to their Guru, that they moved along the path of enlightenment through the reflection of God in that Guru until they reached the point, through their love and devotion, that the Guru within themselves grew and became manifest. That branch of devotion is one of the main branches of Yoga, and it is a legitimate path of reaching enlightenment. However, in this day certain beings have come forth to manifest Mastership directly. You have been told that you are of those beings, for you did not come here to be subject to Gurus. You are self-determining Masters. You do not need anybody, and anybody who says that you need a Guru is mistaken. Teachers are helpful now and then, but you have it all in yourself. You came with it all. In association with other people, you just magnify your own internal learning experience, but you do not give up your self-determination.

This is always a difficult lesson, for if you believe so strongly on a given path led by a particular Guru and then you meet defeat when you go down that path, you feel abandoned. It is an important lesson to learn that you are a God-being, and that although you may have a teacher, you should never deny what is your own, individual Divine Will. [**Kuthumi, Channeling 46, Session 4, 10/29/95**]

The primary responsibility of each is to create from your individual will and to act from the knowing that this can only be allowed in the energy of love, for you cannot separate love and will and power in consciousness. It all comes together in the recognition of the consciousness of self. Throughout the ages there have been many attempts to come across that jewel of truth that will open the door-ways to God-living consciously. But I say to you that there is only but one pathway needed, and that is to be aware in the way in which you are aware because each and every individualized stream of God is different. It is individualized God. There is not one path that is going to work for each and every person for there are as many paths as there are individualized streams of creation of God, and the number of these individualized streams is staggering! No one can tell you how you can be you. Only you know that. There is no Guru, there is no path, there is just you; and there is the need to desire to be God in consciousness that you are. If that desire is appreciated, and felt, and cultivated, then you will see yourself more and more clearly as you look at yourself. Aspects of self-development are valuable in that they can, at the appropriate time, help you in one way or another but do not feel that it is your pathway when it is another's. These aspects are only little bits of energy to help you move within yourself.

There is no Guru for pioneers of God-creation. How could there be? Would you give your power to another being when you are as powerful and when your heritage is the same? It is a community of God-beings is it not? Is not humanity "God-in-action" in this dimension? So how can one be more important than another? If a Master comes through in physicality and says, "I am here to lead you to the path of righteousness of your being..." then remember that as a Master he is more than ready to tell you whatever it is that you are wanting to hear to help move you upon your own path. In fact, a Master will lead you far astray if that is what you need in order to eventually arrive at the end of that path. There are many God-beings of great clarity who are close to living in multi-dimensional consciousness even though they have great blocks in certain areas. However, they feel that their clarity is so great that they will not allow themselves to see those blocks. How could they have these gigantic problems in their energy when they have had such tremendous clarity in their life? And so their unwillingness to see these aspects of themselves created the opportunity to, what would have been considered in this dimension, their down-fall. But it was not their down-fall. It was their salvation. In this way, all lessons lead you to the real you, but some also cause a few detours along the way. Use your discernment to understand what is a detour and what is the path to the real you. And understand that no Guru can do this for you! [**Maitreya, Channeling 51, 2/6/96**]

The absence of a Guru does not mean that you are to be without a teacher. What is meant is that you are all master and student and teacher and pupil. What it means is that I ask you not to be in awe of one who presents energy or information or clarity to you that you do not otherwise have. You would not want those to be in awe of you, and we ask that you give them that service as well. The whole concept of the master-student relationship is one of "greater-than and less-than," but in God, all are equal in quality. This is not to say that each person has the same energy makeup, or the same energy of experience, or the same vessel of experience or the same energy of manifestation. This is not what is meant. What is meant is that in God, all are of the same creation. All have the ability and the opportunity to become whatever is your desire; and whatever is the vessel of your experience you wish to create, it is your opportunity to do so. So while there may be those who have great vessels of experience, it does not mean that they are greater than you. All it means is that they have turned their attention in a different direction than you.

In the realization of Self, you realize your own divinity. If you are of divine origin, then there is no thing of creation of which you are lesser than, because you are "it" as well. How can you be less than what you already are? You have your individualized consciousness and your individualized vessel of experiences but you are also one with all other energy and all other experience. That is why when you meet another in the divine expression of love, in that loving acknowledgment of your God-presence, it is like meeting a part of yourself. When this consciousness is widely felt, and acknowledged, violence will decrease rather dramatically. How many people today purposely hurt themselves? A few do, but not very many. Instead, they ask another individual to do it for them because they are not courageous enough to do it to themselves. But why would you hurt yourself when there is the consciousness that you are one?

It is not that there will not be teachers or students, and that there will not be Masters whose energy is at a certain level of attainment of God awareness. There will be Masters of ever greater God awareness, but it is not "less-than" or "greater-than." It is only looking upon part of yourself that is manifesting in a way which is grand. In the past upon this planet, students have given themselves up through abandonment of Self to their Guru, or to their Master; and through the devotion to that Master, they piggy-backed that energy so that they can gain from the tunneling effect of the energy of that Master to themselves. And it is the Master's great pleasure to do so because that was the way in which it could be facilitated. But now that is not necessary. It is appropriate for you to be in direct communication with your God-consciousness, for you no longer need to communicate through another.

[Kuthumi, Channeling 50, 1/23/96]

Channeling

I may sometimes present a semantic problem in the clarity of my speech because each ear hears differently and each ear needs to hear differently. As a result, the words that are chosen are due to the audience as well as the ability of the channel that the words come through. Remember that every experience of channeling includes the experience of the person who is providing the vehicle for the channeling. No consciousness leaves the vehicle for another to come in and fill that body, because this is like kidnapping and this is not allowed. Even for those who are trance channels, their channeling is a shared participation, and the vehicle is very present. Although some may not think so, they are always very present. The need for their physicality is not only to allow the channeling to occur, but also for the education and advancement of the channel.

It is because the words may mean different things to different people that the clarity will always vary from what you hear, and what you know within yourself is right for you. Believe me, the Masters will be more than happy to provide you with every information you need to fulfill your balancing act of energy. In other words, if you wish to hear from a Master something which leads you on your merry way away from your purpose because that is what you need to accomplish to come into balance, it will be provided. I guarantee it! We will just channel that information right in so that what you need to learn in the most purposeful way will be available. That is why you must always check within yourself to know, and not automatically accept everything that is channeled to you; for you cannot give away your responsibility of clarity within yourself. You must always know within yourself.

I will give you the truth that is best for you as an experience, but you must understand that truth is subjective. Truth for one is not truth for another. You might then ask, "Are there absolute truths?" Well, there is always a deeper truth; but since God is creating anew each moment, then truth is being created as we speak. I can now hear some saying, "Oh, this spoils my conception of the grand truth of the universe!"; but the truths of God are ever-present, ever-available, and as loving and as magnificent as you ever imagined them to be. But just as it is a challenge to know what God is at any moment because

God is ever-growing, it is also a challenge to understand a greater basis of truth. For even in your total clarification of your spiritual being in your physical body to where God is manifest here and now, that is just the beginning. That is just to get the motor running!

There is a grand plan for humanity in which you have a great part to play if you so choose. Many of you will not because you did not come here to experience that. You came to help quick-start this planet and then to leave. Perhaps an entirely new dimension is where you will next be challenged to increase your vessel of God. But whatever you do next, the experience of love which is in this physicality is something that will expand your vessel of Light and Love, and is something that you will always take with you. Love has a quality in physicality that is not felt in other dimensions. So what you gain in this life is a rich reward, for when you take your body into other dimensions, there will be those who will say, "Tell me, please tell me about it." You will have experience that others do not have for Love not only has a special quality in this dimension, it is felt according to the magnitude of the vessel you create for it. That is why you are here. The reward is so great; and if any channeling helps you to realize this, then that channeling has served a very great purpose. But always remember to check within to know for yourself whether the channeler is relating a truth that is a truth unto you. That is very important!

[Blend of St. George and Maitreya, Channeling 47, 11/6/95]

Predictions

Can we ever truly deviate from our path and our purpose? Every moment of now that you are conscious, you re-create your world in that moment, for you create your world marching upon your divine stream of consciousness and you made that conscious decision to be whole in that moment. When there are a series of moments of now in which you create consciously from your own divine space, you create a stream of wholeness in your life that creates more and more opportunities, not less.

So your particular path that you came to follow is what you create it to be. When you were examining the framework of this life with your good buddies in another dimension, you were deciding what this life would be. You looked at the framework of your energy that you have been carrying around with you for a long time, and you decided what would be a wonderful way to get that energy in the light, and to be whole, and to be forgiven and to create the way for others to do it. You created a particular pattern that has been quite efficient, and at this stage in your framework you are not bound by any previous disposition except for those that you have already decided to experience. Other than that, you can create your life in any way that you choose. As long as it is in alignment with your Divine Will, then it is perfectly in alignment with what it is you have defined as your path. But also remember that you wish to create your route, and to move it wherever you wish to go in each moment in time, for each moment in time is a fork in the road, or many forks in the road. And each moment of time you re-create your life out in front of you. It is being re-created each and every moment in time.

So how is it that a seer can possibly tell you what is going to happen in the future if you are re-creating your world with each moment of time? *My theory is that they pick up on the energy pattern and belief system that you are holding in place right now, and from there they see the large probabilities. And if you choose to go in another direction or follow another energy pattern, then that event will change.* You are truly a master, for that was brilliant! A seer can see with great accuracy when people have beliefs in routes or paths that they are to take. They have set them out there, they believe in them, and they follow them. A seer merely looks in and sees what route you have chosen. But where you can trip them up is when you create anew each step. Then they will look out there and see a wide open universe of opportunities which is unlimited. But when seers are so very, very accurate, then you must wonder, "Oh my, I must have created a path that is quite rigid. Otherwise, they could not have seen it."

So what about these seers who have seen what was going to happen on the Earth? There have been quite accurate predictions from hundreds and thousands of years ago of what has been happening on this planet. That happens because the Earth had chosen a route, mankind had chosen to walk those paths, and the great seers could look down those paths to see what was to be. But if a seer tells you

something which is against your very beliefs, then remember that it does not have to be literal. Remember, a seer sees symbols which must be looked at from all angles. One possibility could be that the message is symbolic rather than literal, and another possibility is that the message is a test of your own clarity. The Masters would be more than happy to give you information which may or may not be accurate for you as a method of testing your ability to realize if it is in your divine path or not. The Masters will usually do this in a harmless fashion, but some people might need a major shaking up. As an example, when people give up their power, the Masters are more than happy to shake them in an extreme way so that they can get their power back again. But whatever dire predictions you might hear, the world will make it, and you are a joyful part of that experience. In being conscious every moment, you create the world you came to create. There was but one message as a divine path. That message is to be as conscious as you can be, each and every moment of time. And all that your Father has for you, will become yours; and all that your Mother wishes for you, you shall become; and all that you are, as the Christ Creation, shall unfold as you desire it to be. It is all really quite simple. Try not to be complicated or to follow the predictions made for you by someone else, but simply to be in your consciousness. With that, all will be well.
[**Maitreya, Channeling 53, 5/5/96**]

Astrology

Although there is a whole belief system based on the movement of planetary beings, astrology is truly the science of energetics. It tells how a particular energy is created and formed and the subsequent movement of that energy in the ever-changing environment of the universe. So, astrology is an observation. When that observation becomes a system, it becomes limited.

As it is practiced today, astrology is a limitation. It says that if this and this and this occur with these alignments and energies, then this is what will occur to the individual because the system says it will. But what is not taken into account at that point is the flow of energy at that time. That is like saying that because there is a mountain and a valley and a river and a hill, then the weather will be like this. Well, those are all influences, but they are not what is to be. When astrology becomes an observation of the influences, or an observation of the landscape of your energetic environment for your movement through that landscape, then it has validity; but not when it becomes a limiting belief system.

What is of even more importance is the astrologer being connected within to understand that this landscape is not just by this limited perspective of these individual planetary bodies that they chart. There are influences of dramatic proportions beyond those. The emanations from the Central Sun can overshadow these in any moment of time, and do, on a regular basis. But one schooled in the art, with their own intuition and interaction with the energies of creation, can give an accurate picture and use this system of observation as but one tool. When it becomes a belief system and a structure of rules and absolutes, it loses its freedom. It then becomes limited and humanity becomes a slave to its influences rather than the unlimited creator which humanity is meant to be.

[Maitreya, Channeling 53, 5/5/96]

Doubt

I would like to talk about the re-dedication of each of you to your spiritual path and to the understanding of your life's purpose at this time, for this is a time of breaking old patterns of consciousness, and only by following your divine guidance can those patterns be replaced with the essence of who you truly are.

It is easy to be swayed at this time by events in the world rather than by energy within, for there have been dramatic changes and with those changes it is easy to have doubt and to feel that you are unworthy. When you have doubt as to the level of your spiritual achievements, it is difficult to see yourself as an unlimited being. That is why the re-dedication is important, for most are experiencing the results of their own creations and these difficulties are because of the breaking up of who you are not. In these times of deep release, how many have been free of doubts and frustrations and feelings of unworthiness or lack of progress? How many have doubted the practice of your divine nature?

It is true that doubt will exist on even the most minute level until your ascension. But what level does doubt play in your life? You have heard it said many times "To be a Master, live as a Master." How many are living as a Master, unwavering in your dedication and in your practice of Mastery? Although the mysteries have been shrouded in complexity, the truth is very simple. Live as you would like to become, and you will become it. Remember, this plane is still a plane of slow manifestation for most. Trust that what you are creating will be, and you will be surprised. There is no goal more worthy than to be the Living Christ, and that is what you are. But for your protection you should know that as you get closer to the top of the mountain, the path becomes quite narrow and on the edge of the path is a steep drop-off. And so, care and dedication and attention to your path is required that you not misstep and take a fall, for that fall may not be to just the next lower spiral. That would be unfortunate, for mankind is quite close to the top of the mountain. As you rise higher, be true to that path you have chosen. Your friends are cheering you on as you come closer to the completion of your Earth Journey.

I am the one who comes to spur you on but to warn you that the path is narrow. I have helped many, and I have congratulated them on the completion of that path. I have congratulated several of you when you previously completed this same Journey. In your dedication to service of God, you have chosen to come again and, for this, I honor you. But, nonetheless, you do not have the clear memory of that previous victory at this time; therefore, here I am again giving you the same talk. The major message of this talk is to be attentive, strong and impeccable in each moment. The major admonition of this talk it to learn to recognize when fear and doubt direct your activities, for they are no longer your friends. Instead, they are your prison guards.

As an example, if you dwell upon the fear of potential earth changes, then who is your God? If you trust in each moment in your divine guidance and are attentive to that guidance, you are placing your attention upon your God. Those who have allowed the divine to work at all times within their being can be an unlimited vessel for God's energy to flow to those who would seek it; but energy will not flow where it is not earned. And where it is earned is where it has been created. That is the law. You are created as divine beings and you may live divinely if you so choose.

I have come to bring you the message of peace, and I have come to remind you that if you walk in love, then your path will be made smooth. With love in your heart and peace in your being, your obstacles will not deflect you. Be not afraid or create doubts of who you are, for I understand what you are going through and I understand, as a human, the role that doubt can play in your life. During my physicality I, too, had doubts, but being attentive to the Father's voice within I did not allow myself to stray far. And soon I realized that I did not hear the voice of doubt very often, but only heard the Father's voice. Many have portrayed my night in the Garden as one of self-doubt and, yes, there was some doubt about what the people of that time would miss if I were to go. Doubts often arise because one of the risks of love is attachment, and as long as there is some element of human love, there is attachment. I was attached to the success of the Father's work in the people who heard His words. And so, yet again, I asked "Must this be the way?" As you can see, even at that late date there was doubt, but as my attention turned to the Father's voice I was told, "Fear not. What will be is already written and trust in My plan."

And so, you see, even the few hours before the beginning of my time of ascension, there was some doubt. Do not feel unworthy if you are not living your perfect life as you see it but know that there must be attention to the Father. Only in the attention to your divine energy will you find your correct and true guidance. And as you know, when I say Father I truly mean Mother/Father and Christ for what we all are is Christ in action, which means the son in action, the daughter in action, the child in action, the God in action.

I bring the energy of peace in spirit. Trust in the divine, in the multiplication of love in being, for that is peace. And where there is peace, there is harmony. And where there is harmony, there is celebration of God. And in the celebration of God, there can be no doubt. **[Christ, Channeling 17, 12/7/92]**

Twin Flame/Relationships

Can you explain the concept of the Twin Flame to me? Certainly. The twin flame is a wonderful energetic concept which says that there is the perfect energetic mate for each individual. However, the creation of beings and of souls has followed many different paths in many different systems. Although all existed in God in the beginning, a difference in the soul and spirit energy of beings has resulted because of their initial creation in those different systems. In some systems, duality never existed, and the souls and spirits created in those systems have no twin flame relationship. In other systems there is the creation of an energy that you would call the "twin flame." The twin flame is what is mainly referred to as the complementary principles of creation, or the complementary principles of creating space and filling that space, or the complementary issues of feminine and masculine at that level, with the understanding of feminine and masculine being quite different on that level from what it is on the human level. In those systems where there is the creation of energy with such a clear delineation of those facets of that spirit energy, there is the possibility of splitting into parts; but it is not in the way in which you would assume. It is not where the masculine and the feminine split. It is where there is a coming apart at some point in the creative cycle. This happens to allow multiple experiences at the same time.

But the concept of the twin flame is quite limited because I would say unto you that you, yourself, have existed in multiple bodies on Earth at the same time. So what is your twin flame when there are many of you? There are systems where the spirit energy was created so consciously that there was no need for its separation in the terminology of the twin flame. There are systems where this creation occurred and those spirit energies exist sometimes in multiple experiences, but there is no confusion as to the source of that spirit energy. It is in wholeness. It is not split from its inception which the concept of the twin flame implies. There are systems where the split has occurred, and this has led to the consciousness of twin flame.

But the twin flame concept is greater than this because that same spirit energy can split a thousand-fold times and create soul groups and all sorts of experiences about which you have probably read in your books. But it does not have to be this way either. There are soul energies that are not necessarily formed into groups. Their grouping comes more from God-space, from the process of creation rather than splitting once into creation.

I know this sounds confusing, but the concept is difficult to express in words. Let me try in another way. A spirit energy comes from unmanifest God into creation. It becomes spirit energy at the inception of its arrival into creation. It is Christ-consciousness moving into creation. At different times of creation, that movement out of God into Christ energy was not very clear. In other words, when creation first took place, there was a great learning experience of God in creation, seeing and knowing what it had wrought in this process. And so, there were times of creation of energies that split because there was such tumultuous activity within that spirit energy that it could not remain together at that point in creation. In this way it created a separation of that spirit energy which longs to come together for completion. This is the origin of the concept of twin flame. But I say unto you that there are also spirit energies that have not split, and there are spirit energies that have split into many, many fragments.

Although this is an explanation of the twin flame concept, I would like to present to you the true meaning of twin flame by saying that there is a wholeness within you that is complete. Within you, there is a God-awareness, and that God-awareness knows that it is complete unto itself. It seeks to become whole by taking all fragmentation onto itself to become complete unto the individualized God that was expressed at its creation, and to bring within it the totality of soul experience that it has manifested in creation. That is the true impetus of the concept of the twin flame. It is the returning into wholeness of yourself. There is also the knowing in your spirit-being of others that were created in a very similar fashion. It is like, in some ways, a graduating class from a very special school in which there is the bond of similarity and common goal and common experience. And so there are also spirit-energies of which you are quite similar in your origins. In this way, beings come together in a special way. It is a coming together of those beings within God by a special bonding relationship. But it is rare that there is just one. There are many energy beings that can come together in community of this expression beyond the concept of relationship pairing in humanity, but in the community of energetic experience of your creative process.

Can you clarify this for me? In a given life do you have just one divine partner who is intended for you as your mate? More than you would realize. *Then can you have many partners in a given lifetime and not just one person?* Your life is what you create it to be. There are times when souls come into this life with the agreement to meet up with other souls and to have a common base of experience. It is like you would plan to go on a trip with somebody. You would have an agreement to meet and then you will have this framework that you will move within but then you always have a choice within that trip of what to experience and when to end the trip. Perhaps you would choose to end the trip early, or perhaps even to go in a different direction. It is no more complicated than that.

There are beings with whom you have more divine vibration from the sense only that in the multiplicity of your levels of experience, you vibrate more harmoniously at more levels of experience. It is also shared experience in your energy that comes together in a knowing of old soul friends coming together. It is your choice as to how you create your life each moment in time. There are individuals who will choose to be with one during their whole life experience, and that is indeed a grand expression of love for them. There are others who need to have a multiplicity of experiences in order to know themselves, because until they know themselves, they are not really able to have a relationship of duration.

Most relationships of duration on the Earth are ones of mutual control. There are many that are not in this way, and it is a beautiful experience. What has happened upon the Earth now is because of the consciousness rising within all, there is the realization that there is so much more to experience. There is so much of them unfolding that often they realize their situation is not fully serving them. It is not fulfilling them in the way in which their beingness needs to move. And so there is the shift to a relationship that feels more in service or one that is more creative for movement.

It does not matter to God how you create your life. It is how you create your life that expresses the God within you. If you move each moment in creating from your divine knowing and Divine Will, then whether that leads you to one relationship during your life, or many, is not important. It is what you are doing in the creation of your life each moment in time. Oftentimes there are multiple relationships because there is a flight from the energy to be addressed. In these situations, it would be better to address the energy there rather than to run to some other situation where the energy will still have to be addressed. Oftentimes multiple relationships are flights from divine self coming forth and saying, "This is what needs attention," and there is the movement to move away in order to not address it at that time.

And so it is all in the energy of the motivation of the change. One relationship is not necessarily more holy than many relationships when you look at it from the perspective of love. If there were many relationships in the totality of love and the coming together and the moving apart, is that any grander than a relationship in which there is one that is in the same expression of love? The energy of multiple relationships where there is the avoidance of energy, or the flight from reality, is the situation in which the attention needs to be placed to understand why, and to address the energy of these issues. When there is a total sense that a relationship has served its purpose and that both parties are clear and loving in that understanding, then there is no energy left unbalanced in the separation because in reality there is no true separation. The relationship still exists energetically, it is just not physically present.

You have energetic relationships with many beings, and these relationships can be quite intimate on different levels of dimensionality. When two light beings come together and, in a different dimension, share energy in the essence of coming together, it is a beautiful thing. It is not sex as you would put it here in this dimension, it is merely the coming together to be in love, and it is a beautiful thing. What often unhinges relationships in third-dimensionality is the avoidance of the energy to be addressed.

So, whether there is one relationship, or many, does not necessarily matter. What matters is the energy of the love, and of the honesty, and of the conscious creation within that relationship. It is when there begins to be sexual union that humanity suddenly moves into turmoil. That is because sexuality is greatly misunderstood. The important ingredient is love and honesty and consciousness in a relationship. If the relationship has truly served its purpose, there will be no breaking apart. It will be mutual acceptance of another Journey for each, with love and congratulations to both in the process.

But how many relationships like that have truly ended on Earth in that way? This means that when these relationships end not in this way, there is energy that needs to be addressed first. If you are totally clear within yourself that you have become balanced in your knowing and have addressed all of your issues, then you can move. If the other person does not co-create in the same way, then that is not necessarily your responsibility. But most likely you would not have chosen that relationship had that not been a possibility. Each relationship is a challenge to learn more about you. That is the true purpose of any relationship, be it called a "twin flame" or not! **[Kuthumi, Channeling 51, 2/6/96]**

Photon Belt

Finally, all that you have seen within yourself for you and your environment is coming to pass. Many of you have read books which have called for dramatic changes such as the waves of ascension or the movement into a galactic area known as the photon belt. Are these not one and the same thing? It is just different ways of describing what is occurring.

We have had many discussions here upon ascension and how it is a day by day, step by step movement into you and your being. The photon belt is merely a description of the phenomenon that occurs on a galactic scale to allow such a transition to occur. So you may ask, if we are moving into a galactic emergence of consciousness, what will happen? I would like to describe this in terms of layers of projection of your reality. Since each of you sees reality from the projection of your own energy basis, no one of you here could completely agree upon what reality is. This is also true on a mass consciousness basis. Mass consciousness has many layers. It has layers by region, by country, by hemisphere, by planet and finally, there are layers within the planet. In essence, you create a "reality bubble" around yourself that defines your reality and this is also true on a planetary scale. And so as you move into what has been called the "photon belt," your experience will vary based on how much you have allowed your "reality bubble" to coincide with the energies that are available. It is not automatic that everyone upon this planet will move into higher dimensions and greater consciousness. It all depends on their ability to synchronize with these energies and with this phenomenon. Planet Earth, the grand lady, will do so. She will move, for it is already so. The question is, what will humanity do?

The work that you have done in fulfilling your divine dream will allow you to move into ascension, into the photon belt, into greater consciousness of who you are, into your Light body and all that you have known that is available to you. The coming of the photon belt is not a changing of the laws of divinity. Instead, it is the manifestation of the laws of divinity. This is happening because the consciousness has created it to be so. This could not be so if humanity and the planet itself had not created this opportunity to move through this area of space and into this wave of energy. You have created it to be so, with the helping hand of divine grace, of course.

The length of the period of darkness when we go into this photon belt depends upon the "reality bubble" around the planet. This has been described as the safety net or the safety bubble. This is not entirely an accurate description but we wish there to be a notice of a grand event occurring and to have darkness is pretty dramatic. After this has passed, there will be a new twist on how devices operate. If there is an instrument of darkness that works upon electromagnetic energy, it will not function well, but the electromagnetic devices that have the intention of love and purposeful creation will function well. This is because if you wish to move into the Light, you cannot play the game of intending one thing and acting in another way; for with your intention so shall be your creation.

The entering in to the photon belt will not be a sudden experience except for those who are relatively unconscious. For those who are conscious, you will know all that is important to know. Your Creator never leaves you alone. There is never a lack of what is important for you, and that is true for all. It sounds so ominous, but it is indeed a blessing!

As to when this will happen, I would suggest that you be

careful of any interdimensional time analysis. If you look at time from outside your dimension, it is like looking at a gymnast doing back flips. Pretty soon all you see is twirling and it's hard to know which twirl they are on. You see relative movement. You can tell if there have been a lot of twirls, or if there have been just a few. It is like twirling around in a circle and seeing everything rotate around you. Pretty soon, you're not aware if you've turned five times, or ten times, or twenty times. All you are aware of is what you are seeing in the scenery. And so time estimates are quite relative and no time period is guaranteed. There is too much preparation that needs to take place at this time. There is a great deal of movement humanity needs to perform. There is a great deal of movement within the Earth that needs to take place so that this transition is peaceful and truly loving.

There are many changes taking place within the planet, for the planet is indeed ascending today, as are you. In the ascension process, energies are emitted. As the material properties of the planet change, they emit different types of radiation. There is also a great deal of resonance effect, for there is a tremendous amount of energy impinging upon the planet. It moves upon the planet in a grid system such as the ley lines. These lines are not static as has often been understood. They can move. As these energy vortexes accept this energy, there is a side effect which is electromagnetic radiation. This radiation varies considerably from point to point upon the planet.

However you look at it, or however you see it, there are some interesting times coming for those who are on planet Earth. The "photon belt" experience is just one of many!
[Collection of Space Beings, Channeling 39, 1/9/95]

CHANNELED ANSWERS
TO SPECIFIC QUESTIONS

The explanation of the twin flame concept which we have presented in the teachings is almost too complex for many people to understand and accept. Does the simple concept of a Twin Flame relationship being a blissful, sexual act have any merit? It has merit in the sense that it is symbolic of the relationship of Mother-Father God. However, as we have said before, the concept of the Twin-Flame also allows people to hide out in lack of completeness, because it means that they have to search for another in order to be whole. This is an illusion. The Twin Flame concept, the Twin Flame reality, the joining of Twin Flame souls can only be whole when each is whole in and amongst themselves. Otherwise you would end up with a Twin Flame co-dependent relationship. There is much more on this subject, but possibly it can be held for another time.

During a channeling session with St. Francis at another time, we asked to understand the difference between discernment and judgment. He said that "discernment is where you feel you wish to be"; whereas "judgment is what you think others should do." Is this a fair distinction? Francis has given you a magnificent guideline for life, and in that sense he has been of tremendous help. However, the subject has more depth when considered on its various energetic levels.

Discernment can be rather easily handled. It is the recognition within oneself of the vibration of knowing. However, judgment is not so easily handled, for judgment is much misunderstood. Judgment is often used instead of discernment, but it can mean the same thing. In this case, judgment is discernment.

But judgment goes further. Judgment is the independent assigning of energy by an individual. This is its most accurate description, for when one judges, what are they doing? They are tagging an energy to a created experience. This is very complex in its energetic understanding, but possibly it can be simplified by asking "What happens when one judges? Is this different than when one allows? What is the difference between judgment and allowance?" *There is a vast difference between judgment and allowance.* Are they not nearly diametrically opposed? So what does "to be" mean? It means beingness or allowance. Judgment is "not allowing to be." This happens when one ascribes an energy of acceptance or non-acceptance by calling things "good" or "bad" or "right" or "wrong." Those terms are merely identifiers to relate to that individual whether it is accepted or rejected. What is happening to that individual when he makes that judgment? Do they then become a part of that energy stream? And are they moving to balance it in any way or are they perhaps moving to expand it?

By this reasoning, judgment could be said to be the expansion of unbalanced energy. So another definition of judgment could be the non-productive use of God-energy, but that almost sounds judgmental because the definition cannot be put into words without telling where it comes from.

Is judgment a third-dimensional concept? There is judgment in other dimensions. Many think that because you leave the third dimension, everything becomes God-space and God-love. That is not so. For you see, as above, so below, and believe me, as below, so above. It might surprise you to see Masters quibbling and making judgments about others; but what do you think happens when an evolved being has ascended from the Earth with unresolved energies? Do those unresolved energies just get put off into a storage location? No. It is the natural law of karma that it is ever-present in that being. They can try to shuffle it off but it is always hanging around. And in those dimensions, you cannot hide it. And so these unresolved energies do cause judgments in other dimensions.

From the many examples of judgment which we could bring forth, all would fit into a definition which would be "an expansion of unbalanced energy through a lack of allowance of God's creation." This definition permits the lack of judgment to generate an allowance of God's creation. This definition also allows a feeling of the subtle movement of energy as it moves from being prohibited by judgment to being allowed by the lack of judgment.

As a result of all of this, Francis has given you a magnificent tool for living this life; but if you are truly to understand the full effects of judgment, an understanding of the energetics is desirable.

Why are so many Sea Cows and Manatees dying in Florida? Those beings live in the rivers and the lakes that are in the rivers. The rivers represent the lifeblood of Florida. They support the earth, they support all of the flora and they support all of the animal life. Without that water, that land would be under the sea. These beings live in that water and their spiritual energy cleanses the stream of energy that flows along those waterways. That energy is a focus of the mass energy of that state. In other words, in order to heal the mass consciousness of that state, that energy is pulled into the ground from whence it flows into the waterways because of their great healing flow and the life force of the Mother that flows through them. These animals cooperate with Mother Earth in the cleansing of this mass consciousness energy. They are beautiful, peaceful, loving animals. But what has happened is that the consciousness of this state has gotten so destructive that it is terminating the life of many of these beings, for the task is more than they can take. This is symbolic of the state killing itself. If those animals who are so loving and so healing cannot survive, what is the possibility for you? These animals were specifically created for this purpose. And those in what you term the Devic kingdom that support this life stream are very disappointed, not because they are angry but because humanity has not recognized the beauty of their creation. The purpose of their creation is to beautify and support humanity and Mother Earth. And so these animals can be supported by the recognition of their role.

Are they the same family as the dolphins and the whales in their consciousness? They are of a similar family. The role of dolphins and of whales is of a similar function to what these animals are performing. But there is a difference, and that is that these animals have more of an attachment to the land. They are in closer proximity and they touch the land. That is why they are in the rivers because they are able to live closer to the land. They are a bridge.

What energy did the recent comet, Hyakutake, bring to the planet? What would it sound like if you heard someone running down the street and yelling **Hyakutake** ten times each minute in a loud and distinct voice? What would you think? It would get your attention straight away, would it not? Well this particular planetary form is bringing the energy of the awakening. It is saying, "Hey, I need your attention, because something is coming!" And because you have given me your attention, I will give you the ability to see what is coming, at some level. It is as if you were on a dark ocean and this very, very big boat is coming at you. You want it to know that you are there, and so you send up a flare. This Earth is like this big, big boat, and this flare is like this warning that there is something out there. Now if you are on this big, big boat and you see this flare, you would know that something is about to happen. It has your attention, but you don't quite know what is out there, do you? But you see this flare. It is too dark to see anything else. The flare could come from a land mass, or a small boat, or a great big boat, or something else and so it has your attention. Because it has your attention, you are looking and you are examining and probing to find what is out there. Perhaps you even stop your movement to check it out because it might cause you to alter your course. So now you have the question of what is out there. This comet brought this energy of attention and it brought the awakening to those who would be able to stop, to pause and reflect and to say, "What is out there?" This comet generated X-rays which confused your scientists. Well, what do X-rays do? They penetrate. They do some very energetic energy work. X-rays mean that this comet has some very high rotational energy associated with it. Might it be that the energy of this comet has something to do with the energy that is coming? What happens in a field where there is very high rotation of energy? It changes the rotation of any energy that flows into it because it has such a high energy flux. Well, that is what is coming. The Earth is moving into an area of very high energy flux. What this means is massive amounts of energy movement. This comet is a precursor, an announcement, a bell-ringer, an awakening, a flare.

Will the new comet coming next year be more of the same? It will be different, for it will have more than just this particular rotational energy. It will contain another dimension of what is coming.

SUMMARY

Many of the subjects in this chapter are so short that they tend to present their own summary. These subjects are: Spirit and Soul; Angels; Eternal Damnation; Channeling; and Clarity. Consequently, only the other subjects will be summarized in this section.

In respect to **Gurus**, these teachings state that the self-determining Masters should never give up their own power and allow themselves to be subject to a Guru, for there are no Gurus for the pioneers of God-creation. This does not mean that there are not teachers, for each individual is both teacher and student, master and disciple. All learn from each other and therefore, all teach to each other. Because of this no one is to be in awe of another. There is respect, but since within God all are of the same creation, then no one is to worship another except for the adoration which all give to God.

Since creation is occurring every moment, then **predictions** are meaningful only when a chosen path has been selected and is rigidly followed. If that path is in alignment with Divine Will, then the seer will see that path as the one being followed; but if the path is not in alignment with Divine Will, then that is the path which will be seen. However, whatever is seen by the seer is neither a guaranteed nor a required outcome, for it is subject to change on a moment-by-moment basis. That is the major message about how Creator-Gods create.

In respect to **doubt**, the Christ expressed that he had had doubts when he was incarnate but that by turning his attention to the voice of the Mother/Father God, all of his doubts found themselves at peace. They disappeared, just as ours will if we do the same.

The concepts of **Twin Flame** and divine partnership are complex subjects which do not fit neatly into a summary paragraph. Nevertheless, the teachings do state that the major purpose of either relationship is to return to the wholeness within you that is complete. In this sense, both the twin flame and the divine partnership concepts have a strong relationship to love, but not necessarily to sexual activity in the absence of totally unconditional love.

Discernment was presented as a relatively understandable energetic concept related to the recognition within oneself of the vibration of knowing. However, **judgment** was presented as being energetically more complex as "an expansion of unbalanced energy through a lack of allowance of God's creation."

The **Photon Belt** was presented as one more example of the enlightenment of Earth. It will be a sudden experience only for those who are not conscious of who they are. For those who are conscious, you already know all that you need to know.

SUMMARY and CONCLUSIONS

This chapter is a concise summary of the teachings generated by the channelings presented in Chapters One through Eight. This Summary and Conclusion section is presented as a convenience for future reference.

In regard to **Ascension**, these teachings state that ascension is not a quantum leap which suddenly raises an entity into the fourth or fifth dimension from third-dimensionality. Instead, it is a day-by-day, or even moment-by-moment elevation from pure third-dimensionality in which there is no awareness of consciousness in other dimensions, into pure fourth-dimensionality in which there is an awareness of consciousness in all dimensions. It is this "awareness of the awareness" which distinguishes fourth-dimensionality from the third. Therefore, the ascension from third to fourth-dimensionality is generally a growing awareness of this awareness, and not a sudden and instantaneous shift from absolutely no awareness into full consciousness in all dimensions. This is not to say that the sudden, instantaneous quantum leap cannot happen, for it can happen within the grace of God. However, for most individuals with Free Will, the ascension from third-dimensionality to the fourth is a gradual, evolutionary passage, rather than a dramatic, revolutionary one. Because of this gradual ascension, most fourth dimensional beings would appear to be just like all third-dimensional beings when examined solely with the five physical senses. It is only when viewed from a different set of senses, such as those possessed by a multi-sensory being, that the difference can be noted. Also, because of this gradual ascension, many who are on planet Earth are not fully third-dimensional personalities. Instead, they could be said to be at some higher level, say 3.35 or 3.71, as consciousness in all dimensions starts to progressively develop within them.

In regard to **Creation**, these teachings state that each entity, whether presently incarnate or not, is a creator; and that creation happens each and every moment. Through this creation, God changes by growing and learning to understand more of Him/Herself. One major purpose of our Journey through third-dimensionality is to bring divinity into physicality so that divine creations may be present in all the dimensions including unmanifest God, physicality, and all dimensions in between. In this way creations can exist with feelings and emotions, for they will have been created in a dimensionality in which the experience of feelings and emotions is more evident than in any other dimension. Another major purpose of our Journey through third-dimensionality is to create specifically what God has energized generally. To do this requires creating with divine purpose, for although all creations become a creation of God, those creations which are made with divine purpose increase the awareness of God within the creator and thus increase God; whereas those creations made without divine purpose only rearrange that which presently exists. In this way, creation outside of divine purpose causes competition for existing energy rather than creating from the new energy of the inexhaustible Source. In this way, creation of that which is not from divine purpose creates that which is the worst in humankind, including wars, domination of others and the like; whereas creation with divine purpose creates that which is the best in humankind, including prosperity for all. A final purpose of our Journey through third-dimensionality is the ultimate goal of completing humanity, for until the human family as a whole comes together in united, co-creation of divine intention, it will always be incomplete.

In regard to **Divine Will and Free Will**, these teachings made the definitive point that we chose to come in to third-dimensionality on planet Earth so that we could become a God-conscious being by freely choosing to do so. One becomes a God-conscious being by following Divine Will at all times. Angels follow Divine Will at all times, but they do so because of their environment in which nothing else exists. Humanity has been given the gift of Free Will. This is a great gift, for if humanity can follow Divine Will by choice out of all else which exists, then humanity can become co-creators with God. Humanity can then be trusted to create as God would create, not because nothing else is available, but because humanity has learned to do so by experiencing that which is not-God. In the rejection of not-God by Free Will choice, humanity has had an experience that truly helps God to define itself; for in the experience of being divine, all which is not divine comes up for healing. It is thus identified, experienced and healed; and in the healing, God indeed becomes joyful, for a new aspect of individualized God has been generated.

In regard to **Manifestation and Prosperity**, the major teaching was that nothing would be made manifest in physicality until it had been made manifest in all dimensions between physicality and unmanifest God; and that even then it would not be made manifest unless the creator was clear enough to use the creation for divine purpose. This means that until an entity is conscious of his/her divinity in all dimensions, with no dislocations within the streams of consciousness spanning all dimensions, manifestation in the physical will not take place. Thus the teachings say that the lack of manifestation is generated by a lack of belief in who you already are. The teachings also say that until manifestation can be generated from the inexhaustible Source, any manifestation is only a rearrangement of what already exists. In this way, it is a redistribution of the energy "owned" by another, it does not represent an increase in the amount of prosperity which is available for all, and it will only manifest for a short period of time. Finally, the teachings state that the lack of prosperity is generally because of an enslavement to poverty; and that poverty itself is caused by the lack of belief that the consciousness already exists in all the dimensions between physicality and the inexhaustible energy available from unmanifest God.

The major message about **Christ Consciousness** is that each and every one of us is an individualized aspect of Christ Consciousness because all things which exist in creation are aspects of Christ Consciousness. This is so because the Christ Consciousness is that energy which flows from unmanifest God into manifestation to create all Creation. Another major point of the teachings is that as one becomes aware of his/her Christ Consciousness in this dimension, that then allows the recognition and acceptance of the Christ Consciousness in the next dimension, and the one beyond that, and the one beyond that all the way to the "sound of God" which emanates from the inexhaustible Source of unmanifest God. In other words, the awareness of your Christ Consciousness is the first step into the full divinity that is you. Finally, the Christ Consciousness which is you is your guarantee that you are one with God.

The major message about **Jesus the Christ** was his major teaching which states that anything he did, each individualized being can do—and more! In addition, help is available, not to do anything for you, but to help you to do it. This is not what the Christian Church teaches, but it is what Jesus the Christ taught!

There were many teachings about **Physicality**, including the major teaching that the physical body can be changed, rejuvenated, and made to last forever. In addition, the channelings presented the teaching that one soul may inhabit more than one body in order to gain a variety of experiences, and that there are several types of etheric embodiments. Finally, the channelings presented the teaching that there was no longer any need to learn the lessons of suffering, and that suffering could be eliminated solely by deciding that we have had enough of it.

The short teachings on a variety of **Miscellaneous Subjects** are self-explanatory, and will not be reviewed further in this chapter.

The channelings presented in this book have come from energies which have identified themselves as Ascended Masters. The channelings seem to involve very little, if any, of the ego of the channel. These channelings are different than those presented by other channels, sometimes from the same energized source of an Ascended Master. As these teachings have emphasized quite often, the truth of these or any other channelings is up to the discernment of the one to whom the teachings have been presented.

These teachings are offered in a sense of love and sharing, and not in the sense of being a dogmatic expression of that which you must believe. In that spirit, those who put this book together say:

GOD BLESS!

APPENDIXES

APPENDIX A
A SHORT DESCRIPTION
OF THE CHANNELINGS

Note: With the exception of Channeling 4, all of these channelings were conducted in the Atlanta, Georgia area during 1992-1996. Less than 20% of the channeled material has been presented in this book. Many subjects, especially those which posed a temporal problem such as the Atlanta Olympics, have not been mentioned at all. Nevertheless, the editor decided to make the following list a fairly complete picture of what occurred during these sessions, not to have the reader feel short-changed, but to indicate just how full and complete these channeling sessions were.

Channeling 1 was on April 6, 1992. Melchizedek channeled information about Consciousness, Divine Will and Energy and gave personal readings along with an energy flow.

Channeling 2 was on April 13, 1992. Sananda channeled information on Christ, Peace and Love and gave personal readings.

Channeling 3 was on May 4, 1992. An energy blend of Melchizedek, Isis and St. Germain channeled information about Stargates, Creation and Food and gave personal readings. In addition, the point was made that putting a specific name on an energy that provided information was not really important, for the important part was to feel the energy.

Channeling 4 was on May 16, 1992. It was a personal reading given to Erik Myrmo during great turbulence on an airplane someplace over the United States. The energy level was very high. The Energy was a specific energy, but was not identified. The total subject was Ascension and included what ascension means and how it is to be done.

Channeling 5 was on June 8, 1992. Sananda channeled information about the God-head and Creation and gave personal readings.

Channeling 6 was on August 3, 1992. Kahil Gibran gave a long channeling on Ascension including Divine/Free Will, then gave personal readings and an energy flow.

Channeling 7 was on August 17, 1992. A Blend of Energies led a question and answer session which covered information on subjects such as Love, Clarity, Mastery and Prosperity. During a powerful energy flow, a large mirror which had been securely anchored to a downstairs wall fell and shattered into thousands of pieces. The energy level was very high.

Channeling 8 was on August 24, 1992. Sananda channeled information on Peace, Love and Creation and gave personal readings and an energy flow.

Channeling 9 was on August 31, 1992. Serapis Bey channeled information on Ascension including the Defined Steps of Ascension and gave personal readings and an energy flow.

Channeling 10 was undated, but we believe it was on about September 14, 1992. KL [which stands for Keeper of the Light] channeled information upon Light, Dimensions and Ascension and emphasized the importance of anchoring the Light on planet Earth.

Channeling 11 was on September 28, 1992. The Christ Consciousness channeled information on Ascension and Energy and emphasized the importance of service.

Channeling 12 was on October 5, 1992. A Blend of Energies gave a guided meditation on Ascension and then gave personal readings. Emphasis was made on the need to be prepared for transformation at all times, especially when asleep.

Channeling 13 was on October 19, 1992. Melchizedek and St. Germain channeled information on the Melchizedek Temples, the Order of Melchizedek, DNA, Earth Changes and Maps, and gave personal readings and an energy flow. The session ended with a magnificent prayer from St. Germain on asking for Divine Creation. This prayer has been presented in Chapter Two.

Channeling 14 was on October 26, 1992. Maitreya channeled information on Transformations, Earth Changes, Creator-Gods, Divine Will, Christ Embodiment and Dimensions, then gave personal readings and an energy flow.

Channeling 15 was on November 9, 1992. A Blend of the Energies of Maitreya and Buddha channeled information on Changes in Consciousness, Creation and Ascension, then gave personal readings and an energy flow.

Channeling 16 was on November 30, 1992. Djwhal Kuhl [Master DK], Adama and Maitreya answered questions on topics such as the Christ Consciousness, Eternal Damnation and Anger, then gave personal readings and an energy flow.

Channeling 17 was on December 7, 1992. The Christ channeled information on Ascension, then led a guided meditation on energy, then led an energy flow while he talked about peace.

Channeling 18 was on February 2, 1993. Kuthumi channeled information on the Science and Application of Being and on Creator-Gods, then led an energy flow to a large audience.

Channeling 19 was on February 10, 1993. Melchizedek channeled information on Doubts and Receiving Energy through the Chakras, then gave personal readings and an energy flow.

Channeling 20 was on February 15, 1993. Adama and Maitreya channeled information on Manifestation, Prosperity, Love, Dimensions and Freedom, then answered questions and led an energy flow.

Channeling 21 was on March 15, 1993. Kuthumi channeled information on the Definitions of Bodies, and on Ego, Divine Will, Mastery, Grace and Ascension, then answered questions and led an energy flow.

Channeling 22 was on March 20, 1993. Kuthumi and Maitreya led a ceremony for the Spring Equinox, then channeled information on Creator-Gods and our Journey, followed by an energy flow.

Channeling 23 was on March 22, 1993. Lord Michael channeled information on Discernment, Ascension, Birth dates, Divine Will and the Interaction of Soul and Spirit. He then answered questions and led an energy flow.

Channeling 24 was on March 29, 1993. Master DK and Kuthumi channeled information on Dimensions, on why Channelings do not always correlate, and on Mastery, Freedom and Soul and then answered questions. At the end, Kuthumi mentioned that there was a new color in the room. It was a new shade of gold. It is one of the new rays being introduced. It is the new ray for synthesis of humanity and divinity

Channeling 25 was on April 19, 1993. The Being from the Central Sun channeled information about Doubts, Divine Will, New Age, Ego and the Science of Desire, then answered questions.

Channeling 26 was on May 17, 1993. The Being from the North Star channeled information about Channeling, Divine Will and Physicality, then answered questions.

Channeling 27 was not dated, but we think is was on about May 20, 1993. Adama and Melchizedek channeled information about the Melchizedek Temples, the Order of Melchizedek and Ceremonies to be held on Stone Mountain, then answered questions. Then Maitreya came in to lead an energy flow.

Channeling 28 was on May 24, 1993. Kuthumi channeled information on Physicality, Reality and Divine Purpose. Then Maitreya came in to answer questions, to give personal readings and to lead an energy flow.

Channeling 29 was on May 27, 1993. Maitreya channeled information on Reality, then answered questions and gave personal readings, then led an energy flow.

Channeling 30 was on July 12, 1993. Maitreya, Kuthumi and the

Being from the Central Sun channeled information on Alignment, Mastery, Reality and Free Will, then answered questions. Then the one called The Motivator came in to lead an energy flow that shook things up.

Channeling 31 was on August 31, 1993. Quetzacoatl, Ra and Kuthumi channeled information on the Christ Energy and other Energies, the Ruby Ray and the Opal Gemstone. This was in preparation for several of the group who were taking spiritual journeys to the Yucatan and Peru.

Channeling 32 was on September 20, 1993. A Blend of Energies channeled information on Physicality, Soul, Creation and Christ Consciousness then answered questions.

Channeling 33 was on October 27, 1993. Kuthumi channeled information on Mastery, led an energy flow, then answered specific questions from those who had just returned from their spiritual journeys.

Channeling 34 was on December 6, 1993. Maitreya channeled information on Power and Prosperity, then led an energy flow.

Channeling 35 was on February 21, 1994. St. Germain and Maitreya channeled information on the Elohim Computers, Divinity, and a long session on the Christ, then answered questions and led an energy flow.

Channeling 36 was on May 5, 1994. Lord Michael and Maitreya channeled information on Divinity, Mastery, Modification of the Earth Changes, Christ Energy, Peace, Love and Physicality.

Channeling 37 was on September 21, 1994. Babaji channeled information on the Physical Body then led an energy flow and answered questions.

Channeling 38 was on November 7, 1994. Babaji and Kuthumi channeled information on the Physical Body, Ascension and, in response to questions, the Kombucha Mushroom, then answered questions and had an energy flow.

Channeling 39 was on January 9, 1995. After an introduction by Kuthumi, a Collection of Space Beings channeled information on Time, the Photon Belt, the Future of Medicine, ETs, Sex and Twin Flames, then answered questions and led an energy flow.

Channeling 40 was on January 18, 1995. Kuthumi and St. George channeled information on Time, Living your Life, Dimensions and the up-coming spiritual journey to Rome and Turkey which some of the group were taking. This was our first experience with St. George. Whereas Kuthumi had been a kind, gentle, teaching kind of energy, St. George was a loud, table-thumping kind of energy which stirred everyone up! Then Maitreya came in as a very gentle energy to lead the energy flow and to settle down what St. George had stirred up.

Channeling 41 was on February 2, 1995. Maitreya started the session with an energy flow, then Maitreya and St. George channeled information on Christ, Love, Consciousness, Fear, Healing, the Fourth and Fifth Dimensions, Ascension, Living your Life, and Divine Will.

Channeling 42 was on February 13, 1995. St. George and Kuthumi channeled information on Physicality, Love, Unconditional Love, Poverty, Ascension and Light. Then Kuthumi led a long guided meditation/energy flow on infusing light into the body and answered questions.

Channeling 43 was on April 5, 1995. St. George, Kuthumi and Maitreya channeled information on Emotions, Matter/Energy Interactions, Creation, Clarity, Divine Will and a critique of the Rome/Turkey trip from which some of the group had just returned. Maitreya led the energy flow.

Channeling 44 was on April 17, 1995. Maitreya, Kuthumi, St. George and Sananda as a Blend of the Christ Consciousness channeled information on the Christ Consciousness, Illusions, Symbology, Manifestation, Divine Will and Being/Doing. There was a question session and an energy flow.

Channeling 45 was on August 13, 1995. Kuthumi channeled information on Soul Recovery, Divine Evolution, God-head, Diets and the Atlanta Olympics. There was also a question session and an energy flow.

Channeling 46 was a two day workshop on October 28-9, 1995. Nine people attended. There were four channeling sessions, each 2-3 hours in length. There were a variety of energy-flow sessions. Kuthumi channeled the first, second and fourth sessions. St. George channeled the third session. The first and second sessions presented channeled information on Creation, Manifestation, Divine Will, Dimensions, Cosmic-consciousness, Christ-consciousness and God-consciousness. The third session channeled information on Living your Life, Divinity/Humanity, Multi-body Incarnations, Dimensions, Gravity and Physicality. The fourth session presented information on Divine Will, Love and Ego. There was a long question and answer segment in the fourth session, followed by a private channeling session for each participant.

Channeling 47 was on November 6, 1995. Maitreya, St. George and the Mahatma Energy channeled information on Manifestation, Creation, Jesus, Multi-body Incarnations, Duality, Love, Mahatma, Divine Order and the Atlanta Olympics. There were numerous questions during the channeling, and there was a long energy flow at the end of the session.

Channeling 48 was on November 28, 1995. Kuthumi channeled information on Creating, Manifestation, Prosperity, Divine Will, Creator-Gods, Spirit, Love, Energy Exchange and Encoding. There was a question session and an energy flow.

Channeling 49 was on January 13, 1996. Kuthumi channeled information about himself as an aspect of the Christ Consciousness and gave personal readings to those in attendance.

Channeling 50 was on January 23, 1996. Maitreya and Kuthumi channeled information on Divinity, State of Being, the Various Bodies, manifestation and the Atlanta Olympics. There were questions and an energy flow.

Channeling 51 was on February 6, 1996. Maitreya and Kuthumi channeled information on Divine Will, Master/Student Relationships, Divinity, Prosperity, Manifestation, Multi-body Incarnations, Twin Flame, Christ Consciousness, Ascension and Dimensions. There was a question session and an energy flow.

Channeling 52 was on February 20, 1996. A Blend of Maitreya, Kuthumi, Sananda, and St. George channeled information on Ascension, Creator-Gods, Mass Consciousness and Living your Life. There was a question session and an energy flow.

Channeling 53 was on March 5, 1996. St. George and Maitreya channeled information on Manifestation, Calendars, Astrology, Living your Life, Quantum Shifts, Anger, Clarity, and Suffering followed by an energy flow.

Channeling 54 was on March 26, 1996. Maitreya channeled information on the Christ Consciousness, Creation, Evil, Grace, Ascension, and Physicality. An energy flow followed.

Channeling 55 was on April 18, 1996. Kuthumi channeled information in response to specific questions on Ascension, Creation, Divine Will and Free Will, Manifestation and Prosperity, Christ Consciousness, Physicality, Twin Flames, Sea Cows and Manatees, Comets, and Books on Channeled Information. Only three people were present and the energy flow was fantastic!

Channeling 56 was on May 28, 1996. Maitreya channeled information on Integrity, Karma, Mother Nature, Jesus Christ, and Emotions. An energy flow followed.

Channeling 57 was on May 30, 1996. Maitreya channeled answers to specific questions on Ascension and Physicality, described the ascension of Jesus the Christ, gave definitions for various terms as they were used in the channeled information, and described the energy aspects of the twenty-two beings who had channeled information during the fifty-seven channelings. The energy of each being came into the session, and the three people involved all were tremendously affected by each energy and by the gifts which were given.

Channeling 58 was on July 2, 1996. Maitreya and Kuthumi channeled specific answers to questions on the Devic Kingdom and on Discernment/Judgment. In addition, the definitions of additional terms were presented.

     Note: The channelings continue and so does the increasing understanding of energy and energy flow. However, Channeling 58 was the cutoff point for inclusion in this book.

APPENDIX B
MASTERS WHO CHANNELED THROUGH ERIK MYRMO

     This Appendix describes the energy represented by Ascended Masters who channeled during the sessions presented in *Appendix A*. The first description given after each name is that which was presented by Maitreya during a channeling on May 30, 1996. The part of each description which starts with the word "**others**" is from other sources, some of which may be from these channelings and some of which may be from other New Age literature.

     Adama Adama has the energies of teacher and wily priest. He has been said to have been Plato, but Plato had several energies participating in that incarnation, only one of which was Adama. Adama is a very focused energy. To be the individualized energy that he has been as master teacher in Telos for the past 900 years requires tremendous focus because Telos was not always the orderly environment it has become. **Others** have said that Adama has been the teaching Master in the temple in Telos for the past 900 years and that he previously had an incarnation as Plato.

     Babaji Babaji has the energies of love, compassion, empathy and heart. He is the physical expression of love and honor. Babaji can come and go in physical form whenever he chooses. He is an Ascended Master who is eternal in physicality, because Babaji is the manifestation of the heart of God. There will always be Babaji energy. **Others** have said that Babaji is a third-dimension, living Master or Avatar who is in Puttaparthi, India. He produces physical manifestations of jewelry and bi-locates.

     Being from the Central Sun Being from the Central Sun is one of the Lords of Creation of this universe who participates in different systems as he chooses. This is an Energy whose name can neither be defined nor pronounced in our language, for it is more nearly the sound of solar wind energy than of anything else. The "Central Sun" is the vortex of creation of this universe. From that central vortex of this universe springs all that is in this universe. There are innumerable vortexes of energy throughout the universe that move between dimensions and that move inexplicably to mankind. These are new creations of star energy, black holes and the like. The Central Sun is what the unmanifest moves through as it becomes manifest. [See *Appendix D*]. **Others** have said that the Central Sun is more nearly a source of the energy of knowledge rather than a source of physical energy.

Being from the North Star Being from the North Star is quite simply the energy of direction, and that is the reason for the "North Star" description, because direction is merely the ability to recognize individualized Divine Will. This being is a master teacher from the Pleiades who specializes in helping humanity to recognize what is individualized Divine Will, to understand what is will, to understand that a human being is willful. **Others** have said that this being is another whose name is beyond us, for his energy is not that which can be personalized. The Energy is guided by Divine Will to place the stars in our northern sky and to create and support energy from that region to Earth.

Buddha [Note: When the name "Buddha" was said, Maitreya became quite silent for a long period and the energy flow was very beautiful and satisfying. At one point I said, "I now know what the energy is, but I don't know how to write it down!"] In describing Buddha, you can only describe yourself. Buddha energy is the energy of self-recognition upon the full spectrum of your being. There are no words to describe what the Buddhic energy is, but as self-recognition develops, one will realize that he/she has knowledge of this energy. What happens when there is the recognition of self across the spectrum of an individualized being is that you recognize the energy of equanimity of God. It is the energy of all that is in appreciation and in equality. **Others** have written and said much about the one which Buddhism identifies as the Buddha. A short presentation of the Buddha is presented in *A Personal Pathway to God*.

Christ [Note: Again there was a long pause as the energy came in.] Christ is the movement of God into manifest reality. It is the spectrum of creative God that exists in manifestation and the Christ has innumerable qualities. **Others** have written much on the one which Christianity identifies as the Christ, possibly than any on Earth. Information on Jesus of Nazareth who became the Christ is available from many of these sources.

Christ Consciousness　The Christ Consciousness is merely the recognition of the Christ energy in the state of awareness. **Other** information on the Christ Consciousness may be found in *Chapter Five* of this book.

Djwhal Kuhl [Master DK] [Another long pause] Intellectual wisdom. *Is it proper to say that Master DK is the Master of the Fourth Ray?* DK, like all masters, works on all rays to some extent. In this particular focus of his consciousness he is working with the third and the fourth rays. *So he is not the Master of the Fourth Ray as Alice Bailey stated?* The definition of a Master of a Ray which has been presented is a limited perspective on the movement of a ray into this universe. There are Masters who are specializing in a particular frequency of divinity for this particular Earth experience. In that way they are the Master of that ray, but there are others as well. It is not a structured hierarchy as has been described so often. The structured hierarchy is from viewing what is not physical from a limited perspective. The Master of the Fourth Ray would be a summation of all the beings who are working on the Fourth Ray. Master DK is quite adept at the Fourth Ray, but there are innumerable Masters who have become Masters of the Fourth Ray. If you said that an entity or being was the Master of that ray, then you would not be acknowledging the Mastership of all of those beings who had gained such familiarity with that ray. **Others** have said that Master DK is known as "The Tibetan" for his last incarnation, that he is the source of the Alice Bailey writings, and that he a Master of the Fourth Ray.

Isis [Note: There was a very long pause during which some of the most loving energy I have ever felt was directed around the entire room.] Isis is the name of the being who has symbolized Mother in spirit, the Mother Nature of spiritual energy. Many think that spiritual energy is Father energy, but in truth, spiritual energy is balanced. It is both Mother and Father. Isis entered into this energy flow with you to demonstrate spiritual energy with the quality of the Mother. **Others** have said that Isis has held the office of the World Mother, that she was prominent in Egypt, and that she has had many other names in other cultures.

Kahil Gibran Kahil Gibran is the narrator of spiritual experience, the vessel of spiritual manifestation for multi-dimensional literature. In respect to ascension, Kahil Gibran had what would be termed "a partial ascension after death." **Others** have said that he was a Syrian Lebanese who immigrated to the United States, and that he was a great poet and painter.

Keeper of the Light When there are great energy streams moving into manifestation that are not yet ready to receive them, there are beings who hold the light until it is allowed to move. Many Masters perform this function. All the Masters of Rays perform this function. They help regulate the flow of energy according to divine principle. Keeper of the Light is one of those beings. **Others** have said that the Keeper of the Light is an energy pattern that is responsible for keeping the light steady by continuous concentration.

Kuthumi Kuthumi is master teacher who integrates intellectual and emotional wisdom. He has balanced perspective and is a combination of Christic and Buddhic energy. **Others** have said that Kuthumi is the one who is to hold the Office of World Teacher for the new Golden Age, and one who has had previous Earth incarnations as Pythagoras and as St. Francis of Assisi among many others. In addition, he is defined as the "rays of Christ Consciousness that are manifest in physical phenomenon," and as the one to be called upon when a being is confused about what is the next adventure for spiritual undertaking.

Maitreya [A long pause] I am Maitreya. *I know! Were you in the physical?* Yes, but not at this time. I could not be Maitreya without having been in the physical. [Another long pause of energy flow.] *What words would you like us to use in the book?* [Again another long pause] Christ Consciousness, loving humanity, encouraging humanity to be in Christ Consciousness, in divinity while physical, to fulfill destiny. *Should we forget the information which has Maitreya as the holder of the Office of the Christ and the one who overshadowed Jesus during his incarnation?* Do you think that on my desk I have a block that says "Head Christ?" *Maybe, and maybe Kuthumi has one that says "Head World Teacher!"* These are accurate descriptions of the limited perspective in which those who write the words view our work. **Others** have said that Maitreya holds the Office of the Christ and that he overshadowed Jesus in his Earth incarnation.

Melchizedek Melchizedek is father of universal, divine priesthood with the term "priesthood" in no way defining gender, for it is the divinity that flows through one which determines whether priest or priestess. *Was Melchizedek a human being or is he of the angelic kingdom?* Melchizedek had physicality, but Melchizedek also has angelic energies. However, Melchizedek's beginnings were from the origin. He was from the beginning of what is termed the "Lords of Creation" of this system. Trying to define a "being" as human or angelic really becomes difficult when it is a being whose vessel of experience encompasses an experience such as that of a creator God or another great being. Suffice it to say that the Melchizedek priesthood is a human expression of divine interaction of beings who merely respond to Divine Will. **Others** have written much about Melchizedek. *The Urantia Book* spends a great deal of time describing the Melchizedeks as does *A Personal Pathway to God.*

Michael Archangel Michael is crusader, champion, defender and protector. **Others** have said that he is one of the Archangels, that he has a retreat over Banff, Canada, that he works with the Blue Ray, and that he has never been in human form. He is often designated "Lord Michael."

Quetzacotal Quetzacotal is a massive concentration of Christ energy in this portion of the planet. **Others** have written much about Quetzacotal which has ranged all the way from his being a despotic God of the Mayas and Incas, to his being a Christ embodiment who had as great an effect on the "Americas" as Jesus the Christ had on the Mediterranean World.

Ra Ra is the star energy coming to Earth. *Did he participate with Anwar Sadat?* Yes, but not wholly. What happens when the star energy comes in? It is very powerful and it is difficult for its total power to be accepted. **Others** have said that Ra was called the Sun God in Egypt, and that Anwar Sadat, which means "full of light," was overshadowed by him.

Sananda The energies of Sananda are those of lover of humanity, dedication of self, humanity's expression of love and peace. **Others** have said that Sananda is the spiritual name of Jesus.

Serapis Bey The energies of Serapis Bey are those of dedication, diligence, focus, ascension and stubbornness in the sense of being stubbornly hopeful for humanity. **Others** have said that his focus is on the ascension process and that he is the Master of Ascension.

St. George [Note: As usual, St. George was waiting to make his appearance and so there was no pause as his energy came in immediately with a loud laugh.] My focus is to live life itself in expression, in fullness of what humanity can be here and now. I aim to live life completely and to leave no stone unturned that is in your path, for they have to be turned! My focus is irreverence and total disregard for structure other than what is created each moment from divine interaction. I have total disregard for what is termed "past," for if it is past, it is dead. It is not alive, for what is alive is what was past that is present. That is a riddle! Humanity has killed the past. The past is alive and well in the present except where humanity has killed it! Nowness of life in the fullest. Anything else is limitation. So be it. **Others** have said that St. George has had many incarnations, one of which was Richard the Lionhearted, and that his job is to stand behind the Masters to push the students. In addition, the Masters have said that George has evolved as a father of planetary systems.

St. Germaine St. Germaine is the master of ceremonies, demonstrator of life lived in happiness and joy with the fruitful creation of whatever is needed. *Is it true that he is the guardian of the United States?* Guardian is not quite appropriate. Guardian is more Michael's arena. The violet flame that characterizes my energetic healing is both for protection and for transmutation. And so in viewing the protective aspects of my energy, it can be deemed as being a guardian, but it is not so much guardian as promoter, or as regenerator. I have great interests here even though I have not lived in physical form here as I have in other parts of the world. It is possible that this land will be one of the main genesis points of the Golden Age and so it is here that I have chosen to focus my energies. The possibility exists because this land is new and humanity is able to recognize change here. It is not laden with structured history. The land through its regeneration allows for rapid clearing of mass consciousness. The focus of energy in this area is great, from within and without the planet. And my wish is for the parade of Masters to manifest dramatically here. **Others** have said that he is the Master of the Sixth Ray. He is said to have had a life in Europe which lasted for many centuries, thus demonstrating that it could be done. He is said to have inspired the Rosicrucians, Free Masonry, the I AM group and others; and that he was active in the formation of the United States and appeared at the Continental Congress.

The Motivator The Motivator is an aspect of Divine Will. Different beings have the characteristics of this motivational energy. It is a quality of will that is more massive from the sense that Divine Will encompasses intention, direction, and energy of movement of that intention. The Motivator is that piercing aspect of intention that gains attention. It is the ability of Divine Will to move through the most dense wall for possibilities of recognition. It is the energy of will that becomes "sticky" once it is moving within an individual so that if recognition fades, it begins to stick, and to pull, to gain attention once again. So it has the qualities of piercing as well as grabbing. There is one being who has been termed The Motivator who comes at different times upon the planet during times when great change is needed. It is intended at this time that this energy need not be present in this way, for it is desired that the movement to the New Age be gentle and evolutionary in a transitional fashion of peacefulness.

APPENDIX C
DEFINITIONS OF TERMS USED
DURING THE CHANNELING SESSIONS

These definitions were presented by Ascended Master Maitreya during a channeling session on May 30, 1996 followed by another session for additional terms on July 2, 1996. These definitions differ greatly from those presented in a standard dictionary of the English language. These are the definitions to be used in order to understand the meaning of the channelings. In particular, the understanding of the term "energy" is vitally important in understanding these channelings.

Ascended Master Those beings who have had enlivened physical incarnations upon the Earth to the point that they could move their physicality into a higher dimensional experience. A Master is one who is close to becoming an Ascended Master.

ascension The description of the evolution of a spiritual being. It is the evolution of life at the end.

awareness The movement of consciousness in physical form and in physical consciousness for the purposes of describing awareness for humanity.

balanced energy This is the secret of evolution! Balanced energy is the energy of Self that is the pool of potentiality for Divine Will to spring forth into manifest creation. Unbalanced energy is energy that of itself moves with creative intent to seek balance. Do you see the difference?

channeling The movement of energy in an individual that allows for an expression of information and of energy in a specific way that is provided by partnership with a being or beings who are not necessarily physical.

Christ Christ is the movement of God into manifest reality. It is the spectrum of creative God that exists in manifestation.

Christ Consciousness The Christ Consciousness is merely the recognition of the Christ energy in the state of awareness. It is involved in the movement of unmanifest God into manifest reality.

clarity The allowance of energy without restriction in a particular frequency or aspect of a person's divinity. In the process of developing clarity, the restrictions which prevent clarity are cleared out.

consciousness The ability of the God-head to be aware of itself.

Cosmic Consciousness The awareness of the dual reality of your divinity and your physicality. It is the realization that you are one with God and that your lake of consciousness is interconnected with many other lakes of consciousness and that they are all one. It is the understanding that the enfolding of all that you are into your divinity heals every unbalanced aspect of you.

determinism Determinism is not a term which is often used because it is so greatly misunderstood. Determinism in its purest form merely means that there has been the energy required for the creation of a particular event or other energy occurrence.

dimensions The **First Dimension** is the first principle which is "God is All." The **Second Dimension** is the second principle which is that "God is All and God is aware, or is conscious." The **Third Dimension** is that "God is all, God is aware, God is here, and you are God." The **Fourth Dimension** is that you are God, and you are aware that you are aware that you are God. It is an awareness of an awareness. The dimensions higher than the Fourth Dimension merely reflect a greater awareness of the Third and Fourth Dimensions throughout all dimensionality with finer and finer vibrations as they approach that of God in the unmanifest reality until finally they complete the circle and become the First Principle that "God is All."

discernment Recognition within oneself of the vibration of knowing.

Divine Will The movement of energy from the God-head that is an expression of the desire of God for a particular movement of energy. Divine Will, as it moves through dimensional experience, takes on specific aspects for a particular created experience, but it is up to each individual-ized energy to provide the animation to that movement of Divine Will from the God-head, to provide that coloring, to provide that interpretation, to provide that recognition.

duality Duality merely is an expression of Free Will. Where there is not Free Will, there is still movement within the streams of energy that are flowing. Free Will allows the choice to flow with whatever stream of energy is moving that is within the consciousness of the decision maker. In a simplistic fashion, that is usually described as the physical expression of duality, meaning opposites, but in truth the physical expression of dual-ity is but a very small subset of the whole spectrum of Free Will choice.

ego The energy that has been created to allow operation of a consciousness in the physical realm.

emotions Emotion is the energy of movement in physical form, or the awareness of energy moving in the physical form. The finer aspects of emotions are feelings. Feeling is the awareness of higher dimen-sional energy moving within the consciousness, oftentimes into the physi-cal, but oftentimes not. Emotions are the dramatic movement of that en-ergy in the physical.

energy Energy is God in manifest reality.

energy flow Energy flow is the movement of God in manifest reality.

Feelings See "emotions."

Free Will See "duality."

God Consciousness The spanning of all dimensionality between physicality and unmanifest God. That is what you came here to achieve. In God Consciousness, you achieve a willing co-creatorship with God by the creation of the individualized-aspect of God that you are. God consciousness is that supreme existence in the physical in which you create from all levels of your being, and you are conscious in all levels of your being, and you are truly living as divine God-man or God-woman.

heal or healing To heal is to allow unbalanced energy to move to the fruition of its creation and in so doing become balanced energy.

judgment Judgment is the expansion of unbalanced energy through the lack of allowance of God's creation. Thus a lack of judgment permits an allowance of God's creation.

light body A light body is merely a description of non-physical energies that are responsible for the creation of the physical form.

manifestation Manifestation is two-fold. It is the creation of space and then the creative movement of energy into that space. Manifestation cannot occur without both. That is why it takes both the Mother and the Father aspects of God to have manifestation.

Masters See "Ascended Masters."

Order of Melchizedek The Order of Melchizedek is a group of beings who are realized to the point that they recognize their divine nature and recognize their divine purpose to participate in the further recognition of divinity in manifestation. A being is of the Order of Melchizedek not in the sense of a group on Earth but in the sense of a realized being who understands that the purpose of that being at that time is to participate in a somewhat structured way in the further recognition of divinity throughout manifestation. That being participates in the Order of Melchizedek at that level or in that dimension that is most appropriate at that time. As an example, you might have a being that was a twelfth-dimensional being and a very powerful Lord of Creation who also was in the physical and who chose to focus its Melchizedek activity in the physical while the physical was conscious. In that case it would truly be a multi-dimensional Melchizedek activity. And so as to whether in the physical or not, the physicality would be a sub-set of the multidimensional Melchizedek experience. In reality, the Order of Melchizedek does not mean a structured Order of beings. It means beings who move with the Divine Will that flows to them for this purpose. On Earth, people create structures for the Order in order to have association with other beings of the Order, but perhaps in other dimensions the association is created solely by the flowing of energy. **Others** have said that The Order of Melchizedek was created during a planetary alignment of the first created universe, and that the Melchizedek Order is truly unfathomable to third-dimensional mentality.

overshadowing An expression which presents a mis-conception in that it implies a "lesser than" and a "greater than" relationship. That is not the case. It is more a partnership. These partnerships are important because they allow the opportunity for beings who are not directly in physical incarnation to participate physically. There is so much thought and structure in "lesser than" and "greater than," but how could any part of humanity be "lesser than" or "greater than" if all is of God? That would be denying God! And so what is termed "overshadowing" is a term that we feel is not accurate. Instead, it is more a partnership between those equal in God albeit of different vessels of experience.

personality The specific combination of the energy rays of the individualized energy stream of that incarnation.

quantum shift The spectrum of energy shifts within the universe that occur because there has been the summation of the creation energy necessary for the event to occur in a "sudden" fashion. Because of its "suddenness" the shift seems immediate, but the energy shifts may have been in the "making" for a long period of "time."

Self Self is identity. It is the identity of spiritual energy moving in creation. It is the identity which is applied to the potentiality which moves from unmanifest God into creation.

soul The repository of experience of an individualized spirit energy stream. It is the representation of all that has been for that energy stream in unmanifest reality.

spirit Individualized God that moves *in* God in absolute, and moves *as* God in manifest reality and animates and gives life to the soul and movement of the experiencing bodies. **Others** have said that spirit is merely the finest aspect of your Self that is conscious in those dimensions that lead from unmanifest God.

unbalanced energy See "balanced energy."

unmanifest Unmanifest is the source of all that is, the source of all that will be.

vessel of experience The spectrum of the soul of an individualized being. The spectrum of the soul is what allows the varying movement of the spirit in manifest reality. The greater the vessel of experience, the greater the clarity of the spectrum of God that is manifest.

APPENDIX D
CHANNELED TRIP
TO THE RIVER OF LOVE

During the Question and Answer session with Erik Myrmo on April 18, 1996 when Kuthumi channeled many useful teachings in response to specific questions, the following interchange occurred between L. David Moore and Kuthumi:

Several times you have mentioned the Universal Law of Creation. I have not seen that defined in other writings. Could you please define that for us? The Universal Law of Creation is quite simple. Let me take you to a place and show you. Would you be willing to do this? I wish to take you to a place where you will see a flow of energy that will appear as if it is coming from unmanifest God but what you will be seeing is a river coming through what we shall term the "Central Sun." And I wish you to feel the intention coming from this energy. [Very long pause during the energy flow].

It is hard to leave that river, isn't it? *The sounds were there also!* There is everything there! [Another long pause] There is one word that describes the river from God. *I could choose the word "Oneness," I could choose the word "Uniformity," I could choose the phrase "All the same," or the phrase "In all directions,"* *for the river was all of that and more.* All of those words flow into one word, and that one word is "Love." The intent of that river is Love. That is the only intention that it truly has. It contains all that is. It contains all the possibilities and all that is desired from the heart of God that flows into this universe, for Love is the direction. Love is the motivator. Love is the container of all. It is a River of Love.

That interchange is what was recorded on the tape on that beautiful Thursday evening, but much, much more happened. This write-up is to record the visions which were given to me during the long energy flow when there were no sounds that could be picked up by the tape recorder.

I was taken to a place which I will call "up," even though I realize that the place was really as much "here" as it was in any elevated plane. I was seeing an absolutely huge vista, and it was all in deep darkness. Then, almost as if a light show were being turned on, a magnificent flow of colors commenced. I will call this flow a "river" for want of a better word, but if it were a river, it was more like a flowing river of lava than a flowing river of water, for it had immense depth into which I could see, and not just the upper surface which a normal river usually presents. I have said that the river was a flow of colors, but it could better be described by what my wife has called "flame stitching," for the very vivid colors were in a zigzag pattern such as that used to depict lightening, or such as that which is in the design of the flame stitching made popular by interior decorators a few years ago.

Although there was every imaginable color present in the flowing river of color, to my eye, three colors were dominate. There was a mauve which wasn't really a mauve but which had that hue as best I can describe it. There was a turquoise, which wasn't really a turquoise but again, that is as close as I can come. And there was a white-gold which was neither white nor gold nor a blend of those two colors. Instead it, like the other colors, was beyond the definitions which use English words or which use third-dimensional expressions for their description. In reality, these colors were beyond the experience of this dimension. Although the river which I saw was immense, I had the deep and firm belief that I was being shown but a small portion of what is there.

The river flowed in its immensity into a large sphere which was white-gold, but a different white-gold than the color found in the river. How beautiful everything was and how huge everything seemed to be! The river flowed into the top of the sphere, and out of the bottom came what I will describe as a cubic column. In other words, the output from the huge sphere was a long column which had two dimensions of about the same size, so that a cross-section of the column would be a square. The height was infinite, for the column just kept coming and coming out of the bottom of the sphere as the river of color flowed into the top. The "flame stitched" colors which had been obvious in the river were no longer discernible in the cubic column, for they had been changed. The colors had become individual spheres of color, and there were so many of them that I can only use the word "infinite" to describe their number. These small spheres were no more than dots within the immensity of the column; but although I was seeing a cubic column of immense dimensions, I was told that I was being given only a small portion of the total, for the column was not cubic with finite dimensions at all. Instead, it went on for infinity.

What was most unusual was that I became aware that each dot or sphere of color in the cubic column was surrounded by a sequence of colored spheres which were identical, no matter what direction one looked. This is very hard to describe, but imagine, if you will, that you are a turquoise sphere someplace in the midst of this huge column. You look to your right, and you see a sequence of spheres which are orange, purple, gold, red, and yellow in that sequence. The sequence goes on, of course, but I will use just these five colored spheres to describe the phenomena. Then you look to your left, and you see spheres which are orange, purple, gold, red, and yellow in that sequence. You then look up, and you see spheres which are orange, purple, gold, red, and yellow in that sequence. You then look at a forty-five degree angle first to the right, and then to the left, and then a five degree angle in each direction and on and on and in each and every direction, you see spheres which are orange, purple, gold, red, and yellow in that sequence.

Imagine how difficult it would be to weave an essentially two dimensional sheet of fabric so that at any one point, the sequence of colors would be identical in each and every direction. Imagine how much more difficult it would be to do the same in three dimensions. Then try to imagine how immensely more difficult it would be to do the same in an infinite number of dimensions. The possibilities are incomprehensible to the third-dimensional human mind.

At this point the one being channeled said, *"It is hard to leave that river, isn't it?"* and I responded that, *"The sounds were there also!"* I had not particularly noticed the sounds as I was staring in awe at the sights, but they must have been there. With these kind words from Master Kuthumi, I was brought back from that magnificent sight. On the return trip I was surrounded by millions of red roses and I continued to smell their almost overpowering fragrance as I settled back into the room. After the return I had such a memory of wonderment about the uniformity of the created stream that when asked to use one word to describe it, I chose to use terms which showed its attributes rather than its being. I chose terms such as "oneness" or "uniformity" or "all the same" or "in all directions" rather than the term which causes all of this. That term is "Love."

The next morning, during meditation, I asked how it would be possible to have a creation that from any point, no matter what direction one looked, the color sequence would be the same. The answer came in a flash. It merely said, *"It is simple, because it is alive!"* And I could only mumble, "Oh yes, I see."

Within the River of Love which flows out of unmanifest God into living Creation, that which is created is all the same. It is Love, and as such it is not good on the right but bad on the left; it is not pure in the front but tainted in the back; it is not righteousness above but evilness below; it is all the same. No matter what direction you look from wherever you are, all is the same in every direction around you. That is because it is the Love of God which fills Creation, and there is nothing *but* the Love of God in every direction you look. The differing sequences as you live and move through this living stream of Love may relate to how you respond to this oneness of God, or they may not. I was not given an understanding about that. But what I was shown was that there is no evil, no unrighteousness, no impurity, no non-love within the Love of God. There is only Love; and anything else we see is because of our understanding, and not because of its existence.

It was a profound lesson presented as an almost unimaginably beautiful sight. In the third book, *A Personal Pathway to God*, I presented some personal experiences while on spiritual journeys. In that book I presented the best description I could of the "Void" which I had visited and said that I would try to explain the wonder of it by saying:

I have been there only once, but I believe that it is real;
I loved it and I want to return;
and I have talked with others who have said the same.

With this new experience, I feel that I have been beyond that particular Void, and that what is beyond that Void is even more to be desired than the Void itself. There may be a deeper Void which I have not visited, but I am not certain of that. In any case, beyond the Void which I previously visited, there is a place into which flows an infinite River of Love from unmanifest God. This River of Love is then made manifest in Creation. We can claim our right to be in that Creation not by thinking that we are right while others are wrong, but by accepting that all are the same within the embrace of God, for all are Love. Although it might take an eternity to have all humanity accept that, I believe that it will happen, for that belief is, I feel, the intention of those who truly love God.

APPENDIX E
BIBLIOGRAPHY

Ascending Times, published every two months by Ascending Times, PO Box 100, Simpson, SK, Canada, S0G 4M0.

Bailey, Alice A., *The Rays and the Initiations, Volume V of A Treatise on the Seven Rays*, copyright 1960 by Lucis Trust, published by Lucis Publishing Company, New York [There are other books in this series]

Carroll, Lee, *The End Times, New Information for Personal Peace [Kryon Book 1]*, Copyright 1992 by the author, published by The Kryon Writings, Box 422, 1155 Camino Del Mar, Del Mar, CA 92014 [There are other books in this series]

Essene, Virginia and **Nidle**, Sheldon, *You are Becoming A Galactic Human*, copyright 1994 by the authors, published by Spiritual Education Endeavors Publishing Company, 1556 Halford Avenue, #288, Santa Clara, CA 95051

Hamilton, Virginia, *In the Beginning, Creation Stories from Around the World*, copyright 1988 by the author, published by Harcourt Brace Janovich, San Diego, New York, London.

Klein, Eric, *The Inner Door, Volume One, Channeled Discourses from the Ascended Masters*, Copyright 1993 by the author, published by Oughten House Publications, PO Box 2008, Livermore, CA 94551-2008 [There are other books in this series]

Milanovich, Dr. Norma J. With Betty **Rice** and Cynthia **Ploski**, *We, The Arcturians [A True Experience]*, copyright 1990 by the authors, published by Athena Publishing, 7200 Montgomery Blvd. NE, Suite 220, Albuquerque, NM 87109

Mount Shasta's Directory, A Quarterly publication by Southern Siskiuou Newspapers, 924-B Mt. Shasta Blvd. PO Box 127, Mount Shasta, CA 96067 [Periodical with channeling]

New Catholic Encyclopedia, copyright 1967 by the Catholic University of America, Washington, DC. Library of Congress Catalog Number 66-22292, published by the McGaw-Hill Book Company, New York.

Nolan, Albert, OP, *Jesus Before Christianity*, copyright 1992 by the author. Published by Orbis Books, Maryknoll NY 10545.

Roberts, Jane, *The "Unknown" Reality, Volume 1, A Seth Book*, copyright 1977 by the author, published by Prentice Hall Press, a Division of Simon & Schuster, One Gulf + Western Plaza, New York, NY 10023 [There are other books in this series]

Robinson, Lyle, *Edgar Cayce's Story of the Origin and Destiny of*

Man, copyright 1972 by the Edgar Cayce Foundation, Published by The Berkley Publishing Group, 200 Madison Avenue, New York, NY, 10016 [There are many other books in this series]

Royal, Lyssa and **Priest**, Keith, *The Prism of Lyra*, copyright 1989 [revised copyright 1992] by the authors, published by Royal Priest Research Press, PO Box 12626, Scottsdale, AZ, 85267-2626

Ryden, Ruth, *The Golden Path*, copyright 1993 by the author-channeler, published by Light Technology Publishing, PO Box 1526, Sedona, AZ 86339

Sedona Journal of Emergence!, published monthly by Love Light Communications, Inc. PO Box 1526, Sedona, AZ 86339

Shapiro, Robert, *The Explorer Race*, copyright 1996 by Light Technology Publishing, published by Light Technology Publishing, PO Box 1526, Sedona, AZ 86339

Stevens, Jose and **Warwick-Smith**, Simon, *The Michael Handbook, A Channeled System for Self Understanding*, copyright 1990 by the authors, published by Warwick Press, PO Box 905, Sonoma, CA 95476

Stone, Joshua David, *The Complete Ascension Manual*, copyright 1994 by the author, published by Light Technology Publishing, PO Box 1526, Sedona, AZ 86339.

Urantia Book, The, copyright 1955 and published by the Urantia Foundation, 533 Diversey Parkway, Chicago, IL 60614.

Westen, Robin, *Channelers, A New Age Directory*, copyright 1988 by the author, published by The Putnam Publishing Group, 200 Madison, Avenue, New York, NY 10016

Yarbro, Shelsea Quinn, *More Messages from Michael*, copyright 1986 by the author, published by The Berkley Publishing Group, 200 Madison Avenue, New York, NY, 10016 [There are other books in this series]

Young-Sowers, Meredith, *Agartha, A Journey to the Stars*, copyright 1995 by the author, published by Stillpoint Publishing, Box 640, Walpole, NH, 03608. Originally published in 1984.

INDEX

Note: Major Index references are in **bold** type. Channelings by a specific Ascended Master are presented in *bold Italic* type. Definitions of terms, descriptions of Ascended Masters, or biographys are presented in bold Italic type within parenthesis as *[bold Italic]*. Index notation "[Bib.]" means that the author's book is listed in the bibliography [see pages 269-270].

Other Books by the Editor

Christianity and the New Age Religion

establishes

A Bridge Toward Mutual Understanding
by teaching both Christians and
the New Pioneer element of the New Age
that once they start to learn from each other,
they can travel together
toward Integrated Spirituality!

The Christian Conspiracy

presents
*How the Teachings of Christ
Have Been Altered by Christians*
by showing which teachings
came from the Early Church Fathers
rather than from the Christ.
Most people in the pews today
are following Augustine, Tertullian, Athanasius and Jerome
rather than the Christ, but they don't know it!

A Personal Pathway to God

answers the major question "Where do we go from here?"
by singing
Our Song of Freedom
and showing that humans in all of the
world's major religions have placed restrictions on the
teachings originally presented by the messengers sent from God.
By doing this, they have inhibited spiritual growth. Spiritual
growth is a personal matter
between an individual and his/her God!

Also from Pendulum Plus

THE PENDULUM

AN ANCIENT
AND MODERN TOOL

IS NOW AVAILABLE
IN KIT FORM

THIS KIT CONTAINS:

1. A QUARTZ PENDULUM

2. A COMPREHENSIVE INSTRUCTION BOOKLET

3. TEN CHARTS WITH 3-18 COLORS IN EACH

**ALL CONTAINED IN A CONVENIENT NOTEBOOK
WITH VINYL SEPARATIONS**

These Charts have been channeled from the Masters

The quartz pendulum crystal taps into your higher self to give instructions from the Charts. These instructions from the soul indicate to the presently incarnated personality what is needed in relation to:
Color, Astrology, Chakras, Body Organs, Numbers, Alphabet, Therapies, Causes of Disease, Exercises, Vitamins, Minerals, Herbs, Supplements, Gem Stones, Essences, Aromotherapy, Percentages, Time of Day, Trincarnational Experiences.

The Kit is useful for individual self-evaluation. It is especially helpful for therapists as they work with their clients.

HOW TO ORDER

In the table below, **CNA** represents *Christianity and the New Age Religion*; **TCC** represents *The Christian Conspiracy*; **PPG** represents *A Personal Pathway to God;* **TJK** represents *The Joy of Knowing: We Are One;* and **TPPK** represents The Pendulum Plus Kit.

Book	Retail Price	Pages	Total Delivered Price [one location]		
			1 book or 1 Kit	5 book pkg. or 5 Kit pkg.	20 book pkg.
CNA	$12.95	244	$14.00	$39.00	$140.00
TCC	14.95	360	16.00	45.00	165.00
PPG	13.95	288	15.00	42.00	155.00
TJK	13.95	288	15.00	42.00	155.00
TPPK	29.95		34.95	155.00	

Books are available at all bookstores through
New Leaf Distributing or Baker and Taylor.

Copies at the single book rate, or single copies of the Kit may be ordered on credit card at:

1-800-842-8338

To directly order package sets of books or Kits as described in the table above, or single books or a single Pendulum Plus Kit, please send check or money order to:

PENDULUM PLUS PRESS
3232 COBB PARKWAY, SUITE 414
ATLANTA, GA 30339
Books will be shipped immediately. The Pendulum Plus Kit will be sent via Priority Mail.

About the Editor

L. David Moore was born in 1931. He graduated from West Virginia University and the University of Akron, and then was awarded a Ph.D. in Organic Chemistry from Purdue University.

During an early part of his 30 year business career, he directed technology for the world's leading speciality chemical company, one which specialized in creating remedies for environmental problems. Later, he became Group Vice President and Director of a Fortune 300 company; then Executive Vice President in charge of all operations of a Fortune 50 company where he directed sales of over $3 billion and the activities of some 25,000 employees; and finally, President of a half billion dollar company. After this company was sold, Dr. Moore "retired" to writing books, publishing books and sharing thoughts on spiritual activities.

Dave and his wife Jan have been devotedly married since the mid-1950s. They presently live in Atlanta, GA. They have four children and two grandchildren.

As described in the previous three books, Dr. Moore has had a lifelong, abiding interest in religious activities, primarily those of mainstream Christianity. Lately, his interests have become directed more towards spirituality. His present interests include reading many religious/spiritual works, writing and lecturing on religious or spiritual subjects, and taking spiritual journeys to the many parts of the world he has read about, an activity which has greatly increased his love for his fellow human. As a result of the time spent on those trips and spent in reading, writing and lecturing, his golf game has deteriorate beyond recognition.

About the Channel

Erik Myrmo was raised in Oregon and received degrees from Oregon State University and California Institute of Technology. He has worked in engineering development and corporate management for companies developing high technology communications products for Local and Wide Area networking. He is the father of six children. After enjoying many sports activities in his youth, he now enjoys outings as an avid golfer.

The desire for spiritual understanding and experience has been a constant companion. This has led Erik to an exploration of what IS, regardless of assumptions previously offered.

Through meditation on God, self and the nature of reality, and intensive work to resolve personal energies, Erik has gained a familiarity with a wider consciousness. In this way a natural, conscious communication with God-aligned beings unfolded. As a result, he has experienced the joy of transformational conversations with the Masters.

In this book you will read, see and feel the energy of your self, by yourself, unfolding in your own *Joy of Knowing, in God We Are All One!*

Erik is well known for his spiritual activities in the Atlanta ea. He can be reached through Pendulum Plus by those who are erested in his spiritual activities or workshops.